Julia Monroe
1996

DIANA

ONCE UPON A TIME

DIANA
ONCE UPON A TIME

Mary Clarke

SIDGWICK & JACKSON
LONDON

First published 1994 by Sidgwick & Jackson

a division of Pan Macmillan Publishers Limited
Cavaye Place London SW10 9PG
and Basingstoke

Associated companies throughout the world

ISBN 0 283 06215 0

1 3 5 7 9 8 6 4 2

A CIP catalogue record for this book is available from
the British Library

Typeset by CentraCet Limited, Cambridge
Printed and bound in Great Britain by
Mackays of Chatham PLC, Chatham, Kent

For my parents who made me what I am

For my friends who love me and whom I love

For Ben, my dearly loved son

and for David, partner and special friend,
who never for one moment doubted me and constantly
gave me confidence and support.

I thank you all.

ACKNOWLEDGEMENTS

My publishers, Sidgwick & Jackson, particularly William Armstrong whose faith in my ability to produce a book, and whose encouragement were greatly valued. My editor, Susan Hill, for her guidance and advice, who correctly told me when I had written the text 'You are 90 per cent there, but the remaining 10 per cent is 90 per cent important.' My literary agent, Peter Tauber, who first suggested I wrote the book.

Foreword

My bright orange Citroën Diane edged its way through the London traffic towards Ludgate Circus. Crowds thronged the pavements in the early morning sun on that glorious day in July 1981. London is always busy, usually with people rushing to work, shopping or sight-seeing, a determined set look on their faces, grey masks in a grey world. Today it was different; there were smiles and laughter, the place was bright and full of colour with a wonderful atmosphere that lifted every spirit and made it good to be alive, to be part of the tableau. Even the policewoman, noticing that the tax disc had expired on my car, waved me on cheerily with a gentle reminder: 'When today is over, get it renewed.'

Today the young girl I had cared for ten years previously was getting married and I was on my way to her wedding. The girl I knew then, and with whom I had remained in contact and spent time with in the intervening years, had never had any major ambition in her life. Her aims were a reflection of those shared by so many other young girls – leave school, fall in love, marry and have children. She wanted several, at least three or four, she used to tell me, and to have a large, happy family. Now she was fulfilling the start of her ambition; she had fallen in love and was to marry. There was one major difference between her and her contemporaries; Diana had fallen in love with Charles, Prince of Wales, and was about to become the fairytale Princess that the nation longed for, an answer to so many dreams, an inspiration for those who dare to dream, a reminder that fairytales do come true. Her example offered, for that one day, an escape from the dreary grind of everyday life. Even the pro-republicans and political opposition were happy – they could claim that this marriage was a propaganda exercise by the Government to help people forget the 'misery' that had been cast upon them!

1

I had been thrilled to receive my invitation. There had been great speculation in my family as to whether I would be asked to attend. I had not given it much thought as I knew that Diana, despite all the hundreds who would attend the wedding, had been allowed to issue only a few personal invitations. I had been invited to her older sister's wedding, when Sarah got married at Althorp the previous year, but until the precious card arrived by registered post, I did not know what to expect.

Regardless of inaccurate information published elsewhere, based on incorrect and second-hand facts, I was not one of many nannies. I had been employed to help Diana's father care for the children after the departure of some previous qualified and experienced nannies. I was to stay until the youngest, Charles, went to his prep school, Maidwell. It was me to whom their father, then Lord Althorp, wrote when I had left, saying, 'You made the children happier than they had ever been before.' My pleasure upon receipt of the wedding invitation was very great.

We had a choice of two cars to deck out with requisite labels. The Citroën Diane had no tax disc so how could my then husband and I consider driving it through an area that would contain the majority of London's police force? But the apple green Citroën 2CV, legal, would clash with my emerald green silk suit! We decided to chance the generosity of the police spirit. There was a choice of places where we could join the marked-off route. I wanted to make the most of my fifteen minutes of fame and to savour it as long as possible, so we chose to join the route furthest from St Paul's Cathedral. How the crowds cheered my little car. They were in such jubilant mood, they cheered everything from dust carts to police riders as well as, eventually, royalty. So I took my place, a seat on the main aisle, with a real grandstand view and settled back to watch the world arrive and to view on the TV screens, installed in the cathedral, the Lady Diana Spencer leaving Clarence House on the start of her journey to become HRH The Princess of Wales and, as we then thought, later to become the Queen of England. While I waited and could hear the roar of the crowds outside as yet another well-known person arrived, I had time to reminisce on the path I had taken from the day I first applied for the job at Park House, Sandringham, Norfolk, to my flight back from the Hawaiian Islands, to take my seat in St Paul's.

Chapter One

I sat in a dentist's waiting room at the beginning of February 1971, and idly flicked through the pages of the *Lady*. I had just returned from spending time with friends in Paris and was conscious of the need to find a job, yet not enamoured at the thought of being cooped up in an office, which my training in business law and accountancy decreed. I glanced through Situations Vacant. The boxed semi-display advertisement leapt out of the page at me '. . . ride, swim and drive an advantage'. I loved to ride, indeed I had bought my own horse quite recently with hard-earned savings, and here was an opportunity to incorporate my great love within a job for which I would be paid. The first part of the ad related to job description: to care for a boy of six and a nine-year-old girl and to act as companion to two older sisters. I had no experience with children but that did not daunt me. Nearly twenty-one, the world at my feet, my self-confidence was unassailable. I made a mental note of the telephone number and decided to think about it for a few days. I lived near Great Yarmouth on the east coast of England. Sandringham, where the job was based, was in north-west Norfolk and I did not really fit the description. Having taught a few children to ride did not really constitute 'experience with children or qualifications, desired'. It was an option to be mulled over before I sought an interview and the bother of an hour and a half's car drive to Sandringham.

I pushed it to one side of my mind, but could not totally forget it. The telephone number kept repeating itself in my brain as if urging me to call it. A few days later I succumbed and after I had been out for a ride, I went to a local call-box and dialled the number. The job might have gone, or I might not be suitable; the whole thing seemed far too pie-in-the-sky for me to mention it to my parents, with whom I was living for a short time, so it was better to call from a public phone. Immediately I was connected and spoke to Lord Althorp. I had several coins and every time I had to insert another there was a noise which Lord Althorp questioned; obviously he had not held many call-box conversations. He told me that he had finished all the interviews in London, but as I lived in Norfolk perhaps I would like to come up to Park House for an interview as he had not yet made a decision about the post. A time was set for Tuesday evening at 6.30 p.m. A friend agreed to drive me there as at the time I had no car. So on a dark February afternoon we set off to Sandringham on a journey that was to affect the rest of my life, to a job that, although relatively short term, would have lasting repercussions.

We turned off the Fakenham to Kings Lynn road at Hillington, driving down a minor road with fields on either side, most of their beauty obscured by darkness, but even so I was aware of a change of character in the fields as they gave way to royal parklands. We could feel eyes on us as our progress slowed. The fallow deer silently observed our passage through their territory, ready for flight at the first hint of danger. Rabbits blocked our path, mesmerized by the car lights, and ran a kamikaze course to escape. As we neared the entrance to Sandringham House, the Queen's residence, the headlights picked out the wide grass verges that flanked either side of the road, which unbeknown to me then were to provide such sport for Sarah, Diana and myself in the future. Behind the verges stood the magnificent trees, oak, beech and fir. They were like silent sentinels, as we neared our destination. We passed the royal gates, then went a little further, where the trees receded and the verge became a large green. There stood the entrance to the church and next door, the vicarage. In the far corner of this green, hidden by trees, was the gateway to the drive to Park House, Sandringham.

Park House stood at the end of the sweeping gravel driveway. The house was built of brick and faced with Norfolk greystone, which, because of its rough texture, appeared at first sight to be rather bleak, although its surrounding lawns, trees and shrubs served, rather, to make the approach appear solid and reassuring. It had been built in the nineteenth century by Edward VII, then Prince of Wales, to accommodate his staff and friends who visited him at Sandringham, the estate he bought in 1861. The house had been built as a family home and its initial forbidding appearance belied the warmth and cosiness of the interior.

The house my parents lived in had also been built in the nineteenth century, but although Park House was considered small for the type of home it was, it did have ten bedrooms, whilst our family home boasted just three. My parents had moved with the times and as finances had allowed, so our old home with the open fires had been modernized and extended but it still remained a world apart from the house which faced me as we drove down the drive. I was not overawed by the house for I had not expected that a lord would live in the same type of home as my parents. There was, however, a similarity shared by both homes – they both provided a warm and comfortable family atmosphere.

The drive forked to the left and right. I guessed that the left fork led to the courtyard and rear entrance, so I directed my friend to take the right fork as I did not intend that my first appearance should be at a tradesman's entrance. I was never to regard myself as a servant or be treated as one. We proceeded along the gravel approach to the front door. My friend waited in the car. I knocked loudly. The door was opened quickly by a man in a dinner jacket, whom I assumed to be the butler, but quickly realized was Lord Althorp – he was between butlers at the time. My first thought was, 'Well, he didn't have to dress up just to interview me.' I was soon to realize that the evening dress was not for my benefit: I had been slotted in before a dinner engagement.

He welcomed me warmly, thanked me for coming, immediately putting me at ease. My first impressions were that he was kind, sympathetic and thoughtful. These soon proved to be correct. I followed him into the dining room, passing on the right a large room dominated by a beautiful old desk: it was his study. Little did I realize at the time that within a few months I would be standing in that same room being told that it would be necessary for me to produce a statement to prove the validity of my position at Sandringham and my worthiness of that position. For the present, I was simply absorbing my surroundings. The main rooms had floor to ceiling windows which, I later discovered, allowed wonderful views across the cricket ground and parklands. I followed Lord Althorp into the drawing room. A fire burned in the hearth which was flanked on each side with settees; in the corner stood a grand piano, seeming dwarfed by the size of the room. The walls were hung with pictures, many by famous artists portraying scenes from Norfolk and old England. On the piano and on the small, low tables scattered around the room, stood photographs of his children in lovely silver frames. Before we had exchanged more than a few words it was obvious how proud of them he was.

We sat opposite each other by the fireplace. Vanity had led me to take off my glasses – this was prior to my contact lenses days – so Lord Althorp's features were not very clear to me, but this impaired vision made me more aware of voice and actions. One dulled sense tends to make the other senses sharper. Lord Althorp told me about his family, the circumstances that found him advertising for someone to join it, and how, since his divorce from the children's mother, he was looking for someone to help him care for the children and to bring happiness and stability into the home. His son, Charles, he said, was six years old, too young to have been too badly affected by the divorce, but he was shy and introverted. He would start at his prep school in twenty months' time and although his father was not looking for guarantees, he hoped that the person he employed now would stay until prep school started, to avoid any more disruption. Charles, he assured me, was easy to care for, but he wanted someone who would bring him out of his shell, make him slightly more outgoing, so that he would be capable of coping with boarding-school life.

His youngest daughter, Diana, on the other hand, did not suffer from being an introvert. Lord Althorp told me that until the previous summer term, Diana had attended Silfield, the same day school in Gayton, Kings Lynn, as Charles, but that she had been a little too lively for that school. I did hear that it had been suggested to Diana's father that boarding school might be more suitable and that Riddlesworth, a girls' prep school near Diss, in Norfolk, only an hour's drive away, would be more appropriate for a girl of her character and liveliness. Diana, because of her age, had been the most affected of all the children by her parents' divorce. She had, however, already settled well at Riddlesworth and her father wanted to ensure that the holidays, split equally between him and her mother, should be happy and carefree. No major issue was made of the matter, but during the conversation it became apparent

6

that Diana's rather boisterous behaviour had caused the departure of several nannies and au pairs, one of whom she had allegedly locked in the lavatory. Lord Althorp knew that the contract involved just two years, but these were two crucial years for a child of Diana's age. Moreover, for Charles, the change from a cosy day school to the teeming life of a boarding prep school was an extremely big step and this could be quite traumatic if the child was not adequately prepared beforehand. It was obvious that Lord Althorp realized the influence his new employee would have on his children at this important stage of their childhood, and it could be that this was the reason he had not hastened to make a decision after his London interviews. He was determined to do his best to ensure that these two years should provide happiness and stability to his children.

Diana, he said, had been confused since her parents' marriage had ended. She fluctuated between being bright and happy and being quiet and moody. It was clear, as he spoke, how much he adored all his children. He seemed to be an understanding man who was anxious to do his best for them even though he was not quite sure how to handle them himself. As I spoke to him I felt an instant responsibility not to let him down, so genuine was he in his concern. I felt I wanted to relieve him of some of his worries and assure him that all would be well. Of course I was unable to say this at the time: I was still in the middle of an interview and I had certainly not been offered the job.

Diana's childhood has often been described as golden and old fashioned but full of fun and laughter. I have also read reports in books stating that Diana lay in bed upset, hearing her brother cry and not daring to go to him. This, if true, was certainly not so in my time. Diana dared to do anything she pleased. I set very few rules but those I did impose were reasonable: I expected them to be adhered to and they usually were. The basic code of behaviour had long been established by the children's parents and the previous nanny, Sally. She told me that they had always been brought up to have good manners and to conduct themselves correctly whatever the circumstances and whoever the company. Naturally, I continued to apply this rule and it is to the children's credit that they always showed respect, in that, however much they might be tempted, they never let themselves or the adults down by acting in an uncivilized manner. They were taught to be considerate both in public and private. In the former they never failed and rarely in the latter. To this general rule, I added a few practical ones of my own. As they were getting older, I expected the children to care for their bedrooms and to keep them tidy. This was not something I ever had to remind Diana about, and, as if her room was not enough work for her, she often helped her brother, Charles, with his. I told them that as the mealtimes were set, it was necessary for them to be considerate and appreciate that when people take the trouble to prepare food, they should be conscious of the time and it was courteous to arrive at the table without needing constant reminders. Finally I told them that it was necessary to respect privacy and they should always knock on my bedroom door before they entered the room. I treated them with the same sort of respect. During my interview, even as I spoke with Lord Althorp, I determined that, should I get the job, the children would be free to express themselves, to laugh, confide and feel respect, to gain self-confidence and thus the security that their father desired for them.

Lord Althorp went on to describe the two older girls, Jane and Sarah, who were free to spend their time with whom they wished. They both went to the public school West Heath in Kent. Jane, perhaps the calmest of them all, chose to spend a lot of her spare time with her mother although she always met her father for some parts of the holidays. Sarah, who had free run of the place at Sandringham, spent nearly all her time with her father. A true redhead, fiery, tempestuous, volatile and very likeable, she was the daredevil who egged Diana on, always challenging her to do things Diana had been forbidden. Diana idolized her. Sarah was only five years younger than me. At Park House, Sarah, an accomplished horsewoman and pianist, had everything she needed. Her closest friends, Isabel and Ali-ba, lived nearby and there were no restrictions on how she spent her days. In hindsight, given so much freedom in her teenage years, she acted in a remarkably conservative manner and did not abuse the trust placed in her.

Once the family picture had been presented to me, Lord Althorp asked about my background, and what I had achieved so far in my life and what work I had done. I explained to him that I had no experience with children apart from teaching some to ride, and that I realized this hardly made me an authority on child-care. We discussed attitudes and approaches to certain situations. I told him about my own family life, that I came from a caring, close-knit family and that my own childhood had been secure and exceedingly happy. I talked of my ideals, and books I had read relating to childhood, such as Henry Williamson's novels. Lord Althorp told me that perhaps the most difficult part of the job would be taking the children to and collecting them from their mother in London. In my naïvety I could not foresee any problems with a simple train journey. I did not anticipate the emotional traumas that would be part of the transition periods. When asked, I gave my assurance that, were I to be offered the job, I would do my best to ensure that I stayed for the full length of the contract as I appreciated the need to establish stability in the children's lives.

The only child at home on that day in early February was Charles. Towards the end of my interview, his father sent for him to come down to meet me. He appeared with his nanny, Sally. What a daunting prospect to be presented to someone who might come and care for you. The lad stood in front of me, politely shook hands, mumbled a greeting and I, equally correct, asked him a few banal questions and then enquired if he found it boring being disturbed from his playtime and said that he could escape if he wanted to. This suggestion obviously met with his approval and with a sideways glance at his father to judge his reaction to this rather unusual adult stand, he gratefully complied and left the room with Sally. I saw no reason to make Charles stay longer than necessary. For a child to be surrounded by adults, was not the best way to get to know anyone and I felt that if I got the job we would have plenty of time then to get properly acquainted under more natural circumstances.

The interview neared its end. Lord Althorp, as if to reassure himself that I appreciated all that the job would involve, commented further on Diana's boisterous nature, but reiterated that at heart she was kind and helpful and simply needed gentle understanding. He tried to enlighten me as much as possible on the task ahead without making it appear formidable. I had already decided, if I was offered the job, that I would take it. I was sure no nine-year-old could be that much of a problem. The interview drew to its conclusion. I was asked for my telephone number. As I still had not mentioned the interview to my parents and did not intend to unless I was successful, I told him I was difficult to contact and it would be better if I phoned him at the end of the week, say Friday, by which time he might have made a decision. My interview had lasted about an hour. We made our farewells; I rejoined my friend in his car and we drove off into the night, whilst Lord Althorp made his way to the dinner party. I had certainly enjoyed the meeting but was philosophical about the outcome. The interview had been an insight into another world, but if I was not successful, well, I would just look for something for which I was actually trained. It appeared that, apart from caring for the children, taking full responsibility during their father's regular absences and keeping the nursery area clean, I would also have quite a bit of free time and very generous holidays as I would not be required to work when the children were with their mother. A car would be at my disposal for school runs, outings and personal use. Attractive as it all sounded, it was not a job that would appeal to everyone. There was a need to be self-sufficient, for the setting, although beautiful, was remote and lonely. I would be free often during the day, but committed to work most evenings. This thought did not daunt me as I enjoyed my own company and was much happier in the country than the town. I was sure that, with the riding and walking the dogs, I would find plenty to occupy myself. All I had to do was wait and see whether I would be required. I later found out that sixty-four people had been interviewed. Had I known that at the time, I would have given myself low odds on success – ignorance is bliss. I put the whole evening down to experience and then out of my mind.

Three days later, on the Friday, I returned from the farm where I kept my horse, to be summoned by my father. He owned the local post office–village store–newsagent, and acted as amateur legal adviser and male version of Marje Proops. A foreigner in the eyes of the villagers, he had come from Newfoundland during the war, met my mother, an only child, and married her, buying the business from my grandfather, as he did not wish to be beholden to anyone. Quickly he became accepted by the village for his extrovert, caring manner and his aptitude for hard work. Even at twenty years of age, going on twenty-one, when my father uttered the words, 'Mary, I want to speak with you', my heart would still pound as I wondered what minor misdemeanour had come to his notice. I knew it could be nothing serious, but my idea of serious and that of my parents did not always coincide. In those days my twin brother and I were not exceptions amongst our contemporaries. We held our parents in great respect; that was how we were brought up. We might quietly and inwardly rebel but that would be the only dissent.

So I followed my father into the store whilst my brain raced over all possibilities and could not settle on any. Not for one moment did it occur to me that it might have anything to do with my secret interview; after all, I had said that I would phone Lord Althorp. My father continued, 'I had a rather strange telephone call whilst you were out this morning, something about a job at Sandringham.' It transpired that my father thought I had applied to work at the Sandringham Hotel in Great Yarmouth. I enlightened him, and, bemused by such revelations, he continued to explain that the prospective employer was to arrive within the hour at our home as he was visiting friends nearby in Wroxham and had obviously decided it would be sensible to see where I came from before making a definite job offer. In turn, my father took the time before Lord Althorp arrived to contact the local library and ask them to look him up in *Who's Who*. This served two purposes. It checked the authenticity of the situation and the information provided helped to prepare my father a little about what to expect from this man who was due to arrive on our doorstep.

My mother always went to Yarmouth on Friday morning, so she departed without being informed of what was about to take place. There was sound reasoning behind this decision: my parents were very much a couple who worked together, but the thought of a lord crossing the doorstep would have sent my mother into a flat spin. The vacuum cleaner and duster would have been put into overdrive even though our home was already meticulously clean and tidy, so it would have been a pointless exercise. It has to be added that when my mother was informed later, she was not greatly pleased that the decision to clean or not to clean had been taken out of her hands. So off she went and a short while later a Jaguar turned up which, as no customers who frequented our shop drove such cars, we realized belonged to my probable future employer. He and my father disappeared into the lounge (the best

11

room, as opposed to our sitting room which was for the family), and I was left to attend the shop. Always immensely proud of my father, I had no doubt that he would handle the situation well. By this stage, I was fairly confident that the job was to be mine and that this visit was only a formality. Thus when my father emerged half an hour later and confirmed just that, I was not surprised but nevertheless very pleased.

I went to the lounge and was formally offered employment to care for the Spencer children until Charles went away to school. I promptly accepted, pointed out that the advertisement had stipulated twenty-one years as minimum age, which I would be in two weeks' time and agreed to start immediately after my birthday as long as I could bring my horse with me. Lord Althorp was taken aback but not deterred, as no previous mention had been made of a horse. I had not considered it sensible to apply conditions until I knew that my services would be required. My request was complied with and a starting date confirmed. We shook hands on the deal, proffered thanks all round and said goodbyes, until we met again, during the last week of February 1971.

Chapter Two

Birthday celebrations over, I prepared for my move to Sandringham. A friend in the village offered to drive me there in a horse box. Vulcan, my 15.3 hands iron-grey gelding, was loaded and off we set, my luggage stowed in the groom's compartment. This time the journey was in daylight and the full extent of the beautiful countryside in which I was to live was much more apparent, even though spring had yet to arrive. We took the left fork in the drive to pass by the courtyard which was surrounded by servants' quarters, on to the stables, hidden at the back behind the trees.

Smith, the gardener and handyman, whose wife worked in the house and had been in the family's employ for several years, came to meet me. In his early sixties, he was a sprightly, active man, with leathery brown skin, weathered by years spent outside in the sun and the Norfolk winds which can be bitingly cold. Besides caring for the garden and general maintenance work, he looked after the dogs, Bray, Lord Althorp's black Labrador gun dog, and Jill, the springer spaniel, the would-be gun dog which was returned from training as a total failure, but was very lovable. Smith had seen many comings and goings in his time at Park House and I was aware of him assessing me as I unloaded my horse into the stable he had prepared. I was blissfully unaware, at this point, of all the back-stabbing which could go on among members of staff in this type of household: I understand now that there can be quite a lot of suppressed antagonism between some old retainers and new young staff. I found that although the old retainers were apparently pleasant and friendly, they tended to be, in my view, on the look-out to find fault. This was something that I got used to and chose to ignore – certainly I would have no part in it.

The nanny's position is an in-between one: she is neither one of the downstairs staff, nor part of the family. I had to find my own niche in the household. Lord Althorp used to introduce me, 'This is Mary, she helps me with the children' – I was grateful never to have to endure the word 'nanny' to which I found it hard to relate. The nanny I was to replace, Sally, would stay with me for one or two days to help me settle and get used to the system. Sally and I were as different as chalk and cheese. She was not much older than me, but definitely one of the old school. However, we got on and she helped me a great deal as I found my way about. I unloaded my luggage, waved goodbye to the driver and followed Sally into the house through the entrance that led off the courtyard. Vulcan settled into his stable although in the end his stay at Park House was to be short-lived, as he refused to socialize with the other horses already in residence and I soon had to sell him on to a good home in nearby Downham Market.

The courtyard door opened on to a dark corridor. Off it to the left was the lovely large farmhouse-type kitchen with a range and an Aga. In the middle of the floor stood a scrubbed wooden table. It was a cosy, inviting room where Diana and I would later spend time cooking and making bread on the cook's day off, which was really the only time when we had a free hand in the room. Sarah was forever in the kitchen getting in everyone's way, making herself snacks. One cook, who came not long after my arrival, stayed only a short time as she turned out to be most unsuitable and could never get used to the children having total freedom of the house – except the gun-room – including the kitchen which she regarded as her own domain. The gun-room was on the other side of the corridor opposite the kitchen. It was always kept locked, but I remember going in on the odd occasion and seeing the guns and their victims, the pheasants, hanging. Lord Althorp was a keen shot, who was often invited on royal shoots, and young Charles had a little gun made for him, although at that age he, like his sister, Diana, was too fond of animals to contemplate killing anything.

Next to the kitchen was the laundry room where all the linen was kept. This was where Mrs Smith reigned supreme. Her main role was as housekeeper but she cooked on the cook's day off and acted as go-between in the gossip that ensued from the 'other part' of the house, which lay through the double swing doors. Mrs Smith was a well-endowed, well-covered woman, with thick short wavy, grey hair and was the epitome of a matronly figure. The back stairs that led to what were to be my quarters were opposite the laundry room and next to the utility room, which housed the washing machine and the lines to hang the washing when it was wet outside. This was a narrow, winding staircase, that opened on to the upstairs corridor. Sarah, encouraged by Diana, had even persuaded the little Shetland pony up these stairs. Diana had expressed a wish to plait his mane and groom him but as it was rather cold outside she thought it would give the pony a treat to be in the warmth of the nursery rather than in the paddock. At the time, the housemaid was cleaning the drawing room, so the pony was sneaked in through the back door and persuaded to climb the winding stairs with Sarah gently pulling and Diana ahead enticing him with the proverbial carrot. Giggles and commands of 'Stand still' alerted me to the fact that something untoward was taking place in the nursery and upon opening the door I was presented with the unusual spectacle of a chestnut pony standing in the middle of the floor instead of the usual array of Charles's soldiers. I had to laugh at the comical expression on the pony's face; he, after all, had no objection to the cold outside. I asked them, 'Whatever are you both thinking about?' and told them to get him out immediately. Luckily, he had chosen not to christen the floor and I am sure he was indebted to me for ever for my insistence that he be returned immediately to greener pastures. He certainly needed no carrot to entice him down the stairs! In later years when Diana was a teenager and used to visit her mother in Scotland during the holidays she used to help her to prepare the Shetland ponies for the show ring. Perhaps she had hoped to get in some early practice. When I recounted this incident to Mrs Smith, she told me that before my arrival Romany, the 13.2-hands high bay pony, had been encouraged to venture up the main staircase. When I questioned Sarah about this, she said they had got the idea from the rhyme 'The Grand Old Duke of York', and wanted to find out whether the march up the hill was feasible for ponies as well as foot soldiers. These were not incidents that were repeated. The girls were severely reprimanded and the daily housemaid, Mrs Pertwee, threatened to resign should anything like it happen again.

Our section of the upstairs was, like downstairs, shut off from the main part of the house by a swing door. It was light and airy. I had a large bedroom, simply but adequately furnished, with a lovely feather mattress on the bed. Next to my bedroom was Diana's, a good-sized room full of stuffed animals, games and books. Animal pictures adorned the walls and family photographs stood in frames on her bedside table and on a shelf, including pictures of Diana with her beloved guinea-pig. Her clothes hung neatly in the wardrobe; she preferred to wear trousers and old sweaters, rather than dresses or skirts. At that age she was not in the least fashion conscious and her clothes tended to be somewhat frumpy and practical rather than the trendy things a young girl might be proud to wear. Most of her clothes were bought by her mother but later Diana and I used to go on shopping expeditions together to Kings Lynn. The rest of her clothes were folded neatly in her drawers. None of the children were spoilt for clothes and there were no excesses. Anything that no longer served a purpose was put aside and handed over whenever there was a request for contributions to a jumble sale. It was the children's responsibility to look after their rooms themselves under my supervision. Diana needed no supervision, she was always so clean, neat and tidy, a practical person who proved to be a great help to me about the home. The only rooms I had to clean were those in the nursery wing. I was always tidy, but cleaning was never a forte. It was not beyond Lord Althorp to run his finger surreptitiously along the top of a picture in the nursery and find it covered in dust. He never commented on his dirty finger as the children were happy and that was his main concern. I told Diana how her father had caught me out and to make sure I was not caught again she cleaned the nursery. This practical streak stayed with Diana even after her marriage. She wrote to me in January 1982, 'I do get annoyed at not being able to do my washing and general ironing. I know sister Sarah would adore that situation!' Jane, like Diana, was neat and tidy, but their sister Sarah was the bane of Mrs Smith's life. Her room always looked as if a bomb had hit it only minutes after she went into it, and she worked on the assumption that there was no point in clearing up as everything would only get untidy again. I helped Charles with his room but he had been taught to put things away as he finished with them, so little work was involved.

Charles's room lay on the other side of the corridor, a smaller room, full of books and toys and his army figures. The bathroom which the two younger children and I shared was next to it. Opposite was the nursery, a large room with windows overlooking the rolling parklands. At one end of the room was a table where we ate breakfast and afternoon tea and at the other was a fireplace for the lovely fires we had lit in the winter to make the room cosy. The whole house had central heating provided by great, thick radiators, but the fires brought the house alive. One of my own favourite childhood memories is of arriving home on a dark winter's evening after a long day at school and a cold bus journey, opening the door and being greeted by a fire blazing in the kitchen hearth. I would re-create that scene for the children in the winter and would have the curtains drawn, the sofa and easy chairs pulled up to the fire where we would read and play games, often to be joined by the older girls and their father who found more comfort there in that small room than in the drawing room downstairs. There was plenty of space for games in the nursery, should inclement weather force the children to stay inside – indeed Charles would often have to be persuaded to go outside to play, so engrossed did he become in the battles he enacted with his toy soldiers. History played a great part in the stories that Lord Althorp told to his children, interesting tales that appealed to their imagination yet at the same time helped them to understand their family background which stretched back over hundreds of years, and to teach them to take a pride in the family and its history. Diana loved to be outside regardless of the time of year or the weather and I often had to search for her to suggest that some time should be spent indoors as darkness fell. Like so many children, however much time I gave her, she would always want 'just a few more minutes'. 'Now means now, Diana. Please don't make more work for me when I'm trying to get tea organized,' I would say and she never did. I was impressed from the start by how happy and self-contained the children were and how they always found so much to do to amuse themselves.

As Sally showed me around, she explained some of the ground rules, although it would be up to me to change or add to them as I wished. It was obviously sensible to keep the basic ones set so that the children retained their feeling of continuity, but at that stage, as I had only met Charles briefly and none of the other children, I did not plan to make any changes until I had had a chance to judge the children and see what they would prefer and what would best suit them.

I was lucky on that first day to have a few hours alone with Sally as Charles was at his day school, and I could ask questions about the children and their home and get acquainted with my surroundings before I got involved with Charles. The most memorable thing that sticks in my mind was Sally explaining to me that the two younger children rarely went through the swing doors into the 'other part of the house'. This was how they had been brought up and they expected nothing different. They had always been visited by their parents in the nursery wing. Inwardly I thought that this might not have been so bad when they were babies and toddlers – at least it prevented risk of any damage to the treasures that adorned the public rooms, which would have caused tension. But then and there I decided that one of the first changes I would try to make was to have the family more integrated as a family, particularly as Jane's and Sarah's rooms were on the other side of the swing doors. I had no idea, on that first day, of the opposition I would sometimes face, not from Lord Althorp, but from the other members of the staff some of whom may have felt I was rising above my station. Conscious, of course, that there were supposedly different classes in life, I had, nonetheless, never regarded one as any better than another, just different. The only 'station' I knew about was connected with trains. I had much to learn about social attitudes.

Downstairs, as well as upstairs, the other side of the swing doors presented a very different picture. Stone floors downstairs gave way to carpet. The first door on the right was to the pantry, lined with cupboards and shelves. The butler's trolley was kept there, as was all the silver, crockery and glass for the dining room and it was rare that anyone but the butler went into this room. Opposite lay the door to the dining room. The butler's pantry, like the gun-room, had small windows as it lay on the chilly north side of the house. The nursery was above the housemaid's laundry room and shared the same views as the dining room. As I had seen in the drawing room on the night of my interview, the dining-room windows also reached from floor to ceiling. The whole room was decorated in a pale, sea-green colour with matching curtains, and the walls had pictures depicting coastal scenes, all with individual lights. It was a quiet, relaxing room, giving a feeling of peace. Unfortunately, the ambience portrayed by the colour scheme did not always guarantee that peace remained and in my time at Park House it was certainly the setting for some scenes that could scarcely be described as peaceful! The first meal the children shared with the then Lady Dartmouth, who later became their stepmother, was in that dining room: on that occasion, I would have felt more relaxed if I had been sitting in the middle of a minefield. Yet, on my first day, that was a situation I was unable to visualize. From the moment Sally showed me the dining room, I loved it. The beautiful pictures compared well with the beauty that lay outside the windows. The view had a sense of timelessness, the lawns, cricket pitch and the rolling parklands with their lovely old English trees. It was, perhaps, on first gazing at that room, that I realized life here would be entirely different from anything I had known before, a way of life that, because of 'progress', will soon be experienced by only a few. The children and I were to share some wonderful happy times in that room, both with their father and during his absences. It was to be the scene of much laughter and jollity, often at the expense of the dour-faced butler, Betts, who, with his wife who took over the kitchen, joined the family after I had been there some time.

From the dining room, the corridor opened into the main hall. It was here that I had arrived for my interview. The main door to the house was to my right and opposite was another door, leading into the garden. This door was often used when we had visitors, to save everyone walking around the house to get to the principal garden area. In the middle of the hall was a large winding staircase, ideal for making dramatic entrances although such an opportunity never presented itself to me. However, it was not unknown for Sarah, Diana and me to slide, at considerable speed, down the banisters, something I had always wanted to do and never before had the opportunity! When Diana and Charles began to spend time in the evening with their father in the drawing room, they always looked such tiny figures trolling up that stairway in their night clothes on their way to bed.

Across the hall was the entrance to the drawing room and next door was the study. In the daylight, I could really appreciate the double aspect from the drawing room. It shares the same views to the south as those from the dining room and the nursery, but its westerly aspect overlooks the tennis court and the woods beyond – exactly the same as from the study. Besides the settees on which we had sat during the first meeting, the room was full of occasional tables and easy chairs. The inevitable display of family photographs stood on the tables and on the grand piano and now I had a chance to study them. They were taken of all the children through their different ages and showed just how proud Lord Althorp was of his offspring. A variety of books and country magazines were scattered around to invite the visitor to relax in these pleasant surroundings and to feel at home.

The study, a room I hardly ever entered, was dominated by the large desk where Lord Althorp sat, with his back to the window, writing his weekly letters to the girls in their boarding schools. From here he sorted out the affairs of the boys' clubs that he patronized, and administered the land that he owned in the area. I went into the study only once during my time at Sandringham and that was when I was summoned by Lord Althorp to be told that I was to be the main witness at the High Court in London, when the children's mother would apply again for custody of them. Following Sally as we toured the house, I had no inkling of the drama that would later unfold in that room.

We went upstairs, via the back stairway. It was unheard of at that time for us to use the main staircase but I was able quickly to change such outmoded ideas. Through the swing doors we went to Sarah's and Jane's rooms. The two guest rooms, one blue and the other pink, both with their own bathrooms, were also in this part of the house, as was Lord Althorp's room. It seemed so sad to me that such a lovely home should have known so much unhappiness. The house was large by the standards my friends and I were used to, but it was not enormous. It was a manageable size, cosy yet with plenty of space. Jane's room was kept clean and tidy, but she spent very little time in Norfolk, preferring to be in London or Sussex with her mother. Even though so little used, it was kept well aired and had no feeling of neglect about it, so when Jane did arrive, it soon came alive. Sarah's room had a lived-in air about it the minute she set foot in the house. In a few moments, all Mrs Pertwee's hard work would be destroyed. I never envied her her job. A cheerful woman from the nearby village of West Newton, her bright disposition proved invaluable in her determination to stick to her post. Horses in the house, guinea-pigs escaping, the place showered with rose petals blown off the walls and through the open windows and garden door when the children's uncle, Lord Fermoy, landed his helicopter on the back lawn, all just when she may have thought the housework was finished for the day, were only a few of the extra tasks she had to cope with along with her daily routine.

To complete the tour of the house, Sally showed me the entrance to the wine cellar that lay beneath the house. That door, which closed off the stairway from the back corridor, was, like the gun-room, always kept locked, the butler retaining control of the key. Not always a convenient state of affairs, such as on the day that Princess Anne popped round after church with no prior warning. Little alcohol was drunk in the house, so none was left on display. Consequently, when someone turned up unexpectedly if it was the butler's day off, as on this occasion, it proved rather embarrassing not to have anything on hand to offer the guest.

I had now got my bearings inside, so we went outside, although, of course, I already had a general idea of the grounds. Lord Althorp was away when I arrived and that in itself gave me a bit of time and freedom to settle. A short way up, the gravelled front drive forked to left and right. Left led to the courtyard, servants' quarters, garages, stables and tradesmen's entrance while the right led to the entrance in front of which the drive opened up into a large circular area, allowing plenty of room for cars to turn round. This area was fringed with large bushes and shrubs backed by woodland. The entire drive was sheltered from the road that ran through the estate and from the prying eyes of any visitors or picnickers who loved to visit the area. Who could blame them? It would be hard to find a more lovely place for a day out and the fact that Sandringham was the Queen's winter home was also a draw. Park House, however, needed to be private, and dense undergrowth and foliage helped to achieve this. To the right of the house, the lawn started and further to the right was the hard tennis court. The lawn stretched round to the back of the house and widened into a considerable sized garden, separated from the parkland and cricket grounds by a small wire fence. One of Mr Smith's tasks was to keep the lawn in trim and this he did with great pride, sitting upright on his sit-on mower. To the far end of the house, still facing the park, outside the servants' quarters, was the open-air swimming pool. Such a thing was unusual in those days and a great attraction to the children and to their friends, which was the reason Lord Althorp had it built in the first place. The pool had a slide which doubled as a diving board. Diana and Sarah, particularly, made excellent use of all the facilities Lord Althorp ensured they had at hand and all the children were free to invite friends whenever they wished to come and stay or visit. They had a childhood of freedom and few restraints in a setting that allowed the individual to develop an independent character. None of the children abused this freedom, but theirs was a lifestyle much envied by their contemporaries.

Beyond the pool lay more lawns and then the paddocks. I was to look after the horses while Sarah was away at school. Besides the Shetland pony and her pony, Romany, she had a Connemara/ thoroughbred called Peppermint which I used to exercise. Later I sold Peppermint to an excellent, loving home, near my parents, where she lived to the grand old age of thirty. She was replaced by a larger chestnut for Sarah to compete with and hunt.

Sally finished the tour and it was time to go to Gayton to collect Charles from his school, Silfield. We had the use of a blue Simca 1100. The school was about seven miles away. The drive was through the Sandringham estate towards Wolferton and then we turned on to the main road towards Kings Lynn; it was very pleasurable. Wolferton was where the royal family used to arrive by train from Kings Lynn but this station is now closed and has become a private house. The road from Sandringham to Wolferton is lined with rhododendrons which in June are a mass of colour. The Queen's small private home, Wood Farm, is at Wolferton and this is where Prince Philip used to keep his polo ponies and the stallions stood at stud nearby. Members of the family often stay there, particularly if it saves the big house from being opened.

Sally introduced me to the headmistress and said that in future I would be looking after Charles. We returned to Park House with Charles sitting in the back of the car, answering my questions about his school politely. I did not press him much as I guessed that, in time, when I was alone with him, we would gradually build up a rapport. He must have felt confused that yet again someone was leaving and a new person starting. When Lord Althorp visited my parents' home, he sensed that they had provided stability and warmth, that mine had been a country childhood, cosy and secure, and that is what I was well placed to give Diana and Charles. I wanted to establish the same feeling of security as I knew it would benefit them far into their adulthood. Park House lent itself to such an atmosphere. The rooms were large, but comfortable and cosy. The children, I quickly realized, had been brought up in the old-fashioned way, with ideals clearly stated and clearly defined lines between good and bad. Manners were very important, but love, kindness, generosity of spirit and discipline were paramount. I did not want to change this but wished to establish a more relaxed regime, to encourage the children to act in a responsible manner because that was what they wanted to do and not because it was expected of them. Lord Althorp's letter to me on my departure shows that I achieved this, when he wrote 'You made the children happier than they had ever been.' When Diana was engaged, she supposedly said it was the first time in her life she had ever felt secure but I think that was poetic licence, inspired by her deep love for Prince Charles. Diana had a happy, secure childhood. From the time I met her and shared that time with the family, I saw that she was helpful, laughing, exuberant, loved by both her parents, the apple of her father's eye; these characteristics do not suggest insecurity. I guided her through those crucial years of development, encouraging her to share her thoughts, her fears, her hopes with me, giving her support and, I like to think, sound advice. Their childhood contained almost all the ingredients of a stable, secure, loving home. Once the parents had split, there was no shouting in the house, no raised voices, no angry words (I'm not saying there ever were any – I was not there), just a steady routine, a gentle way of life and controlled freedom. Whatever Lord Althorp's private thoughts about the children's mother might have been, never once did he speak against her to the children. They were free to make their own comments without feeling disloyal or needing to be secretive.

Sally and I decided that the rest of the first day I would be free to settle in and the next day I would work alongside her, learning the routine so that the changeover caused as little disruption as possible.

Chapter Three

I was lucky to be able to meet the children one at a time, so I had the chance to get to know them as individuals rather than have to learn to cope with them en masse immediately. Charles was six when I started work at Park House, his seventh birthday due on 20 May. Both in his looks and his ways – he was quiet and serious – he took after his father. He bore a striking resemblance to a portrait of the young Lord Marlborough. It was typical that he, a boy, should have beautiful golden-blond hair – red, if you were to listen to Sarah, who loved to tease – while Diana had to make do with her rather mousy colour.

Charles was a bright, articulate little boy, well mannered, but shy and introverted in company, although well capable of holding his own in conversation, particularly with his sisters who were all protective of him, yet unable to resist teasing at times. I quickly grew fond of him; he was a loving child who gave me no problems. Naturally, he had been very young during the last troubled years of his parents' marriage and any acrimony had been kept well away from his ears. I loved our evenings together when he lay in his little bed, and we sat and read and talked together. If Lord Althorp was at home he came, without fail, to read the bedtime story; however busy he might be there was always time for the children who took precedence over any other business. It was these times when their proficiency in history grew: he talked about it enthrallingly so they never became bored. Indeed, Charles went on to study history at Oxford. When Lord Althorp was away, I read adventure stories, the classics in easy form, such as *Robinson Crusoe*, *The Swiss Family Robinson* and others bound to appeal to active imaginations. Aesop's fables, Greek myths and Enid Blyton school stories were on the agenda when Diana joined us, but her powers of concentration did not equal those of her brother. She was much happier

24

doing things rather than sitting still for any length of time. It was always so peaceful and quiet in the room with only the sound of birdsong as from the safety of our four walls we shared adventures in imaginary lands. We were happy in the new worlds to which books gave entrance. Diana's favourite was the Never-Never Land of Peter Pan, Wendy and their four-legged nanny. Books are the root of all knowledge, of dreams and escapism. Even at that age Charles was a fluent, avid reader, but as a child it is still enjoyable to have someone to read aloud and share stories with. Whether I was on my own with Charles or if his father read to him, it was always I who went in to hear him say his prayers. Diana and Charles said the same prayers, The Lord's Prayer and then a personal prayer to bless everyone they knew. In Diana's case, it also included a list of all her pets, both past and present. There were no sleepless nights: it was an active, full, healthy life that we led at Sandringham. Illness, stress and pressure did not exist to spoil the harmony of our days. The majority of the usual childhood illnesses had come and gone before my time.

I was always an early riser. I liked to get myself organized before I got caught up in the day. I also relished the small period of peace in the early morning. Charles got up at 7.30 a.m. and just had a quick wash as I supervised the baths in the evening. He dressed in his school clothes which I laid out on the chair beside his bed the night before so that there would be no mad rush in the morning, working on the theory that organization is in partnership with calmness. I set the table in the nursery the night before, ready for breakfast which I collected from the kitchen. I only prepared the actual food on the cook's day off. Cereals and jams we kept upstairs in a cupboard in the nursery. When I started at Park House, Lord Althorp ate breakfast alone in the dining room, joined in the holidays by his older children and soon by us when I changed the system. However, to start with, he was alone and he came upstairs to see Charles just before we left for school. By 8.30 a.m. we were in the car heading for Silfield, Charles looking smart in his uniform. He loved school and it would never occur to him to say he did not want to go. In the car we went over tables and spelling, so he was well prepared for his tests, an exercise I was to repeat many years later with my own golden-blond-haired son Ben.

Looking back, I've often thought how similar in character and colouring the two boys were – it almost seemed, later, as if I were doing a re-run.

Sally left during my first full day at Park House and I went alone to Silfield to collect Charles from school at 3.30 p.m. Parents of other children were very polite and friendly towards me and the mothers whose sons were friends with Charles introduced themselves and said that we must make arrangements for the boys to spend time together. When we got home from school, at that age Charles did not talk about what had happened in the past or what might happen in the future; he talked, as most children do, about what had happened during the day. I always ensured that Diana and Charles knew as soon as possible about where they would spend their holidays, so they could see and look forward to firm, happy plans.

Charles and I settled into an easy daily routine. We kept ourselves to ourselves and I did not mix with the other house staff except to exchange greetings. It was still early in the year when I started at Park House, so by the late afternoons it was cold and I made sure a good fire was burning brightly in the nursery, ready to greet Charles when he arrived home from school. With the curtains drawn against the darkness, it presented a warm welcome. When Sally left, I had a few days alone with him and immediately established an easy-going relationship that was to prevail the length of my stay. Lord Althorp returned one Saturday afternoon when we were playing in the garden. I had climbed a tree and was hiding from Charles during a game of hide and seek when Lord Althorp came into the garden in search of us. Lurking among branches had not been the place I would have envisaged for our first meeting since we had said goodbye at my parents' home. Clambering down the tree, lacking a certain elegance, I called for Charles to abandon the search. Lord Althorp told us that Diana was due home the following weekend for the start of the Easter holidays, and suggested that it might be a good idea for me to collect Diana from school so that I had some time alone with her. Car journeys often present an ideal opportunity to talk and take the first steps towards a relationship. It has to be admitted that while I acknowledged the principle that it was a good idea, I also viewed the thought with some trepidation. Sally had been with me when I met Charles; now I was being asked to go to a strange school, sort out the end-of-term procedures and meet a nine-year-old girl with whose exploits the staff had taken, I thought, a certain delight in regaling me. It was mostly due, it seemed, to Diana's high spirits and pranks that my predecessors had left. When I asked the staff for examples of their insinuations I was told of two separate incidents, neither of which should have happened, but both harmless enough compared with the often intolerable and unacceptable behaviour of today. On one occasion, mentioned earlier, Diana in an attempt to delay her bedtime, had considered it a joke to lock the nanny in the bathroom and there she had to wait, fuming, until Lord Althorp rescued her when he came upstairs to bid the children goodnight. The other involved an au pair who had forbidden Diana to go outside as the weather was bad. To get her own back, Diana had gone into her room – that in itself was forbidden – taken some of the girl's underwear and managed to throw it on to the roof where it stayed until Smith fetched it down. Diana and Charles went outside to watch – and I'm sure to have a final laugh – so Diana's objective was achieved. I certainly had one or two reservations about Diana, although I made sure that the staff gained no satisfaction from the knowledge that their tales caused me any unease.

I was sure that Diana and I would get on fine together as long as I made good use of the car journey and established the basic format of our relationship from the outset. It was apparent that high-handed authority was not the way to tackle Diana and, in any case, I hoped that she would see me as a friend and confidante – after all, she had a mother and I was not trying to replace her. I simply wanted to be a person she would feel able to relate to. On the basis of this, I hoped to make a good relationship based on love and respect, at the same time giving help and guidance, which in itself would dispel any need for rebellion or a repeat of the childish pranks at the nanny's expense. I certainly had no intention of being the recipient of these or any other bright ideas she might come up with, fired by her rather vivid imagination. Diana, I was told, had a lively, outgoing nature and tended to be rather mischievous. As her father explained these aspects of her character to me, I had the feeling that he was displaying the true English trait of understatement. I wondered how far her mischief-making would extend with me. I certainly did not want to dampen her spirits, rather to guide her excess liveliness into more useful channels. Most important, I hoped that she would not have a disruptive influence on Charles – I was yet to learn that he was not easily influenced – and that the calm we had enjoyed so far was not about to come to an abrupt end.

Saturday arrived, and my main thoughts on waking were that this was the day I was to meet my second charge, for the first time and alone. I dressed with care, finding it strange to put on smart clothes when mostly I dressed in jeans and sweaters. I enjoyed the chance to dress up and did not want to let Diana down in front of her friends. There really was no need to feel uneasy. I was very confident of my capabilities and sure we would get along, yet, I reflected, I expect others before me had thought that and look what happened to them. I had promised Lord Althorp I would stay until Charles went to prep school and I certainly did not want to let him down. His love for Diana was so apparent whenever he spoke of her that I knew he desperately wanted her to be happy during the holidays at Park House and that our relationship would be one of the key factors. So, setting off to Riddlesworth I had mixed feelings, conscious that the journey did not just involve collecting a girl from school, but that the future of my job rested on our first impressions of each other.

I found my way with no difficulty. It was only about an hour's drive from Sandringham. I followed other cars up a long driveway and found a spot to park. Diana had been told by her father that I would come to meet her. I had wondered how I would find her, but she was waiting for me. She came towards me, very polite, and shook my hand. Certainly, her demure approach belied all the tales I had heard, and it was difficult to imagine that this nine-year-old, hair hanging loose to her shoulders – she had already pulled off the restraining band to celebrate the start of holiday freedom – with the lovely rosy cheeks and downcast eyes could be the cause of so much mischief. In later life, during the early years of her marriage, that same downcast, demure approach was to fool many people who did not realize what a strong character it hid.

I immediately felt a little relieved, although she was hardly likely to be a problem as soon as I set eyes on her, and I knew very well that good manners instilled at a very early age can be deceptive. For many years, Diana's eyes were downcast when she met anyone new. Both Charles and Diana had real problems about looking people in the face when they were speaking. It was a habit that with Diana I was never able to break completely; she did improve but I think she partly used it as a shield to hide her feelings. Sensitive and, at the same time, strong-willed, she was genuinely shy and it always took time for people to discover the real Diana.

The first greetings over, any awkward moments could quickly be brushed aside in the usual rush of activity to collect the trunk, tuck-box and guinea-pig. Riddlesworth allowed their pupils to bring pets if so desired, to ease the stress of being away from home and to give a responsibility and occupation during free time. Diana looked after her guinea-pig, Peanuts, with love and care, even winning the prize for best-cared-for pet. Somehow, we managed to load everything into the Simca and set off on the journey back to Sandringham. Now, with all the hustle, bustle and activity over, and settled into the car, Diana sitting next to me, was the real testing time. I chatted to her about school and she, like Charles, made no reference to Sally or to previous nannies, or why they left. Both children appeared to take this in their stride and it did not seem to unsettle them. The most important thing, their home base, remained constant, as did the care of their parents. Diana told me about her school, how she had settled, her friends, one who lived nearby, Alexandra Loyd, daughter of Julian Loyd, the Queen's Sandringham estate manager. They lived in a house in the park, near West Newton. Although not a close friend – Alexandra was much more studious than Diana – they were close enough to spend some of their holidays together. I asked about other friends whom she might like to invite over during the holidays. Annabel Fox, whose family then lived at Amner Hall, was her favourite local friend. Amner Hall later became the Norfolk home of the Duke and Duchess of Kent. I told Diana what Charles and I had been doing and how much he was looking forward to seeing her. I was conscious, as I spoke, that I did not want to make too much of an issue about our activities, in case she should feel as if she was intruding, but I think this was me being over-sensitive, as I was so determined that Diana should settle down well. Park House was the only home Diana had ever known – she had even been born there – and I'm certain that intrusion was the last thought that would have crossed her mind.

In a sisterly way, Diana grimaced at the thought that Charles was keen to see her. No one likes to admit wanting to spend time with a younger brother, but in reality she was extremely fond of Charles and there was no antagonism between them. Their totally different personalities complemented each other and avoided any danger of competition. Diana, exuberant, out-going, non-stop chatterer and organizer, was not threatened at all by her quiet, pensive brother, who knew his own mind but would go for the least line of resistance as far as his dealings with Diana were concerned. Diana asked me when her sisters were coming and I told her that Sarah was expected home shortly, but that she would see Jane when she visited her mother. Diana told me she could not wait to be grown-up like Sarah so that she could do what she wanted, and it was clear from the outset how she idolized her eldest sister. I had yet to meet Sarah and hoped from this comment that any headway I made in my relationship with Diana would not be destroyed by a sister who was obviously quite an influence – good or bad, I had to see.

I decided to change the subject and move on to the safer ground of what subjects she enjoyed at school. She loved Physical Education and ballet and had wanted to be a ballerina as she grew older, but she already knew she would be too tall. She had ideas of being a nurse, preferably caring for children. Diana was always drawn towards the defenceless, be they animals or human. I asked what school subjects appealed to her and, with a mischievous glint in her eye, the first hint of a break from her polite, demure attitude, she told me she really enjoyed her biology lessons. I was naturally led into asking what she found so interesting in these lessons and Diana explained they had learnt about the reproduction of rabbits – not something, I felt, that she found especially exciting in itself, but certainly a good opening gambit towards the conversation she really wanted to have, concerning marriage and babies. Her parents' divorce was obviously on her mind and intertwined with her thoughts on marriage. Her only ambition, she told me, was to fall in love, get married and have lots of children, but with the divorce clearly on her mind, and all the hurt that it entailed, she added she would never marry unless she was really, *really* in love. It did not matter who the person was, but she would never risk marriage unless she was sure of her feelings, because, if you are not really sure you love someone, then you might get divorced. 'I never want to be divorced,' she said. Of all the Spencer children, Diana, because of her age, was the most affected by her parents' separation. Although she often displayed a happy-go-lucky, couldn't-care-less attitude, because of her sensitivity she was conscious of the hurt that both her parents had suffered.

By the time I arrived to live there, the house had settled down again, with a good, secure, calm atmosphere. Like many children whose parents have divorced, Diana liked everything clear-cut: in her eyes, a family should be a family – mother, father, brother and sisters – and they should all live together under one roof. I told Diana that was the ideal way, as portrayed in her story books, but real life did not always work like that and sometimes people could be happier when they were apart. I said nearly everyone thought they were in love when they got married, but people change, particularly if they marry young, and as they mature they might not always feel the same way about their partner. Often too, I said, until you live all the time with someone, you do not really know them, so there could never be any guarantees. I told her not to be in any rush to get married. She was very young with time to enjoy herself and wait to see what would happen in the years ahead.

Diana asked about my parents and if I had brothers or sisters. She was interested in the ideal family unit and asked if she would be able to come to visit my parents. I told her that although there wouldn't be time in the Easter holidays we would go together in the summer.

We arrived at Park House and the journey had gone much better than I had hoped. The ice had been broken and we had quickly settled on topics of interest closest to Diana's heart and had a really sensible chat. I had not expected the content of our first talk to be as direct, even adult, as it was, but was pleased that we immediately seemed to relate to each other, and that no subjects would be taboo. I had chosen to speak to Diana as an equal, not down to her as a child, and she seemed to appreciate this approach.

Diana leapt out of the car and rushed off to see the dogs, horses and the Smiths. Mr Smith helped to unload and the beloved guinea-pig was settled into his cage.

On our return, Diana's father, hearing the commotion our arrival caused, came to greet us. I used to think how uneasy the first exchanges were considering they loved each other so much. Now, after my own son has been away at boarding school, I can appreciate the huge change between school life and home life. For weeks the children are away in a world that has nothing to do with parents. Then, in the matter of hours, over a journey, it is all change and on both sides it takes a little adjustment and relaxing naturally. Time and again I have seen parents and children, obviously thrilled to see each other but struggling to reach common ground. Still, I had been surprised to learn that, even during the holidays, the younger children did not eat with their father and I did not approve of this. Everyone would benefit if they all saw more of each other and mealtimes were the ideal opportunity for talking together without outside distractions. The whole thing would be more natural. I planned to wait until Sarah arrived and then to suggest a change. Diana's father was a true gentleman. He had no airs or graces and I was sure he would agree to any idea that would create a better family rapport.

The day after I had collected Diana from school, Sarah arrived. The housemaid had spruced up her room that morning and made the bed, while mumbling to herself that she wondered how long it would stay tidy. It was, however, obvious that, despite all the mutterings of the staff, they loved to have Sarah in the house. She had not been home long before I realized why. Suddenly the house, now full of children, came alive and there was never anyone more vital than Sarah. Although she was old enough to realize that her father would do anything for her, she did not abuse the privilege, but she made full use of the facility . . . Music played loudly from Sarah's room. The house echoed to her charging up and down the front stairs. Self-centred, like so many teenagers, but so likeable, she could get away with anything. It was easy to see why Diana idolized her. Sarah shared Diana's love of animals, tennis and swimming but, unlike Diana, she was a competent, fearless horse-woman. This became a common interest from which our friendship grew. Lady Fermoy, the children's maternal grandmother, was a well-known concert pianist who had met her husband Maurice Fermoy, twenty-six years her senior, when she was a student at the Paris Conservatoire of Music, where she was considered to be both accomplished and gifted. Sarah was already quite proficient and gave many a great deal of pleasure when she chose to sit and play the grand piano, always by ear as she inevitably had misplaced the sheet music. Diana had not yet taken her first tentative steps in her piano lessons so her improvisations had some way and some years to go to catch up with Sarah's ability.

When Sarah first arrived, apart from the polite greeting I had come to expect from all members of the family and some gentle teasing of her brother and sister, she took herself off to organize her holiday, contact friends and to make her arrangements to ensure she got maximum benefit during her break from school. Sarah clearly was not the type to sit about doing nothing.

I did not meet Jane until later, but she was by far the calmest and quietest of the three girls. Jane chose to spend more time with her mother, for two principal reasons. Much as she loved her father, life in the country did not hold the same appeal for her as life in London where her mother lived. Jane did not share Sarah and Diana's enthusiasm for outdoor country pursuits, preferring to read and spend time visiting the galleries and museums of London and to shop. The second, more minor point was that, always fair, Jane acknowledged that Sarah spent more time with her father, so to maintain a balance it was better for her to stay with her mother. Most of her time at Park House was spent in the summer when she could share her love of swimming with her brother and sisters. She related to Charles as Sarah did to Diana. Sarah, Jane and Charles were all academically very capable, whereas Diana's leanings were much more towards practical things. All the children got on very well together and there was little bickering to spoil the atmosphere. Perhaps, because they lived with just one parent, they showed a sense of responsibility towards each other. Sarah loved to egg Diana on to do something she had been forbidden, knowing very well that the combination of mischief and the wish to oblige Sarah would inevitably lead to Diana's downfall. It is wonderful that, years later, Diana feels happiest with her sister, Sarah, as her lady-in-waiting.

I loved the contrast between term-time, when Charles and I

were mostly alone, and the holidays when there were so many comings and goings. When I recounted details of my job to friends they all thought it sounded fantastic which it really was, when I look back on my time at Sandringham and recall one glorious day after another. I suppose there were days when it rained, but I don't remember them. We were happy and self-sufficient. It would not have been everyone's idea of a perfect job. But I was my own boss, well respected by Lord Althorp, who, realizing I could cope, left me to get on with no interference. I had good holidays, plenty of free time, my car, and the sports I loved, riding, tennis and swimming. The children were no problem and a pleasure to be with. We did live in the middle of the country estate and it could be lonely. But I, too, was very self-sufficient and loved to read and write in the evenings. As Lord Althorp was often away, it was not possible for me to go out much, although I was allowed to have friends to visit. Nevertheless, many people would have found the life lonely, so the extremes between term-time and holidays were a pleasant change.

The staff were very attached to the children. Jane they regarded as the most thoughtful, Charles, an easy, obliging child. Sarah they loved, but took great pleasure in complaining about her ways and all the extra work she made. These were affectionate complaints and the staff would not have had her otherwise. Diana, too, they were very fond of. They loved to recount her antics and were always on the look-out to see if she would get up to any more tricks. Diana made them laugh and she never forgot to ask about their own families. In her girlish way, she sincerely cared about them. Diana had many friends. She was generous-natured and open-hearted with no side to her at all. With his children around him Lord Althorp appeared to be a happier man. He never led them to think they were any different from any other children. This must be one of the reasons that Diana finds it so easy to relate to everyone.

It was because of the happiness Lord Althorp evinced when he had his children at home, that once the Easter holidays had started I suggested to him that it would be a good idea, now Diana and Charles were no longer little children, that everyone ate lunch together in the dining room. The same for breakfast when the two older girls were at home, although during term time it was more convenient to eat in the nursery. Lunch, once established in the dining room, became a fixture. This gave everyone more contact with each other and contributed to a more normal family life which is what he wanted. I thought it time to do away with the 'upstairs, downstairs' pattern as far as the children were concerned. Lord Althorp readily agreed with my suggestion that it would be much more pleasant to have the children with him and make full use of the lovely dining room.

The staff, from the old school, including Betts, the new butler who had recently started, were rather taken aback by the idea, although Mrs Smith took quite a pleasure in the hesitation with which Betts greeted my innovation. She thought it would cut him down to size as she considered he had rather grand ideas about himself. Betts, certainly, was not happy at the prospect of having to wait upon children. Later he was to become even more dismayed when he discovered that this service was also expected of him even when Lord Althorp was away. Sarah, Diana and I were to derive great pleasure from these meals. The idea, presented and approved, was implemented immediately and proved to be a great success, helping to break down uneasy barriers between the father and the children. As they now saw more of him, it was much easier for them all to communicate and their relationships became much more relaxed. Before lunch downstairs became a permanent feature of everyday life, the children would only eat in the dining room when there were visitors; thus the occasion was often tense. Otherwise the only meal Lord Althorp shared with the children was when he joined us for tea in the nursery. These had been uncomfortable occasions with an unnatural, stilted conversation instigated by the father with the children replying in polite monosyllables. I determined to put an end to this as soon as I possibly could and the unnatural atmosphere caused me to put forward my suggestion for change quicker than I would otherwise have done. Still, once implemented, when Lord Althorp did come for tea, as the children were now used to eating with their father, conversation flowed much more easily.

So the house was usually full and rang with shouts and laughter. For all the children it was a golden time, at least during the period I lived there, with the divorce well behind them; a childhood full of love and free from petty restrictions. Many children would have envied them. Easy as time goes by and the child grows older, to listen to other stories, not always to remember accurately, but to confuse truth with fiction, to read psychological meanings into situations that did not exist. Yes, the parents' marriage had broken up but the home was not broken. It was full of people, not least their father, who really loved and cared for the welfare of his children. They were cocooned and guarded from the realities of the world and allowed to enjoy their childhood largely free of cares and worries experienced by so many other children whose parents are still together. For the Spencer children, there were no financial worries and that is the root of many of today's social problems.

We settled to enjoy the Easter holidays. I was totally unaware of the cloud that was forming over my head, one which would erupt at the end of the school holidays, and disrupt the peace I had so quickly found at Sandringham. It would not affect the children, who were to know nothing of it, but the experience would stay with me always, as I was summoned to the High Court as the main pawn in the parents' struggle for custody of their children when old wounds were again re-opened and I was called upon to answer for my actions and defend my job and my capabilities.

First though, the Easter holidays.

Chapter Four

I t was the first full day of the Easter holidays. Even upon waking, the atmosphere in the house felt different. A family home, it exuded a charged, vibrant feel. From the outset I learnt to say 'goodbye' to my luxurious solitary early mornings, because Diana – completely the opposite to her young brother who was content to lie in bed and dream until I asked him to get up – was up and about at first light, anxious to get on with all her self-set tasks. She liked to be on the move and was determined not to waste one moment of her precious holidays by lolling around in bed.

After a quick wash and pulling on any old clothes (she was not then in the least bit interested in what she wore), the older the clothes, the more practical and suitable for the outdoor jobs that lay ahead, she was ready for the day. Most important was the need to attend to her guinea-pig and to assure herself that it had survived the change in environment and had not suffered withdrawal symptoms from the lack of a school bell announcing freedom for its young owner and subsequently care, attention and food for itself. I went to greet her to ask how long these pre-breakfast duties would take. I can remember consciously making a point of keeping our conversations as natural as possible, as if we had been having chats for months and that this first day was nothing strange or new. I wanted to establish an easy-going atmosphere that allowed no room for tension or discord. Park House was Diana's home, I knew she did not want change and hoped that all would be the same with no hassle and I was determined that she should realize at once that this was the way it would be. There would, however, be some practical changes and I told Diana that for the first morning only, we would eat breakfast in the nursery, but afterwards we would do so in the dining room. Diana questioned me about this, slightly dubious as to whether it was a change for the better, remembering the somewhat stilted teatime sessions in the nursery with her father and wondering if it would be the same at breakfast; when I said the more meal-times that were spent together as a family, the more relaxed they would become, she was happy enough. Her mischievous spirit grasped the positive side of the situation and took delight in the prospect that the cook would not be enamoured with the change, favouring more traditional arrangements. I told Diana that upsetting the cook was irrelevant and not the point of the exercise; spending more time with her father was the important factor. I was keen to generate a light-hearted, fun atmosphere in the home and in our relationships, but not have it directed against other people.

During this exchange, Diana tried to be polite and stand still to listen, but clearly she had one thing on her mind: to get outside. I gave her half an hour for her immediate tasks and told her I would like her to help me in the kitchen to carry the breakfast to the nursery. She liked to help and I thought it good that she should be involved in our daily routine from the start. Released, she charged off along the corridor, down the back stairs and through the door leading into the courtyard, slamming it behind her in her rush to get outside. The first two weeks were to be spent with her father and then the next two weeks with her mother before returning to Norfolk and school. Diana never told me about her stays with her mother.

I went to check the horses. They seemed contented, so I wandered over to the hutches to discuss the welfare of the guinea-pig. He was certainly a fine looking specimen reflecting the care lavished upon him. Diana said she was ready to help me, so I asked her to run and see if brother Charles was up and about and if he was not to tell him breakfast would be ready in a few moments so he had better hurry. Given the opportunity to issue an order to her brother, Diana was off like a shot and I called after her that we would meet in the kitchen. She was always so willing to help me in any way that she could. There was never any rebellion or defiance.

In the kitchen Diana chatted away about plans for her holiday and I asked her if she spent her time in a similar way when she was with her mother. I wanted her to be aware that there was no taboo subject. I told her I would contact her friends and make arrangements for them to visit. Diana in turn would be invited to their homes. She preferred that they came to us, as she liked to be on home ground with all her familiar things around her. The way we lived was very relaxed, offered few restrictions and a great deal of freedom which was never abused but was very character-forming. Diana loved her home and she loved Norfolk. In a letter from Diana in December 1978, long after my work there was finished and the family had moved to Althorp Hall, she wrote, 'We all miss Norfolk terribly as that's where our roots are . . .' Even three years later in another letter, written when she was Princess of Wales and had returned to Norfolk for the winter stay at Sandringham House, Diana expressed her love for the county. 'How I envy you living back in Norfolk – we spent two weeks there,' and said how sad she was to see her childhood home empty and forlorn. It is wonderful that it has now been put to such good use as one of the Cheshire homes giving holidays to the handicapped and as much happiness, it is hoped, as when we lived there.

The temporary cook, a small, neat, grey-haired lady, gave us our breakfast trays with all the items needed to take upstairs. The children were happy with cereal and toast, along with an assortment of spreads. This meal was not a prolonged affair as we were all keen to get on with the day. We discussed the general routine for the holiday. Lunch we would eat in the dining room at 12.30 p.m. and tea in the nursery at 5 p.m. I told Diana and Charles that they had to go to bed by 8 p.m. Diana said that as she was older she should be allowed to stay up longer. I agreed that in deference to her years, she could keep her light on for an extra half an hour. In the event, the days were so full and active that no one ever complained about going to bed. I told them I expected them to keep their rooms and the nursery tidy and that if they helped me, I would do all I could to comply with their wishes as I would have more time and by us all working together we would all benefit. Mrs Smith had the task of going through the trunk, so it had been left in the linen room. She also did all the washing and ironing. I just had to collect all the clothes that needed washing and leave them in the utility room. I told Diana that at some time we must prepare a list of clothes she would need to replace ones she had grown out of but that need not be done immediately as it was better for Mrs Smith to get everything clean first.

Mrs Loyd telephoned the first morning to make arrangements

for Diana and Charles to go to her house for tea. I was also invited as she thought it would be an opportunity for her to introduce me to the girl who helped with *her* children and who did some work about the house. Not many people in similar jobs to mine were quite so lucky as I and expected to care purely for the children with no extra domestic duties thrown in. The longer I stayed and the more people I met, the more I appreciated just how lucky I was. I also felt my job was made easier by being the only woman in charge of the children when they were in Norfolk. My word was law. I did not have to consult with a mother and could always use my own judgement so there was never any risk of conflicting opinions. Lord Althorp had had the confidence to offer me the job and he had the belief that I would do the work well. He trusted in my abilities and left me to my own devices, although I am sure he observed from afar. It was kind of Mrs Loyd as it gave me the opportunity to meet someone of my own age and I readily accepted the invitation.

The breakfast things cleared away, I told the children they were free to do as they wished. I wanted to give them a chance to settle with each other and with me. I did not want them to think that I intended to monopolize every moment of their time. I was always on hand if I was needed. Diana chose to spend some of her time with Sarah, but their age difference meant that they had separate interests and although Diana hero-worshipped Sarah, she did not spend so much time with her that her own character was influenced. Sarah was also aware that her father and Charles were happy with me, so there was no need to put her younger sister up to any tricks. As the holidays wore on, Sarah and I got to know each other and enjoyed each other's company. Our mutual love of horses was a great help in forming the basis of our relationship.

It was not long before I followed the children outside. Like Diana, I preferred to be out rather than in. They were watching the antics of Diana's guinea-pig which she had released from the cage and allowed the freedom of the great outdoors. Diligent surveillance was required as the large ginger cat, named Marmaduke, stalked nearby anticipating an easy target and a quick mid-morning snack. I told them I was going to walk the dogs and they said they would like to come with me. This pleased me and I suggested it would be an ideal opportunity to look for a suitable place to make a den, an essential part of every child's holiday, a hide-away and a base for any number of games. They thought this was a great idea. Charles could visualize it as a good headquarters for his army encampment and Diana quickly decided it would make an ideal alternative home and immediately thought of all the items she could put in to make it comfortable. So we set off on our exploratory walk with me reminding Diana that she must not take anything from the kitchen without first asking the cook.

The cook left at about this time. There were thus a few days when we had no cook and Mrs Smith stood in and worked in the kitchen to prepare the meals, a job she had always carried out on the cook's day off. Lord Althorp tried to make these days as easy as possible and was often out to dinner. I remember clearly the mantelpiece in the drawing room and the huge number of invitations that stood on it. When I first saw it, I could not believe that one person could get so many printed and engraved invitations, which previously I thought were reserved purely for marriages and perhaps christenings. In my experience, a telephone call or a quick note were more common. Lord Althorp was obviously a very sought-after and popular dinner guest. He had many loyal friends who stood by him throughout his single years after the departure of his wife.

Diana and I planned to help Mrs Smith as much as possible and one morning we experimented with bread-making. The large Aga that stood in the fireplace in the kitchen was ideal for this with its different oven temperatures. The results of our labour did not compete with those of the local bakery but Diana's father loyally chewed his way through a few slices, declaring them to be 'a remarkable first effort'. No parent could have given more encouragement and helped build the confidence of his daughter than that given by the children's father.

A few days into the Easter holidays, the new cook and her husband, the butler to be, Betts, arrived. It was one of the butler's tasks to look after Lord Althorp's clothes. I had never met a butler before and found it difficult to imagine that anyone would be happy to spend their life, in this day and age, waiting on someone else; it just seemed so menial. None the less, he fitted into my image of a butler. This was only based on ideas gleaned from books and plays written at the turn of the century. He reminded me of

Jeeves. With his pompous attitude, he was an ideal butt for Diana's jokes. I was amused by many of her remarks, but I did not let myself appear to condone them.

On that first morning we had put on Wellington boots as we intended to walk in the woods and parkland, and the undergrowth remained very wet as it was rarely allowed to experience any warmth from the spring's intermittent sun due to the dense foliage from the trees, which still failed to prevent the penetration of frequent showers. So we remained very wet as we walked in the long grass in the park. We called the dogs, Bray, Jill and Suski, the old keeshond (Dutch barge dog), and with Smith's instructions to make sure we did not allow the dogs to chase any of the pheasants or partridges, we went on our way. We passed by the tennis court, with its net hanging limp and folded over and where a few sturdy weeds pushed their way resolutely through the hard surface. Tennis, along with swimming, was classified as a summer activity, the cold Norfolk winds acting as able deterrents to any premature enthusiasm. So we entered the darkness of the woods. Diana chatted on, as exuberant as her brother was quiet. Suski trotted quietly behind us while Diana and the other two dogs rushed backwards and forwards, examining the foliage for any signs of wildlife. In the woods it was always so quiet and peaceful except for the scramblings of mice and other wood folk as they rushed for cover, aided in their race to safety by the boisterous proximity of Diana and the dogs. I suggested that it might be a better idea to have the den nearer to home rather than in the depths of the woods; perhaps somewhere suitable could be found in the huge shrubs that bordered the woods, so they would be closer to amenities and not too far away from the house to make carrying goods a difficult task. We found a badger's sett and several birds' nests. I warned them against touching the eggs, otherwise the mother bird would desert the nest.

As we walked, I told Diana and Charles stories from my own country childhood, how my twin brother and I used to spend our holidays when we were their age. I said we had no woods so near to us, but we had an orchard, separated from the road that led to our village shop, by a high hedge. How one of us used to climb a tree for look-out duty and tell the other one who was lurking behind the hedge with a plastic bottle full of water waiting for a poor unsuspecting customer to walk by. How on cue they got liberally soaked. Diana had the comics that I had loved in my childhood, *Bunty* and *Judy*. I told her how I used to love the story of the *Four Marys* who were at boarding school. This story still ran in the comic so Diana knew what I was talking about. One episode described how they wrote the words 'Beware of the Avengers' everywhere. As a child I had told my brother of this and, not knowing what the word 'avenger' meant and being too impulsive to waste time to try and find out, we wrote it in chalk on the floor of a neighbour's garage which was rented from my parents. We then forgot all about our prank until a few days later, playing in our barn, the local policeman walked in and asked us if we had any idea who the 'avengers' might be, and we said, 'Yes, us.' We had to follow him to our home where a discreet word in my parents' ears, followed by a sharp reprimand, were punishment enough to ensure there would not be a repeat. Such innocent stories of childhood fun, when the local bobby rode around the village on his bicycle, before the violence and crime of today's magnitude could even be envisaged. I privately thought the man who called in the policeman must have had a guilty conscience! Charles and Diana loved my stories, especially Diana who could empathize with the mischievous tales from my own childhood with her own idea of fun.

Diana asked about the schools I had gone to and I told them of the little village primary school where children between five and eleven years old were all in one classroom and how we gathered around a large open fire in the winter to keep warm and to do our lessons. 'Does it still exist?' she wondered. I told her 'No'. Like so many schools as the population of the village got smaller it was closed, sold and converted into a private home. Diana told me of Silfield, but spoke little of it, for she obviously connected it to the unsettled period in her life when the relationship between her parents was not good. Much as they tried to hide their differences from the children, even youngsters are sensitive to the atmosphere around them and Diana was happy to put that part of her life behind her when she had settled well at Riddlesworth. Little was to be gained from resurrecting the past. Silfield was a small family school which taught on similar lines in which Diana had been initiated by Ally, the governess. Gertrude Allen had taught Diana's mother, her brother and sister a generation earlier when she had been in the employ of the Fermoys at Park House. In those days they called her 'Gert'. To Sarah, Jane and Diana and to the ten to twelve other children, including the local doctor's son, she was known as 'Ally'. She came every weekday morning from her cottage in Dersingham two miles away to teach them in the downstairs room set aside as the classroom between the kitchen and the drawing room. All the children were allowed to work at their own pace, necessary because of the differences in their ages. Each day started with a roll call and it was here in the classroom at Park House that Diana was introduced to history for the first time and heard stories of kings and queens. At Silfield the three 'R's and discipline, combined with a selection of outdoor activities, team games, netball and rounders. Diana, once she had got used to being around more children, mixed well, was cheerful and bright and, I was told, did not appear to carry scars from the changed life at home. Riddlesworth, similar to Silfield in the principles it emphasized, was larger and, being boarding, provided a twenty-four-hour family school atmosphere.

As we moved deeper into the woods, I instructed them never to come there on their own; it was perfectly safe, but I could just imagine how difficult it would be for me to find them. We saw grey squirrels leaping from branch to branch, tree to tree, only the silent shaking of the leaves giving indication of the inhabitants they could hide. I told the children about the woods we played in as children, when we went for Sunday outings with our parents. In these woods, a fairy was meant to hide in a clearing in the middle and if we managed to spot her it was considered to be very lucky. Diana wanted to know if I believed in fairies and had I ever seen the one in the woods? She was at the age, on that strange bridge between childhood and adulthood, still deriving pleasure from childhood ideas yet pleased to be able to think as an adult. All the time she was growing more aware of older attitudes and her inquisitive mind was keen to find out the secrets of womanhood. In reply to her question of whether I believed in fairies, I told her of a vision I had as a child, when, as I lay in my bed, I was sure I saw a chain of fairies dancing at the top of the stairs that led into my bedroom. I was convinced it was real and not a dream.

My stories appealed to Diana's imagination. Charles listened, but asked few questions, preferring to let Diana take the limelight.

It was as if he knew he had me to himself when Diana was away, and in the meantime he was content to take a back seat. At the time I thought what a marvellous mother Diana would make as she always threw herself wholeheartedly into everything and I could imagine with her own children she would remember and, even as an adult, still relate to childhood thoughts and pleasures.

Woodland gave way to the park, acre upon acre of rolling, undulating grasslands, interspersed with oak and beech trees. It stretched from Sandringham to West Newton and to the road that led to Wolferton. We turned and looked back, up a slight hill, to see Park House, the cricket grounds and the paddocks. To the right stood the vicarage and the church which attracted so many visitors, particularly during January when the royal family were in attendance. Further to the right, from the parkland view, stood Sandringham House with its beautifully laid out gardens, its well-kept lawns, rockeries and a large lake. It was a very popular place for tourists to visit when it was open to the public during the summer months.

Diana pointed out the Loyds' house that lay further down the park towards West Newton and where we were to have tea that afternoon. We turned and walked back to the house across the parkland. In the distance we could see the horses grazing in the paddocks. Charles told me that his father wanted him to learn to ride and that he was keen to do so, but Diana, much as she loved animals, said she was not in the least bit interested as she was too nervous. I told her that in that case there really was no point, there were plenty of other things to do and as even the quietest horse is able to sense fear and may act out of character it would not be worth the risk. Later it was to prove that, even though I had put no pressure on Diana to ride, indeed had advised against it, she was keen to have a go especially as it was a hobby so enjoyed by Sarah and myself. How many children fall into this category, that when not forced to do something, choose, of their own free will, to do just that? Diana was no exception to the rule.

The parkland was beautiful in the early spring, so green and lush. Larks rose from the ground, singing their hearts out as they soared towards the heavens. Pheasants and partridges, hiding in the grass, rose at our feet but not due to any encouragement from our dogs whom we kept under strict control following Smith's instructions. Game birds sent the dogs into fits of excitement but we had to keep them quiet and calm as it was the nesting season and it was considered a grave sin to disturb the birds at such a time. It was very important to let them survive in the spring so they could be shot during the winter! I told the children that my brother and I had been taught to use an air rifle as children, only for target practice or to shoot tin cans off a wall. Diana said that her father had had a gun made for Charles, but Charles was very reticent on this subject, it was obvious that shooting tin cans was acceptable, but shooting birds was a different matter altogether. However, it is a part of English country life and Charles already knew it was expected of him to become proficient with the gun but he shared with Diana the dislike of unnecessary killing.

We neared the house and here we saw the swallows taking time off from building their nests in the eaves as they joyfully skimmed low over the swimming pool, quenching their thirst in flight, to return again refreshed to the task of home-making. So we returned to Park House. The walk had been enjoyable and entertaining, even though the main objective, that of finding a den, had not been achieved. We decided to postpone that event until the morrow. In the meantime we were hungry and it was time for lunch.

Lunch that first day of the holidays was to set a precedent for the future. It was the move from nursery to dining room, a step from childhood to adulthood. From the outset it was a success. Sarah joined us and Lord Althorp was clearly thrilled to have his family around him. He certainly had no regrets that his solitary lunches had come to an end. Betts had yet to appear on the scene, so Mrs Smith had placed the food on a hot trolley and we helped ourselves. There was a very relaxed air, which had never really been achieved during Lord Althorp's visits for tea in the nursery. A large, well-built man, he always looked out of place at the nursery table. Here in his natural environment, with Sarah enlarging on her plans and Diana and Charles recounting the events of the morning, the meal passed in a very affable manner.

After lunch, I suggested some time spent indoors and told them they must change before tea at the Loyds. Both were very willing to amuse themselves, so I did not have to spend all my time with them. However, I took the opportunity quickly to go through with Diana the clothes she had grown out of and which could be put aside for the jumble sale. This chore finished, Diana decided to reorganize her room in the way she wanted it for the holiday. I found Charles in the nursery; he really appreciated his quiet times there, involved in an imaginary war with his soldiers, so I sat and read until it was time for our departure.

At about 4 p.m. we drove to the Loyds' house at West Newton. The children went off to play and I met the nanny, an Australian girl with whom I immediately got on well. She helped to care for the children, but she also had work to do in the house. She was working her way round the world and really seemed to be happy to have the opportunity to have a job in such a lovely environment. It would make a good tale for folks back home! We had a nursery tea of sandwiches and cake.

I never could really get used to the idea of a them and us situation and was extremely pleased that we had made a compromise at Park House. One of the things that I learnt during my time at Sandringham, was that people with 'old' money were much more natural than those 'nouveau riche'; they were the real snobs, not the old titled gentry. The other revelation that came as quite a surprise to me, was that money certainly does not necessarily bring happiness. I never met any truly happy adults in all the time I was there. Perhaps there might have been some, but they did not appear to be any such people. Those with no money might well say, 'Give me a chance and I'll show you how to be happy', but money brings its own problems. It was quite a shock to a girl of my age then to acknowledge this fact as I had always worked on the assumption that having money would solve all problems. In fact, it does not and actually goes a long way to create others. It is, of course, wonderful not to have the constant worry about where the next shilling might come from. The inhabitants of Park House and the other homes I visited during my time at Sandringham certainly did not have that worry.

We only stayed for two hours, just long enough for the children to play and have tea. The Loyds' son, Charles, was older than Diana's brother and there was a younger sister of three years and, of course, Alexandra, but apart from sharing the same school and the fact that they lived near to each other, they had little in common and Diana was always pleased to return to her own home. I did make arrangements for Alexandra to visit the following week along with her nanny. We did not make too many outings, as two weeks is not a long holiday and Diana preferred to have free time rather than be too organized or her days fully committed. She did try and persuade her father to ask Smith to prepare the swimming pool, but it was far too cold and he told her she must wait for her next break from school.

The first day was over and the plans and priorities for the holidays had been established. Top on the list was to find a suitable setting for the den. I told Charles and Diana to make a search and choose one or two suitable venues, then I would come and inspect them and together we would make a choice. So began the search for a den for Diana to transform into an outdoor home. They were spoilt for choice with the many ideal spots available. They were both determined and enthusiastic to find a good spot and it was not long before my advice was sought. A group of large, overgrown shrubs with a clearing in the centre and a natural formed roof overhead, where the branches had reached out and joined, proved the ideal choice. Closed in on all sides, as if walled, it prevented spying from enemy and adults alike. It made the perfect hiding place, a sanctuary for them to enact whatever roles they chose to play. I suggested they clear the ground area that would be the floor while I went to telephone Annabel Fox's mother to ask if Annabel would like to come over the next day along with Giles, one of Charles's friends. Clearly the girls would derive fun from preparing the den while Charles would be able to use it as base camp for his games.

As promised, I made the arrangements along with further plans for the following week when the invitations would be reciprocated. I would have a two-week break when the children went to their mother so I did not take time off during the first part of the holidays. It did give me a bit of a break when the children went out for the day, otherwise, if their father was at home, I might go off for an hour to ride, but I never went far from the house if he was away. I shared with the mothers the journeys to and fro, preferring to take Charles and Diana to their friends, but to deliver their friends at the end of the day in case they should tire of each other's company, when it would be up to me to end the visit. In fact this never happened. In such a natural playground, children would have to be very difficult and bored not to be able to amuse themselves for a few hours.

However busy Diana was she never skimped the care for her guinea-pig, Peanuts. She had little time to spend on inanimate toys such as dolls, preferring to get feedback from living things. She was sure the guinea-pig should become domesticated but I would have disagreed with her. Charles's hamster, a considerably smaller pet, did live in his cage in the house. Diana called it favouritism towards the smaller animal. I told her the guinea-pig was used to living outside at school and it would not be right to change its environment completely by bringing it indoors, as it would only make it more difficult for Peanuts to settle outside again. This argument seemed to settle the matter. I liked all animals, but believed that they must be kept in their place, and in this instance that place was the hutch. It was soon to be clear that Diana did not agree with my sentiments for not long after we had this discussion, when I was otherwise occupied, the guinea-pig made a cameo appearance in the nursery. 'Just to give it a break,' said Diana. 'It's bored being outside in its hutch.' 'Can a guinea-pig get bored,' I asked myself and gave instructions for it to be removed immediately. It had already proved that being house-trained was not one of its accomplishments but it did appear to understand my instructions, for it took the opportunity of the open nursery door to make its escape along the corridor heading for the great outdoors. I told Diana if she was not careful it would disappear outside. The fear of losing her beloved Peanuts persuaded Diana the right course of action was to comply with my wishes and put it safely back in its cage.

It was a typical English spring with the weather constantly changing. We spent as much time as possible outdoors. Sometimes the children chose to walk the dogs with me, but sometimes I walked alone. Our walks gave us the ideal opportunity to talk. Diana never tired of tales from my childhood. I told her that during the long summer holidays we always had a central theme and some of the children from the village would join us; my favourite had been the year we had a circus. Charles said he really liked the clowns in the circus, while Diana was fascinated by the high-flying trapeze artists. She was curious to know how well I got on with my parents, and if as a child I had often got into trouble. I said that every summer we loved to help with the harvest in the fields owned by my parents, which were behind our house. It was in these same fields that we would fly our kites. This was one of my favourite pastimes. I used to wish that I could fly free in the sky like my kite, just an ordinary windjammer, as a child's drawing of a kite would show, not a complicated two-string version. I made the tail for my kite from strips of newspaper and string. Diana was interested to hear the story of how my kite got me into serious trouble with my parents because, one fine windy day, I flew it in the fields just before the corn was cut. They were so angry that I had trampled the corn that I was sent to my room. Thus were the misdemeanours of the 1950s punished – how times have changed!

We talked about dreams. Diana told me that when her mother first left her nights were very troubled but she could not remember any real dreams, she was just sad, but there were many people in the house and the deep sadness soon passed and once she could see both her parents properly again, she was all right. Diana wanted to know about my dreams, but I said that I had forgotten most of them. The only one I could clearly recall, and that because I had dreamed it so often, was set in those same harvest fields where I had flown my kite. In my dream, I would have to run and run until my feet left the ground and I soared upwards into the sky, higher than the clouds, I was able to fly down low and then swoop upwards again. Diana had never had such a dream – apparently it is a common one – and she wondered if I still dreamt it. I told her that I had not for several years. Many years later, in 1990, I wrote to her and reminded her of the 'flying dream' and said that I had just returned from a trip to Kashmir and while I was trekking in the Himalayas with my son, I had the same dream, but in a different setting. At the time I was so surprised that upon waking I wrote it down, lest I should forget, and I recalled the talk Diana and I had had so many years before. Perhaps Diana did not remember our talk, because by the time I wrote to her she was too caught up in the reality of her disastrous marriage to pay any regard to dreams and talk of childhood.

Diana loved to talk about what she would do when she grew up. She wanted to know if at her age I had any plans. When she said she would like to care for children, either as a nurse or a teacher, because being a ballet dancer was not a realistic idea due to her height, I told her my mother would have loved me to have had the same ambition. When I used to be questioned by her friends on 'what do you want to do when you grow up', I would send her into despair by announcing that I wished to be a gypsy or to join a circus as a bare-back rider. The only basis on which I chose these 'careers' was that I felt they would enable me to travel. Diana wanted to know why I was so anxious to leave home. Had I been unhappy? I assured her that this was not the case; mine was a secure, happy home but I just wanted to be free. She, experiencing insecurity in her young life, could not relate to this, as my childhood, with its tight family unit, seemed to her to be ideal.

Like the majority of children Diana was very competitive. We set out a hopscotch square in the courtyard and had great fun seeing who could complete the square first. Sarah would often join in and there was much hilarity. Tall for her age but quick and nimble, Diana proved a worthy competitor. There used to be so many games that gave much pleasure and fun which we seldom see practised today. What happened to them? Perhaps their disappearance is due to the fact that they are not computerized! Therefore apart from our walks, full of light-hearted conversations and stories, we played hopscotch, held competitions with hula-hoops and skipped, the hard-floored courtyard proving a good base for these activities near to home.

Naturally, at times it really did rain; then we were stranded indoors. With a bright fire blazing in the hearth, through the windows we watched the rain falling over the park in a sheet which obliterated all thoughts of sun and walks, making us feel closed in, safe and secure in the warm world I tried to create. These times gave us an opportunity to indulge in one of Diana's loves, that of play-acting, dancing and singing. When I was a child I too used to love to act and sing but I was always too shy to do this in front of my parents. Remembering this, I encouraged Diana to act out whatever role was on the cards for the day. I told her how I used to hide away with my second cousin in the old thatched barn on her father's farm and how we used the stacked straw bales for our stage and took turns to act out our songs with only the other person for an audience. Diana's audience was only slightly bigger than mine – her brother – and he was a rather indifferent spectator.

Diana's preference was to sing and dance, but she threw herself completely into her roles.

I told the children that in the old farmhouse where my cousin lived there was a ghost. Neither Diana nor Charles were sure if they believed in ghosts. Diana thought they might exist in really old places but said she would 'die' if she saw one. Charles thought it was a 'load of rubbish', possibly just to hold opposite views to his sister. Diana was curious to know if my cousin had ever seen the ghost. I explained to them the practice of exorcism and how this particular ghost had been shut away in a cupboard. For many years the house was ghost-free until, unwittingly, one day the cupboard had been opened and the ghost was again free. Soon after this occurrence, my cousin saw the ghost at the end of her bed. Accused of being over-imaginative by her father, she insisted it was true and persuaded him to sit in her room one night. With bated breath, the children waited for the outcome of my story and were amazed when I told them that her father too saw the ghost. Once I had recounted this story, I was rather afraid that it might create disturbed nights, so I hastened to assure them that there was no ghost at Park House, they did not just appear, everyone would know if one existed.

With both Charles and Diana I tried to instil and share my love of poetry, hoping that the beauty of the words and the pictures they conjured up would fire their imagination and would help to introduce them to the world that lay outside their safe cocoon. They had plenty of opportunity to be aware of this world. Their father did his best to bring them up to be similar to other children. They were taught to appreciate the life they had, free from financial stress. They did not lack the essentials, but neither did they take anything for granted. They were very conscious that for so many people life was very different and the main task of each day would be to survive and get through to the next. In no way did Lord Althorp spoil them with excessive material possessions.

The children had close ties with the royal family, but they were not royal, so they had plenty of opportunity to mix freely and have a relatively normal upbringing. This has stood Diana in good stead in her married life and formed the basis of her instinctive way of communicating with everyone. This is because she understands them, their hopes and their fears and the day-to-day pressure of everyday living. Through her own experiences of a happy child-hood, even though it was touched by trauma during her parents' separation; through the experience of her own marriage break-down, she has personally experienced emotions that afflict so many. Thus in all spheres of life she has either personal examples or a natural understanding of ordinary people to help her conduct her duties with warmth and sincerity. It is because of her natural, open manner that people relate so easily with her. There would have been no better person to shape a future People's King than Diana, with her natural understanding of the public, fashioned as it was during her own childhood.

Charles did not take part in the singing and play-acting. He called Diana a show-off, which she was, in a way. She loved to play to an audience, mostly having to make do with her unimpressed brother and myself. In many areas, Diana did not excel. Her academic achievements were negligible so she sensibly glossed over this and concentrated more on those subjects in which she was more confident. These tended to be practical and sporty, such as her swimming, and they supplied an excellent platform for her talents. Her natural instinct told her when she could get away with little pranks, or when it was better to simply fade into the background. No one has ever pretended that Diana was academic-ally bright, but another of her attributes — her disarming honesty and her ability to laugh at herself and her own failings — has defied anyone who tries to mock this lack of qualifications. Her abundant common sense, which is not so common and in many ways is much more valuable than other qualifications, has stood her in good stead from childhood through to adulthood.

In the evenings and before bedtime, we sat by the fire reading and talking. Diana had been initiated in the art of cats' cradles — making complex patterns with wool and fingers — at Riddlesworth and she was keen to practise her skill with me. I also showed her some of the patterns I remembered from my own childhood; there are certain things that never change. We played board games, Diana preferring draughts to the chess her brother played. She found that game too slow and tedious and it required too much thought if it was to be played properly. Very rarely did we watch television, there always seemed to be so many more interesting ways to spend our time.

The day after the site of the den was found Diana was up and about as early as usual, excited at the prospect of Annabel spending the day with her. She had not seen her friend since the previous holiday and there was a great deal of news to catch up on. Annabel was delivered at 11 a.m., about the same time as Charles's friend Giles arrived. I told the children they would be expected clean and tidy, ready for lunch by 1 p.m. otherwise the time was their own. Diana immediately took Annabel off to see the den, followed by Charles and Giles. The boys sensibly decided that equipping the den was more of a girl's task and, although unspoken, it was accepted that Diana's success rate at obtaining the items required would be higher, she seemed to be able to make the person to whom she made her request feel as if she had done them a favour by asking them to help her. The boys went off, happy to be on their own as in company Diana could tend to get 'bossy' on her home ground. The den, although meant to be shared by both Diana and Charles, immediately became Diana's territory and she appointed herself in charge, issuing orders as to where items should go and sending people to fetch things while she stayed and organized all, liking to think she held command. 'Go to the kitchen and ask cook for another plate,' she might demand of Charles. Her brother would promptly tell her to go herself. Guests, far too polite and not wanting to offend Diana, would rather pluck up the courage to face the cook than let Diana down. Charles had an army outfit as did Giles, so commandos were the order of the day with a tree trunk near the swimming pool acting as the look-out tower.

Diana and Annabel made an inventory of the necessities required for the den and went in search of Mrs Smith, who they felt sure would help furnish them with the necessary items. Mrs Smith complied with their wishes and proved as willing to help as had been hoped. Perhaps she thought her assistance would keep the girls occupied and out of the house and hopefully out of mischief. An old rug, cups, cutlery, vase for wild flowers, to add a homely touch, some plates and off they went. At lunch, they told Lord Althorp their plans and invited him to see the den now that it was complete. I asked where they would get the flowers and as it was a small vase, suggested we went on a search for primroses. Parts of the woods were blanketed with flowers of different colours depending on the time of year. Snowdrops, crocuses, anemones

54

and a carpet of blue in May and June with the bluebells, while in March and April, large patches of yellow appeared across the park when the daffodils danced merrily, stirred by the wind under the trees. To find the primroses, I said it would be better to look along the banks and hedgerows in the park. I loved spring, it was my favourite time of the year and always seemed to be full of hope; it was wonderful to see everything green again after the dismal grey gloom of winter. Lunch over, the boys did not want to join in this expedition and went back to their game. We put on our boots, the long grasslands of the park boggy with constant showers, and set off in search for the small yellow faces of spring – the primroses. We were lucky and soon found some clumps of flowers, many hidden in the undergrowth that with recent rains had grown at a frantic rate, almost, it seemed, in an attempt to obscure all the beauty. Some were protected by nettles and we decided there were plenty of others in less risky places. I told the girls to pick the primrose stems as long as possible and to make the flowers into little posies surrounded by their wide green leaves. The bunch for the den was soon gathered, but Diana thought that Mrs Smith might like some for her flat, a kind, instinctive gesture on Diana's part, typical both of the child and the woman. Annabel decided she would like to take some home to her mother. When these were collected, I persuaded them to take only what was needed and leave the rest to grow wild and free in their natural habitation, as wild flowers never last long indoors.

On our return to the house I left the children to their own devices and organized the tea in the nursery. The day had been another success and all the children were tired but happy. During every holiday friends would visit and add another dimension of pleasure to an already contented environment, which is the over-riding memory that I have carried with myself during the years since I lived at Sandringham. In the same way I always recall that the weather was fine. Obviously there was rain, in fact the records show that it often rained, likewise there must have been days that did not run so smoothly and were infiltrated by moods, but they were too insignificant to have made a lasting impression on me.

Chapter Five

The days passed by peacefully. One of the only bones of contention was the attitude of some of the other members of staff towards me. Most were old retainers and I did not fit into their idea of what a 'nanny' should be. My main concern was the children and I always felt relaxed wherever I was, upstairs or downstairs.

The butler, who arrived soon after the start of the Easter holidays, did not take too kindly to me, resenting the way in which I mixed with the people 'upstairs'. Lord Althorp gave him instructions that regardless of whether he was with us or not when we ate in the dining room we were to have the same treatment even though our meals were simple. Sarah and Diana took great delight at Betts's discomfort and his obvious abhorrence at having to wait on just 'children and the nanny'. Only his knowledge that he had a very good job which he did not wish to jeopardize, prevented him from expressing his feelings on the subject to Lord Althorp. He was bright enough to realize that any sign of antagonism towards the children was a sure way towards a hasty exit unless, of course, it was justified. Lord Althorp was a very fair man and in that event he would sympathize and try to amend the situation. However, the girls did not waste a chance to lord it over Betts and had he been more amenable to me, I could have found it in my heart to feel sorry for him as the joined forces of Sarah and Diana were truly something to be reckoned with. As it was, although I tactfully pointed out to the girls that this was not really the correct way to behave, I did not persist as I rather tended to side with them and thought Betts could be brought down a peg or two, his manner was so arrogant. The rest of the staff could not resist a private giggle behind closed doors, but neither did they lose the chance to criticize me for what they took to be my slack approach to the girls' behaviour. I learnt very quickly to ignore all such comments. We

56

This page and following two pages: Diana growing from a toddler into a young woman. (*Press Association*)

Me, with the new owner Pauline, saying goodbye to Sarah's horse Peppermint as she leaves for her last home. Lord Althorp borrowed a hunter to replace her for the remainder of my time at Park House.

From right to left, Charles and Sarah Spencer with John, a friend of Charles, and the Spencer dogs, Jill, Suski and Gitsie. They are sitting on the bonnet of the blue Simca that I used to fetch the children from school.

Above: Sarah accompanying us on a trip to the Norfolk seashore with the dogs Jill and Gitsie. The little girl in the background is Mrs Loyd's youngest daughter with her nanny, Barbara.

Left: Charles and friend Giles playing soldiers in the garden at Park House.

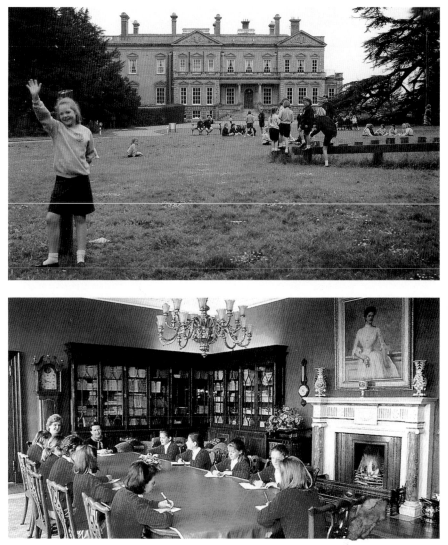

Above: Riddlesworth Hall, the prep school Diana attended while I was in the employ of the Spencers. (*Courtesy of Riddlesworth Hall*)

Bottom: Diana would have sat to write her letters home to me and the family at this table. (*Courtesy of Riddlesworth Hall*)

Top: Earl Spencer outside Althorp Hall, which he inherited in 1975. (*Press Association*)

Bottom: The late Earl Spencer gave this to me to remember my time with the family. Each of the names of the four children is engraved on it. The fifth disc carries the name of Park House and the dates I was employed there.

were so happy, there was so much to do that we had no need to make an issue of such a situation. We only wanted some light-hearted humour at lunchtime.

However, Betts's wife did produce good, hearty, wholesome meals that were thoroughly appreciated and enjoyed by all. The children ate everything that was put in front of them. They were not encouraged to be fussy, nor were they forced to eat what they might not like. Meal times were a chance for everyone to get together and catch up on news, not to have protracted conversations about whether something should or should not be eaten. Very little alcohol was consumed in the house. We all, including Lord Althorp, drank water with our meals, served in large glass jugs on the table.

One of our main outings that Easter holiday was to a local fair and jumble sale in the village hall. It was for this sale that Diana and I had sorted out all her old clothes to make a contribution. Lord Althorp, Charles, Diana and I all went in the Simca. We rarely travelled anywhere in Lord Althorp's Jaguar; he tended to use that for longer journeys, for his visits to London or to his parents' home, Althorp Hall. He was not very car-conscious and was certainly not concerned with making an 'appearance'; he cared more about easy and convenient parking and, of course, the Simca was much more economical. I was pleased to have an opportunity to wear some smarter clothes and managed to persuade Diana to wear a skirt and sweater instead of her favoured trousers. Charles, dressed in checked Viyella shirt, corduroy trousers and sweater, bore a striking resemblance to his father.

The fair consisted of the usual variety of stalls: one selling homemade cakes, biscuits and bread – we had not made a contribution – another full of locally grown produce, one of preserves and homemade wines, the delights of dandelion or nettle far out-weighing any of the best that the French might produce, if the vendors were to be believed! There were stalls encouraging people to roll a coin or throw a dart to win a cuddly toy, a stall selling knick-knacks and ornaments along with joke toys, the kind usually to be found in any seaside resort shop. The atmosphere was happy and carefree with everyone pulling their weight to do the best to boost village funds. Rotund, cheerful women, their clothes protected by pinafores, produced cups of tea and coffee and orange juice for the children, along with an assortment of cakes and sandwiches. Charles and Diana were free to wander and explore. Both had brought their pocket money with them and searched for gifts to take to their mother when they visited for the second part of their holiday. Diana also could not resist buying yet another cuddly toy to add to her collection.

Before they were sent off on their own, we had wandered around the room together. Lord Althorp, a tall, portly man, had towered over many and most were aware of his presence. Obviously very well-liked and popular, he knew many people by name and we spent much of the first fifteen minutes shaking hands as we were introduced first to one and then to another person. I was extremely relieved and pleased that in every instance I was introduced as 'This is Mary, she helps me care for the children', and the dreaded word 'nanny' was never used. It was a name that I would never be able to relate to and never needed to due to Lord Althorp's diplomacy. It is difficult to describe my dislike of being called 'nanny'. To me it conjures up visions of a person who has planned to make this a career, which is very worthy in itself, but not something that I had ever considered. The choice being made, real nannies then go to a college and become qualified or/and gain years of experience in their chosen field. They are often treated as a somewhat second-class person – working for a family but never treated quite as family, allowed to wield power in the nursery and highly respected in all probability by their employers, but never regarded as equals. Someone in uniform, part of a system, a type of servant. Twenty years on, this picture has greatly changed and the majority of nannies are now as I was then. My dislike stems from the way things were all those years ago and it is to those years that I relate.

I returned from looking at one stall to find them talking to an older man, introductions obviously over. As I stood there, the gentleman said, 'And this must be their sister?' which Lord Althorp absent-mindedly affirmed. Diana giggled, but then kept a straight face, but as soon as the man had moved on, I hoped she would not mention the subject as I was a little embarrassed. What a hope. She repeated it to her father – Diana could not resist an opportunity for a laugh at other people's expense as long as no malice was involved. Lord Althorp merely replied, 'Oh, did I?', which rather took the wind out of Diana's sails. As always when the children were introduced, they politely shook hands but still tended to look down. Charles, with whom I had spent more time, had greatly improved and usually managed to look up when gently reminded, but Diana still hovered on the border-line, trying to do as she had been asked but finding old habits hard to break. Eventually we left and drove back to Park House, our sanctuary, where we knew that within minutes the calmness and serenity of the surroundings would envelop us after the hectic excursion just experienced. Diana must often feel the same now, that at the end of her royal duties she has her own home to retreat to where she is able to derive comfort from its familiarity.

The children did not want outings or entertainment every day. They were happy with their own and each other's company. Surrounded by people all the time at school, they relished the peace their home gave to them. We did not have many visitors staying at Park House; certainly Lord Althorp went out to dinner on many more occasions than he entertained at home. During the Easter holidays though, some friends of the family from Denmark were expected for the weekend. We all duly attended lunch in the dining room on the Saturday, the atmosphere much more relaxed than it would have been before the move downstairs. This was because the dining room was no longer related to tensions and unease. Lunch there was now an everyday occurrence, the only extra dimension on this particular day being the Danish visitors, very easy-going people who did not exclude the children from their conversation. Sarah told them about the horses, especially Pepper-mint. They politely said they would like to see her. As lunch was finished, Sarah excused herself from the table and said she would go and fetch her and bring her up to the house. Diana asked if she could go with her.

I was rather surprised as Diana seldom spent time with the horses but I assumed she wanted an excuse to leave the table. We all retired to the drawing room. Normally it would be at this point that the children and I would leave Lord Althorp to his guests, but we decided to wait a few moments until Sarah arrived with the horse. Suddenly there was a commotion in the hall and into the drawing room – that beautiful room which could have proudly graced the covers of any magazine – walked Sarah, horse, metal shoes and all. The look on the guests' astonished faces and the bemused look on her father's face will not be easily forgotten. Surprise turned to laughter as Lord Althorp gently remonstrated with his mad-hatter eldest daughter. 'Sarah, I said UP to the house, not IN.' To say that the Danes were slightly taken aback is a true English understatement, but when they returned to their own country, their thank-you letter said that out of all their experiences during their visit to England, the sight of a large grey horse walking into the drawing room would remain the most memorable. It later materialized that the reason for such outlandish behaviour was that Diana, to liven up proceedings, could not resist the opportunity to dare Sarah to actually go inside, recipient as *she* so often was, of Sarah's dares. Sarah had no need to agree, but how could she let her younger sister get the better of her? She took up the challenge. It must be mentioned that such pranks were not commonplace and there was never a repeat of this incident. The children respected their home and appreciated the work done by the house staff to keep it in good order.

Alexandra and her nanny, Barbara, came for the day in response to the invitation of the previous week. Charles had another friend over, John, and again, apart from lunch and tea, the two groups played separately. Lord Althorp was away for the day and as it was the cook's day off, Barbara and I prepared the lunch and decided to eat in the nursery as Sarah was also away to visit friends. Diana immediately took Alexandra off to see the den that she had prepared with Annabel the previous week. In the intervening time, Diana and Charles had used it as a base for their games, but not for the game that Diana and Alexandra would play. They immediately got themselves involved in make-believe families after Alexandra had duly expressed her approval of the 'shrubland' home. Even in our first car journey together from school, Diana's conversation had made it clear how much her ideas and views on life focused on love and marriage. One point never altered, her little girl's certainty that without one there could not be the other.

It was the memory of Diana's girlhood ideals, the knowledge that all her dreams and aims were of a happy marriage and lots of children, that made me so sad and angry when her marriage collapsed through no fault of her own. She was cheated of her very simple ambitions, a happy family life. It is to her credit that she has used her considerable will power and strength of character inherited from her mother, Frances, whose own parents and grandparents, especially on her father's side, were renowned for their strong characters and dominant personalities. They were very vibrant and assertive, completely individualistic. Diana's maternal grand-mother, Ruth Fermoy, formerly Ruth Gill, came from a military background and was as strong-minded as her husband. The com-bination resulted in a force to be reckoned with in their daughter Frances and in time in her youngest daughter, Diana.

She has used the subtle strengths to overcome the disappoint-ment of a failed marriage, made all the worse by her predominance on the world stage, and to thwart the courtiers who would like to push her into the background. Using common sense, integrity and will power, she has shown that nothing, not even the destruction of her childhood dreams, could floor her. It was the same as when she was a child, the tougher the challenge, the more able she was to cope. There were times when Diana felt she had so much to do, especially prior to going away either to her mother or back to school and she wondered how she would fit everything into the time. Nothing was actually so dreadfully important, but that's not how she saw it. When dramatics came into overplay as 'pressure' built up, I told her to take one step at a time, that nothing was impossible to achieve. It was important to see the aims clearly and then work steadily towards them. To try and think of everything at once might make the task seem impossible, so she should work steadily through putting all attention on the matter in hand. I asked her to remember that no one is any better or worse than anyone else in life, just different. There are good and bad points in all people. I told Diana, when she said how difficult she found it to look up when she was speaking to people, not to let them intimidate her, or even imagine that they were, just look them in the eyes as if to say, 'It doesn't matter who you are, I'm Diana'. To practise that line of thought at all times and she would be surprised how soon she would find it had become a natural way to behave. To remember at all times that regardless of what title they might hold or position, they were just ordinary people, all with their hopes and fears, attributes and failings.

In the afternoon I took Charles and his friend John for a ride on Charles's pony while Diana took Alexandra to the place we had collected the primroses so she could take some to her mother. I noticed during tea, when Alexandra talked about school, that Diana, although happy there, obviously did not want talk of school to intrude in her thoughts during the holidays. As with most of the days spent with friends, it ended at about 6 p.m. to allow the children some quiet time on their own before bed. Sarah had returned with her friend Isabel, and Diana always liked to spend time in their company in the hope that she would glean more inside information on 'being an adult'. Sarah was very tolerant of her youngest sister and always made her welcome, but never hesitated to tell her to go away when she had had enough, or, being a teenager, wished to indulge in more private 'girl's talk'. This always infuriated Diana who felt it was just this sort of talk that she should be party to. It would be here she could pick up scraps of information to be passed on in whispers to the other girls in her school dormitory after the lights had been turned out. She would come back to me at those times with the child's classic cry of 'it's not fair', to which I would reply that life is tough when you are a younger sister but that she would grow up all too quickly and she must understand that Sarah needed a quiet time with her friends just as she, Diana, did with hers.

Two days before we were to leave for London for the second part of the holiday, the children's maternal grandmother, Ruth, Lady Fermoy, invited us to tea. I wanted to leave these two days free to make sure all last-minute jobs were done. Lady Fermoy lived nearby in Hillington and we went with Lord Althorp, who had retained a very close relationship with his mother-in-law, perhaps even more so since the divorce from her daughter. She had a beautiful home, furnished in excellent taste, and was a close friend of the Queen Mother, who was Sarah's godmother. Lady Fermoy was very involved in music and art and played a constructive part in the annual Kings Lynn Festival, which had been founded by herself and her late husband. The Queen Mother would often stay at Sandringham during this period and support her friend. Lady Fermoy was a refined and elegant woman and I was pleased to see how well-behaved and relaxed the children were with her. She gave guidance to Lord Althorp on the care of the children after the divorce and encouraged him to send Diana to Riddlesworth, a school that had been suggested by another caring friend. Lord

Althorp had been hesitant, wondering if it was wise to send his daughter away so young and after the disruption of his failed marriage, but he was persuaded that a new environment was just what was needed. Lady Fermoy later explained this to me when I saw her at Park House. Lord Althorp had made it clear to Diana that she was not going away for any reason other than for her own good and reports have not been correct when this situation has been psychoanalysed with the conclusion that Diana was left feeling unwanted because she was sent away. It is so easy to take circumstances out of context and reach a wrong conclusion, albeit more sensational. No child could ever have been made to feel more wanted than Diana. Both parents had plenty of time for her. She was never pushed aside with the words, 'I'm too busy now.' Diana in turn treats her sons with the same sensitivity towards their feelings. She makes sure they benefit from the most valuable asset that a child can receive from the parent – time. Diana realized there was little choice but for her to go to another school. It was not right she be taught at home – she was too old for that and it would have been too insular for her. Silfield, the day school, was no longer suitable, so she accepted that Riddlesworth, near to home and where she knew some girls already, was a fair choice. There she was treated well, settled quickly and was happy. The staff at the school took great pains to understand their pupils. Diana and Lord Althorp both described to me how the decision had been reached and it was clear that Diana suffered no repercussions of feeling unwanted. Lady Fermoy talked to the children about their activities during the holidays, what they intended to do with their mother and about summer term at school, putting emphasis on the sport and swimming side for Diana's sake. The two hours passed pleasantly and quickly. I found it interesting to visit another home as my days were spent mostly at Park House.

From the time I arrived at Park House I gave Charles a riding lesson on his Shetland pony about twice a week. It was a very low key affair. We walked across the park and occasionally I had to run should the pony feel inclined to break into a trot. Sarah and I often rode together across the park, jumping some of the permanent cross-country course, and we would explore further that part of the estate which lay across the road opposite to Park House. We made good use of the wide green verges used by day trippers for their picnics. As the days grew lighter I liked to ride early in the evening if Lord Althorp was at home or early in the morning. I never rode during the day when the children were about, until one day towards the end of the holidays when we made an exception. Sarah suggested a ride across the park and Diana said she would like to come. I was rather surprised at this. Charles decided to join us too so a quiet ride was assured. I led him from my horse while Diana rode Romany, the New Forest pony. We never ventured beyond a trot because of Diana's nervousness. I have never been able to understand why Diana chose to come with us, except that she tried to emulate Sarah in so many ways and possibly she hoped to overcome her fear of riding. Romany had been Sarah's pony and was very safe. We had a lovely ride, laughing and telling jokes, with Sarah setting Diana impossible dares that she had no intention of accepting, such as jumping a ditch. I was pleased to see Diana on a horse and managing well in a quiet, steady fashion.

Park House came into view, and then disaster struck. Romany tripped with his hoof in a rabbit hole. He regained his composure very quickly but Diana, perched not very steadily on his back, fell. Luckily the pace was walk so the fall was gentle. Although upset and a little shaken, she was on her feet immediately. No damage done, and I told her it would be better if she mounted again to ride the last little bit home, so she would not be nervous in the future. Diana did not wish to remount. I wanted to insist because she was not hurt and I saw no reason to dramatize the situation. Had I insisted, I am sure Diana would have complied with my wishes just to humour me and I would have walked beside her. Sarah, however, advised against this. She was aware how close the children were to seeing their mother and knew from past experiences that Diana apparently could not then be relied upon not to make a mountain out of a molehill just for effect and to draw attention to herself. The more time I spent with Diana at Park House the less often she was to act so, until she grew out of this form of childish behaviour altogether. The decline of this type of behaviour coincided with the growth in her self-confidence. Taking Sarah's advice, we led the pony home. Diana did not ride again until she was married and had riding lessons with Captain Hewitt, by which time the memory of this little fall had grown out of all proportion.

It was a pity that the incident had to happen to spoil an otherwise successful ride but it was very minor and I put it out of my mind. I did, however, first take the precaution of telling Lord Althorp and he too, mindful that if he was not careful there could be problems, suggested it would be wiser to take Diana to the doctor for a check to make sure nothing was wrong, then no charge could be placed on us for carelessness. The doctor confirmed that there was no damage. Diana was a little bruised and shaken up by the fall which unfortunately had cancelled all her brief newfound confidence. She certainly revelled in the dramatics of the situation and was somewhat disappointed that a sling was not required. We returned home, relieved that no harm had been done. Diana declared she would never ride again. I told her I thought she was making a great deal of fuss over a little fall, but that certainly there was no need for her to ride if she did not wish to. I recounted the saying that it is necessary to fall seven times before you can be regarded as a rider and jokingly added that I could not stand the strain.

So our part of the Easter holidays ended rather dramatically but with no lasting effects – or so we thought at the time. The last day was spent packing and tidying up. The children did not have to take much with them for they had clothes at their mother's home but naturally they wished to take some of their favourite items. The den was tidied up and a makeshift door erected to keep out visitors. Goodbyes were said to everyone and Smith was issued with minute-by-minute instructions on how to care for Peanuts, the guinea-pig. I prepared for my first break away since my job had started and early the next morning Lord Althorp took us to Kings Lynn station to catch the train to London.

In hindsight, I can only speculate on the many thoughts that must have passed through his mind, the sadness tinged with bitterness he felt and managed so successfully to hide as he said goodbye to the children and saw them off to visit their mother, the wife he had loved who had left him. He hid his feelings and he never spoke a word against his wife to his children. His behaviour was absolutely correct. Not for Charles and Diana, the bickering between estranged parents, the feeling of being used as a pawn in a game of chess as each tried to outwit the other.

At the last minute, shyness struck and the goodbyes were

hurried and awkward. In their young lives they had not had too many goodbyes and they still had to learn how to handle them without embarrassment at public displays of affection. A pity, because their stiff behaviour did not reflect the depth of feeling for their father. Or perhaps the very shyness did, in an introverted way. However, the excitement of the train journey lay ahead and at the end a change of venue for the next two weeks. Their mother had decided to take them on a skiing holiday and like all children, with their inherent ability to switch from one situation to another, they had already shut Park House from their minds and were looking towards the next chain of events. The train journey was extremely pleasant. For me, it was a new experience as we travelled first class and ate in the restaurant car. The children read the comics we had bought on the station and talked about the forthcoming skiing holiday. We also discussed the time we had spent at Park House and they said how much they had enjoyed the freedom. I asked if they were happy with the new eating arrangements we had instigated. They thought it was a great improvement and that it felt more like being a natural family.

I had been told that their mother would meet me at the barrier at Kings Cross. This was to be the first time that we had met. We arrived; the children naturally excited on the one hand, yet slightly reticent on the other, hurried me forward to introduce me to their mother. Had I not been told who she was, I would have been able to guess as she bore such a resemblance to her own mother, Lady Fermoy. A polite smile on her face did not reach beyond her mouth. Her eyes were cold as she formally shook my hand. It was no more or less than I had expected so I was not disappointed. There were a few formalities and then I handed the children over, confirming the time and date I would collect them to return to Norfolk. I kissed them goodbye and walked away feeling rather strange to be on my own, free of all responsibilities, but I knew I would be pleased to see them again at the end of their holidays.

The two weeks went so quickly and in no time at all, it seemed, I was back at Liverpool Street station waiting to collect the children. I felt as I had done the first time I went to school to meet Diana, a mixture of trepidation and anticipation, as I wondered what their reaction would be at the end of their holiday. I hoped

66

they would be pleased to see me. They arrived on time with their mother and to my surprise I saw that Diana had her arm in a sling. Her mother indicated that Diana had been brought to London with her arm unattended when all the time it had been fractured. I knew that the doctor had checked her after her fall from Romany and that Diana had used her arm in such a way that should not have been possible if the arm had been seriously injured.

None the less, I did not want to get involved in what could be a rather unpleasant conversation and it was obvious the children might get upset at the way our reunion was going. Diana stood looking down at her feet and I felt sorry that they should have to listen to this. To curtail the conversation, I demurred, accepted the messages that had to be passed on to Lord Althorp and the children said their farewells, thankful now to get on to the train. I can truthfully say that the worst parts of my job were these transition times. The train journeys to London were not too bad but the meetings with their mother were always slightly tense and the journey back was never very relaxed as the children prepared for yet another change. If the journeys to Norfolk meant the start of their holiday at Park House they were fine, but if it meant the end of the holiday and preparing for school then they were more difficult. During this first train journey back, Diana told me that she had had a fall whilst skiing and that it was during the check-up after this fall that the fracture was discovered. I made a mental note to relate this conversation to their father, but did not discuss it any further with the children. Instead we talked about the rest of their holiday.

It was on these journeys that Diana seemed most unlike her normal self, the emotion of the transition making her reserved and pensive, her thoughts obviously on the parent left behind. She tried to test my loyalty by melodramatic comments but I was always very careful and diplomatic about what I said in case it should be repeated. Without fail, as soon as we arrived back at Park House I would remind Diana to phone her mother and then leave her to her own devices. In no time at all, she was back to her happy self. She had a very sunny disposition which never took long to resurface as long as she was not pressurized. Charles never seemed to be affected at all. They were both always pleased to see me, but he never played such games. Diana used all the feminine wiles, especially for her poor father's benefit, thus ensuring that she was not the only one to feel unsettled. After he made them welcome to be home he would normally retire to his study and leave me to restore equilibrium in the house. This never took long as Diana only acted for effect, and without an audience there was very little point.

With just two days left at Park House before Diana went back to school, we spent our time quietly, making last-minute checks through the trunk and sewing on one or two more name tags. Peanuts had survived Smith's ministrations and was dutifully prepared for his return to school. Walks with the dogs, sorting out her bedroom, choosing the cuddly animals that were to accompany Diana to school were the tasks with which Diana occupied herself. Diana grew more subdued as departure time approached, but she clearly looked forward to showing off her arm to her friends. Lord Althorp took Diana to school so we said our farewells at Park House. The holiday had been a success. We had fitted in a tremendous amount and most importantly we had formed a very good basis for our friendship. I knew that the next time Diana came home there would be no feeling of trepidation on either side.

Charles and I prepared to settle into our quieter life. Sarah had already left and suddenly Park House seemed large but we were self-contained and had no trouble returning to the pattern we had established before the girls appeared on the scene.

Lord Althorp returned from Riddlesworth and asked me to come to the study. I had never been summoned there before, so I guessed it must be about something serious. He looked very subdued and asked me to sit down. He told me that the children's mother was to re-apply for custody of the children and then became really embarrassed as he had to tell me that she was basing her re-application on the fact that she did not believe I was competent to care for the children. He hastened to assure me that this was a view he did not share and how pleased he was with the relationships I had already formed with them. He told me that the case was to be heard in the High Court in London in the beginning of July but that before then I would be interviewed by his solicitors and would have to present a statement. I told him I appreciated it was nothing personal. I did not feel upset and I was sure all would be resolved.

I hated to see him embarrassed on my behalf and tried to make as light of the situation as possible. I did wonder what would happen to my job, but decided to follow the advice I gave Diana and take one step at a time.

Chapter Six

The house seemed very quiet with the children back at school. Charles had returned to Silfield, so again I was on my own during the days. Lord Althorp, after taking Diana back to school and breaking the news to me of the impending court case, disappeared to London for a few days. One of his jobs was to see the lawyers who would prepare his case. I tidied our part of the house sorting out the chaos created by the children during the holidays, putting everything back in the right places and having a general spring clean. I put aside clothes, books and toys that took up useful space. When I had tried to do this with Diana, she had insisted that this, that or the other might be useful later, so I had better keep it. Once out of the way I knew the items would have been forgotten by the time the summer holidays arrived.

After such an eventful holiday it was remarkable how quickly Charles and I reverted to the way of life we had established earlier. We settled quickly into the school routine. Charles was bright and school presented no problems for him. Once I had the nursery wing organized again, and with Charles at school, I did initially miss the hustle and bustle of the holidays. I turned my attention to the horses and decided that as I had free rein with Peppermint and could ride her daily, it was time I sold Vulcan on. I advertised and a good home was quickly found, leaving me free to explore the surrounding countryside on Sarah's trustworthy horse, very fast, reliable and kind.

I wrote regularly to Diana telling her stories about the antics of the dogs and other news from Park House. It was only three weeks before she would return for her first exeat (weekend break from school). I knew I ought to relish the peace and quiet, because when Diana came home the weekend would be hectic with her trying to cram as much in as possible. Besides my riding, I walked the dogs, deriving great pleasure from the beautiful countryside. As he was still a young dog, Bray was meant to have a certain amount of routine instilled in him, so that by the start of the shooting season he would not disgrace his master. For this reason Smith often chose to walk the dogs, always complaining, perhaps with some justification, that Lord Althorp really ought to have his dog with him at all times even in the house. Instead he scarcely saw him during the summer but expected complete obedience in the hunting field during autumn and winter. As I liked to walk every day and I was not always able to take the dogs, I decided to ask Lord Althorp on his return if it would be possible for me to have a dog of my own. My horse had gone, so I saw no reason why he would not comply with this request. When I approached him on this subject, he immediately agreed. He wanted to make sure that I was happy at Park House. He said that if I found a puppy, he would buy her for me. He realized that if I felt settled his children would be the ones to benefit.

In my next letter to Diana, I told her about the impending new arrival and she wrote back and asked me to get a keeshond as Suski was getting old and would soon die. Birth and death carry a certain fascination for children who often accept such inevitable events with strong emotions that are quickly forgotten. I repeated Diana's request to Lord Althorp. Until I went to Park House, I had never even heard of keeshonds, let alone seen one, and because I knew so little about them it was not my immediate choice of dog. I have since discovered how kind, loyal, lovable and obedient is the breed. For myself, I had already decided on an Afghan hound and had started to scan the local papers to try to track one down. I only wanted a pet, so the pedigree was not important. Lord Althorp, now made aware of Diana's preference, realized that Charles had a birthday in May and he decided that a keeshond puppy would make the ideal present. For many years there had been keeshonds in the family and as Diana rightly pointed out, Suski was getting old. Now, instead of looking for just one pup, we would search for two. I found mine first in a village near Kings Lynn, a twelve-week-old black bitch. I called her Amina and brought her home, gave her a basket for her bed in the nursery, listened to her crying all through the first night and refused, with difficulty, to give in to her. She never cried again.

Park House looked lovely now in the fullness of spring.

Everywhere was so very lush, the bright fresh green that heralds new growth, rather than the worn, dusty green of late summer as the countryside prepares itself for the advent of autumn. The air was freshened by light showers and the sun was warm on our faces when we took shelter from the wind. Smith seemed to be constantly sitting on his lawn-mower in an attempt to prevent the grass from growing more than an inch above ground level. If he was not roaring up and down the lawn he could be found, scythe in hand, fighting the nettles and weeds that grew at such an alarming rate. The growth effort of the flowers and shrubs faded into insignificance against such competition.

When Charles came home from school now, we would take Amina on the lawn to play with her and to start her training. A long-legged, ungainly little thing, she strongly objected to the lead when it was attached to her collar, much preferring to gambol along behind us. No sooner would I have her standing on four legs, than two would collapse beneath her. Upright again, she would collapse the other two legs. She would eventually tire of this game and with one hand on the lead and the other firmly ensconced on her behind, I would gently propel her across the ground. It might have looked a peculiar method of training on the lead but it achieved the desired results. She eventually capitulated and acknowledged it was easier and more dignified to walk unaided by such props. For the first six months that I owned Amina, she nearly convinced me that she was deaf. The more I called or whistled for her attention, the more she ignored me. Worse than that, she would deliberately set off in the opposite direction. Charles soon tired of being my assistant in the thankless task of trying to cajole an apparently deaf, disobedient Afghan into a hound who would accept basic discipline. Diana, during her first exeat, had much more patience as we stood a few yards apart and tried to entice Amina to run to either one of us. Young as Amina was, she quickly realized that Diana was a soft touch as far as helpless animals were concerned. She would collapse on her back with her four legs flapping wildly in the air, yelping her head off as if trying to embarrass us by convincing those within earshot that she was the hapless victim of gross mistreatment. It was times such as these that I was grateful we lived in the middle of nowhere. Diana tried gently to persuade her to stand up, but usually she had no more success than I. In time we were to make great strides, gradually working our way into intermediate dog obedience class. Even the instructress was surprised, as her previous Afghan pupils had never progressed beyond beginners!

Lord Althorp found a litter of keeshond puppies of fine pedigree. Charles, his father and I went to collect Gitsie, an adorable bundle of fluff. She soon shared an equal place of affection in my heart with Amina and I was so pleased that Diana had suggested another keeshond. Gitsie was Charles's dog, shared with Diana, but because both children were at school, she attached herself to me. Even when they were at home, other interests meant that not all their attention was focused on Gitsie especially, as is the case with most children, when enthusiasm and interest waned as the dog became older and lost its puppy appeal. As independent as Amina was – she preferred to flop lazily on a heap of sand that stood in the courtyard – Gitsie became my shadow. She followed me everywhere, breaking all the rules by her insistence to be with me at all times, even in the house. Left outside, she attacked the back door with such ferocity that we had little choice other than to comply with her wishes.

When my job at Park House ended, Lord Althorp wrote to me and said that soon I would be receiving a gift to thank me for my work. I desperately hoped it would be Gitsie. In due course a lovely gold bracelet arrived with five gold discs, four bearing the name of one of the children while the fifth and largest had the name 'Park House' engraved on it and the dates of my employment – a much more practical memento of my time there and one that would endure the passage of time. Naturally I was very appreciative to receive such a thoughtful gift, but I can still recall a certain sense of disappointment. I knew I could not have Gitsie, she belonged to Charles. As Diana had rightly foretold, Suski had died, so Gitsie was the remaining keeshond. I did have Amina with her wild, independent spirit, whom I had grown to love. We had by now reached an understanding and I did command a certain amount of respect unless her attention was drawn to the antics of a rabbit two miles away! Throughout her life, she maintained her disdain for other human beings. Should any stranger attempt to stroke her black silken head, she simply looked down her long aristrocratic nose at them with an arrogant stare, stood up and moved to my other side. Amina moved with me wherever I lived, even coming with me to Istanbul and finally back to England, quarantine and Norfolk, where she died before I moved to London as if she knew that the city would not be suitable for her who loved the freedom of the wide open spaces.

Gitsie stayed at Park House and when the family moved to Althorp Hall on the death of the children's grandfather, Earl Spencer, she went with them. It was from there that Charles wrote to me in 1978 to tell me that eventually she had to be put down because of cancer. Some time after her marriage Sarah wrote to me and amongst the photographs she included with the letter was one of her keeshond, Digby. It pleased me that the family had remained loyal to the breed.

Lord Althorp spoke to Smith and persuaded him to leave the lawns in order to prepare the pool ready for Diana's first exeat. North-west Norfolk is quite wild and the late spring winds were still keen. I could not imagine anyone being enticed to swim, but Diana wished to and her father had promised. Smith rolled back the cover that had been put over the pool to protect it from the winter and to prevent too much dirt or leaves from falling into it. He moaned about having this extra work. As far as he was concerned, so early in the year, didn't he have enough to do without this extra task? In all likelihood it would rain all weekend and then his time would have been wasted. Wasn't it enough that the grass did not know when to stop growing to give him a break? But the complaints were good natured. He and his wife had known Diana since she was born and loved to see her happy and enjoying herself, glad that the sadness that had prevailed for a while at Park House during the difficult times in Lord Althorp's marriage had been dispelled and replaced with light-hearted banter and laughter. They too would make sure they played their part to add to this brightness and if this meant that Smith should forsake his lawns to prepare a pool while the wind still blew cool, well, so be it. Diana was at her most exuberant and liveliest when she was swimming and diving and no one could fail but feel happy to see such pleasure so clearly displayed.

In the last letter that I wrote to Diana before her exeat, I told her that we had acquired the two new puppies, my Afghan and, as she had suggested, a keeshond. I recounted some of their early

74

exploits and told her I looked forward to her help with the training. I also told her that her request had been granted and the pool would be ready for her if she was mad enough to use it. I would, in any case, remain a spectator as I was not that brave or foolhardy. I never complied with Diana's beseeches of 'Oh, come on, Mary, come in, it's *really* warm'. Firstly, I did not believe her, quite justifiably, for often I would insist she left the pool as she turned more and more blue while still trying to convince me that it was warm! Secondly, I did not trust her, for in the water she knew she would have the better of me. Certainly I could swim, but not as strongly as the Spencer girls and I was never quite sure what tricks Diana might get up to. For these reasons she never persuaded me into the pool except in the warmth of the summer and then only after I had extracted a promise from her that there would be no pranks. The receipt of my last letter gave promise of a lively weekend ahead and Diana cruised through the last few days of school.

Lord Althorp returned from one of his many trips several days before the exeat. It was to be a busy few days as the solicitor would be at Park House to take statements from the people who would act as witnesses on Lord Althorp's behalf, in the impending court case. There was a considerable amount of comings and goings at the front part of the house, but it did not disturb us. Charles, in any case, was at school during the day and as I was not involved I paid little heed to all the activity. The solicitor also visited some people in their own homes to procure as much favourable evidence as possible as to the suitability of Lord Althorp as custodian to his children. The statements came from friends who could vouch for the happiness of the children at Park House in the care of their father and myself.

Before the solicitor left, just before Diana's exeat, I was asked into the drawing room to meet him. The outline of the case was again explained to me, this time by the solicitor, and so was the part that I would be required to play. He told me that he needed to ask me many questions and from my answers, he would put together a statement for my approval and signature. There was, he said, a possibility that I would have to issue a second statement depending on the comments made by the children's mother, but that would come later. Lord Althorp left me alone in the drawing room with the solicitor and his assistant. This initial meeting had no effect on me, the full implications of the case had yet to hit home and I treated the interview in the same way as I would have done had it been for a job, giving concise, straight answers. Later in the day I was called back, read through the statement and signed it. From the outset, in the study, I had been warned by Lord Althorp that there would be such intrusions into our lives during the late spring and early months of summer. I did what I had to do, to the best of my ability, then promptly put the interview out of my mind.

To add to the pleasure of that home weekend, Sarah arrived the day before and our quiet, ordered lives were again thrown into the organized chaos of the previous holiday. Putting aside the pressure and stress that must have been caused by the necessary but unpleasant meetings of the previous few days, Lord Althorp collected Diana from school while I collected Charles from Silfield. I had looked forward to the weekend. Pleased as we were to now eat our meals in the dining room, the table did seem very large with just Lord Althorp at the head and Charles and I on either side of him. It was even larger when Charles and I were alone, and it was at these times that lunch in the nursery did not seem such a bad idea. However, having initiated and established the move downstairs, I did not intend that we should revert to the old ways.

Regardless of how many people ate, the dining room table was always immaculately laid with silver, glasses and linen table napkins. To this day I regard linen table napkins as the most telling part of a table setting. To use them shows that certain something which paper serviettes can never achieve. Naturally at Park House there were always people to launder and iron them or Mrs Smith would add them to the bag of laundry that was collected every week and returned a week later, immaculate. Much easier to use paper ones, but what a world of difference. The full complement of silver cutlery would be laid and the children learnt at a young age about the correct knife and fork to use with each course. Betts's wife, the cook, always made sure she prepared the children's favourite dishes and provided an excellent choice of puddings, apple snow and strawberry meringue being two of the most popular, as well as plenty of fresh fruit which varied according to season. She would always ask them, especially Diana, if she was only home for two or three days, if there was anything she would particularly like, but Diana, as the other children, was easy to please and would eat anything. With Diana and Sarah in the house, Charles on holiday for the week and Lord Althorp free from the first stages of preparation for the court case, we determined to make the most of every minute.

The forecast promised a fair day for the Saturday, so against our better judgement we decided to believe it and planned a swimming party to celebrate the first official use of the pool for the new season, and surely Smith's efforts had to be seen to be appreciated! Against all odds – as forecasts are notoriously inaccurate – our optimism was rewarded. In a way, but the best possible way, it was wrong. Fair turned out to be the kind of lovely warm late spring day which we always hope means the promise of a long hot summer, the sort of day when the pastel colours of the English countryside are at their best. They never make the technicolour shades of blue and green that are found in the Mediterranean, but on such a day when even the larks soar higher, the blackbirds sing all the sweeter, the thrush works harder crushing snails on to stones to feed to its young, and even the robin puts in an appearance to prove it is not just a winter companion, there can be no better place on earth to be than England. The swallows had arrived after their long journey from Africa and celebrated their safe return to familiar ground, and their escape from the guns of hunters who imperil their flight over parts of Europe where these beautiful birds are regarded a delicacy, by swooping low over the pool, excited by this unexpected mass of water in the middle of a garden and so conveniently placed near the eaves where they nested. They skimmed, snatching at the insects who bravely defied Smith's efforts to produce a spotless pool. Such valuable assistants should not be criticized for the mess that consequently surrounded their nests, mostly built into the eaves of the Smiths' upstairs flat. To complete the picture, the cuckoo, whose first toneless notes are eagerly awaited every spring – the date of its arrival compared with previous years, to record the real start of spring, not necessarily 21 March – while to actually see him would be a disaster, an omen of impending bad luck; had changed from intermittent song, to a continuous, joyful, 'cuckoo, cuckoo'. 'Listen,' I said to Diana. 'Listen to the cuckoo', and together we repeated the rhyme taught to every child in the land as soon as they are aware of the existence of this bird: 'In April the cuckoo comes, in May he sings all day, in June he changes his tune, in July he prepares to fly, in August go he must.' Diana and Charles compared dates as to who had heard the cuckoo first that year. Diana had heard it in the nearby woods as soon as she returned to school, while Charles claimed he had heard it in the woods near the house before she went back. Diana hotly denied that this could possibly be true, as she always preferred to be the first in such cases. I told them it was of little importance as long as they had both heard it and quelled a rare argument before it could start.

England on such a day is wonderful and our part of England, our cared-for green lawns and gardens; the adjoining cricket field and pavilion, calling to mind men in white flannels and cream teas accompanied by the drone of unseen insects on a hot summer afternoon; the rolling parklands with the ancient trees that had graced the landscape for countless years, paying silent homage to the royal family and other landed gentry; the dark, watchful woodlands, keeping secret the lives of their inhabitants, supplying cover for the gentle fallow deer that sheltered in the shadows, tense and taut, their large doleful eyes fearful, ready for flight in the event of danger – it must have been instinct bred into them, for in the safety of the Sandringham estate, no danger lurked – and overlooking all, Park House, a real English country home, its greystone blending into the surroundings, effusing grace, continuity and security. The Victorian dwelling has the 'Sandringham blue' door marking it as royal property. This was our England, evoking a sense of timelessness and serenity that we could not imagine ever to be shattered or changed, a picture of England similar to those recorded in books and on the screen, to be shared there by many, but in reality experienced by so few. I will always be pleased that I could share in this life, albeit for a relatively short period that will not ever be forgotten.

On the Saturday morning, Diana was about as early as I had expected she would be, so as not to waste a moment of her precious home weekend. Even so, as it was not so long before the longest day of the year, the sun had pre-empted her and had already started its climb, its warmth increasing as it rose higher in the sky. Before breakfast, Diana visited the den to make sure that nothing untoward had happened to it during her absence. She opened it up and put it straight, ready for use when her friends tired of swimming. The previous evening, I had telephoned the mothers of Diana and Charles's friends and arranged for them to come over in the early afternoon. Sarah had already spoken to her friends and made similar arrangements. It would certainly be a mixed age group but there was room for everyone. Lord Althorp had to go to a memorial service but would join us later for tea outside if the good weather lasted. Diana spent a few moments after breakfast chatting to the Smiths who were keen to know how the first weeks of the new term had progressed. As it was the swimming term the reports were very favourable. Diana, always very fair and helpful, realized there was quite a bit of preparation for the afternoon's fun, and willingly gave me a hand tidying and making beds – all the clearing up after the children had returned to school for the summer term had been muddled in a matter of minutes and I wondered why I had troubled to do it in the first place. To Diana, this was not work, she was by nature domesticated.

There was a light, early lunch with their father in the dining room. Betts was left to clear the table in peace. Lord Althorp departed for the service and I told the children to rest in their room for half an hour to digest their meal and make the most of some quiet before friends arrived. Charles complied at once. When he was at home at the weekends, this was a general rule and we both enjoyed a relaxing thirty-minute read. Diana, eager to get into her swimming costume and start the afternoon fun, did not relish the delay. I was extremely firm with her and told her that if she went into the pool at once, not only would it be bad for her so soon after a meal, but it would be the end of her afternoon swimming as she would not be allowed in again and would be able only to sit and watch her friends enjoying themselves. I rarely had to speak thus to Diana. On this occasion she was just excited that the pool could be used and she would have an audience. Laughing, joking Diana immediately became a sullen little girl with a scowl on her face as, muttering to herself, she went to her room. I followed her. I did not want the afternoon spoilt by a childish mood, although I doubted it would last long, as the arrival of her friends would dispel the gloom and, as I wrote earlier, she had by nature a sunny disposition and seldom bore a grudge. I gently reminded her how rare it was that I laid down the law, so that when I did, it was for a very good reason and I expected my wishes to be adhered to. I told her how much I enjoyed having her at home and how I appreciated all her help, but that there were times when I did know best and this was one of them, 'so please don't spoil it by being moody after all the trouble I've gone to'. I purposely spoke in this manner to place the onus on her, as I knew Diana did not like to feel she had offended or upset anyone. This approach never failed to work the few times I had to employ it.

Half an hour later outside, all cross words were forgotten as the swimming pool beckoned welcomingly in the warmth of the afternoon sun. Everyone had arrived with, besides swimming costume and towel, a variety of accessories considered part of the essential equipment for messing about in the pool, to be added to the variety of playthings that we boasted. Few had much intention of serious swimming; that was left for class lessons. Now it was self-imposed competitions, mostly instigated by Diana who knew she stood a good chance of winning unless she was against Sarah whose age gave her the edge. Who could dive the straightest and quietest? Who could race dive the furthest? Who could swim for longest under water, do a handstand, a backward somersault – or as a Portuguese acquaintance once called it as he fell off his motorbike 'a salted summer'? Charles and his friends often did not bother to compete, knowing there was little chance of success, but Diana's friends, playing the perfect guests, would rise to the challenge only to be outshone on every count. They accepted defeat graciously, acknowledging it as a foregone conclusion.

Sarah, to infuriate her young sister and to put her in her place if she thought she was 'getting above herself', would issue a challenge that Diana could not refuse without losing face, and cheered on by the others they would each execute a number of near perfect dives, while we acted as judge and jury. Sometimes, luck and skill were on Diana's side, but more often Sarah had the advantage. Not to be outdone, nor wanting to lose her self-esteem, Diana would then perform her pièce de résistance: climb to the top of the slide, pose, a slim silhouette in black school regulation costume against the azure blue of the perfect summer sky, before gracefully diving into the waters below. This stunt was half-heartedly forbidden by her father, but the dare-devil side of Diana preferred to focus on the other half, a weakness in his pride for his daughter, who looked so perfect as she entered the pool causing scarcely a ripple.

I lay by the pool making the most of this opportunity to relax and to sunbathe. I was a sun fanatic; at the merest hint of a bit of warmth my first free moments would find me outside, face upturned to the sun, letting its rays send a feeling of well-being coursing through me. This was in the days before the skin cancer scares. Now older and wiser, I would not expose myself to such a danger. Relaxed as I was on my sun lounger, I did not let myself doze off, very aware that I had several children in my care and I could not risk any accidents through neglect of my duties. Nonetheless, it was extremely pleasant to soak up the sun and to listen to the children laughing and teasing in the background. The two pups, Gitsie and Amina, cavorted around my chair and by the pool as Diana unsuccessfully tried to entice them to swim.

I was suddenly aware of a buzzing noise in the distance that had nothing to do with the bees. The buzzing grew louder and more persistent. I opened my eyes and saw a helicopter flying above and inwardly cursed this mechanical metal object for disturbing the peace of the lovely afternoon. I noticed it did not fly over and continue on its way; instead it seemed to hover overhead like some giant bird waiting to swoop on its prey. Of more immediate concern to me, it was blocking the sun! I turned my eyes back to the children who were far too engrossed in play to pay any regard to a mere helicopter, and the next thing I knew, the noise had intensified dramatically, caused by the sudden descent of the helicopter on to the back lawn, its whirring blades generating a strong wind which had so far been absent on this day. It created havoc with the roses that climbed the back walls of Park House, sending a myriad petals flying through open windows and french doors to settle over the floors and furniture and on the stairs, which had all been so conscientiously cleaned by Mrs Pertwee.

At this unexpected intrusion into their afternoon, the children did stop their antics to gaze in wonder at the surprise arrival. A helicopter landing on the back lawn was not an everyday occurrence and did cause a certain amount of interest. Sarah immediately put an end to the speculation by announcing that it was their uncle, Lord Fermoy.

As Lord Althorp had not yet returned, it was my place to go and welcome our visitor. Dressed in bikini top and shorts, I walked towards the helicopter as Lord Fermoy emerged through the open door. If it was an unusual sight for the children, it was, for me, equally unusual. Nothing like this had previously happened in my life. As I crossed the lawn towards Lord Fermoy, the helicopter blades were still rattling around, their speed decreasing all the time, the whirr becoming less distinct. I could picture myself in scenes similar to those I had seen on film, particularly in James Bond adventures, when a helicopter lands on a special mission and a woman walks towards it. I arrived at the helicopter before my rather vivid imagination took too strong a hold. The reality was that I was not an Ian Fleming heroine and Lord Fermoy was certainly not James Bond! I introduced myself and explained who I was and that Lord Althorp was away for the afternoon. Lord Fermoy looked rather taken aback. I accounted for this by assuming he had not anticipated Lord Althorp's absence. It transpired that his surprised look was caused by me. Apparently, as he later explained to Lord Althorp, he thought I was a guest, and could not believe it when I said that I cared for the children. He said he 'envied' the children having a 'nanny' like myself, 'they were not like that in my day'. Sarah told me that he meant most nannies had to wear uniform; bikini and shorts were not their usual attire!

Introductions and explanations complete, we walked towards the swimming pool to meet Sarah, Diana and Charles, who, remembering their manners, had left their friends and were coming to greet their uncle. A few pleasantries and we made our way back to the pool. I offered him some refreshment. I sent Diana and Charles to the house to ask cook for some cool drinks and about fifteen minutes later Lord Fermoy left, asking us to tell Lord Althorp he had called by – 'dropped in' would have been a more appropriate phrase. We hardly needed the reminder, such an incident would not be easily forgotten. The children and I walked with him to his helicopter to see him off. Farewells made, the machine sprang into life shattering again the stillness of the afternoon and causing further mayhem amongst the roses, as its blades picked up momentum and it heaved its heavy metallic body skywards. The event had certainly caused an unexpected diversion in the afternoon's fun. Lord Althorp arrived home later in the afternoon in time to have tea with the children and to see their friends off at the end of a happy day. Diana's preparation of the den that morning had not been necessary, for the pool had claimed all the children's attention. Lord Althorp was amused by the account of Lord Fermoy's visit, but he was not surprised, saying it was the impulsive sort of thing he would do.

Sunday was spent quietly. Diana was slightly subdued, tired after all the fun and excitement of the day before and aware she had to return that evening to school. She was content to play quietly with Charles and to collect one or two more items she wanted to take back. We talked about school and how she was managing with the work. I told her to try to do her best in everything. It did not matter what marks she got as long as she knew she had tried her hardest, that was the most important, not only in subjects she enjoyed, but to put effort into less favoured ones. It was hard to get Diana to admit she enjoyed any class subjects. Swimming and sport were the only things she admitted to liking. Others, such as biology and English, were awarded an 'all right'.

Charles's sports' day at Silfield was to be our next gathering. I suggested on the Sunday before Diana went back to school that she could use her skills to help Charles practise for some of his races. Silfield, a junior school, still had fun sports' days with good spectator races, such as three-legged, egg-and-spoon and sack. Not until prep school do the more serious races start with pupils recording their times, keen to beat their personal bests. Heated debates on advantages and disadvantages of placing feet in the corners of the sack or in the middle are replaced by talk of minutes and seconds.

Diana, regarding herself as above such junior races, was nevertheless eager to help her brother improve his technique. With the aid of one of my old belts, I tied their legs together and with my 'On your marks, get set, go', they were off down the lawn, a rather ungainly sight as Diana was considerably taller than Charles, making for a lop-sided pair. The puppies considered this great fun and raced along beside them, barking and causing a real hindrance by trying to snap at the loose end of the belt. Jill, the spaniel, attracted by all the noise, chose to forget she was full grown and supposedly responsible, and rushed to join in the fun, bringing the practice to an abrupt end as her enthusiasm brought the already unstable children crashing to the ground in a heap of flailing arms, legs and dogs. Diana's fit of giggles did nothing to help the situation, it simply rendered her helpless and incapable of extricating herself and her poor brother, who, due to the belt, had no choice but stay with his sister until the giggles subsided and she got herself under control.

The dogs, beside themselves with excitement, flopped over the children, licking exposed limbs; the more they were fought off and told to stop, the more enthusiastic they became. I managed to undo the belt, not an easy task as the knot had pulled itself tighter and tighter. At last, Charles gratefully stood up while Diana tried to suppress another fit of giggles. This rather abortive attempt to improve Charles's style persuaded him that he could manage the other races without his sister's help.

Diana returned to school at the end of a very happy home weekend. She was sorry to leave, but looked forward to being reunited with Peanuts, who I am sure had missed the attentions of his devoted young owner. In the event, Diana did not come to Silfield sports' day as it did not coincide with her free time. Charles performed well and did himself credit, but it is doubtful whether that Sunday practice was of any benefit to him. Lord Althorp and I went to the sports' day. Clouds scurried across the sky, but the threatened rain did not materialize. Smartly dressed parents – many of the women in hats – watched their offspring perform to the best of their capabilities. Everyone was very friendly. I was never treated in a condescending manner. It was an afternoon of hilarity and laughter, but none of the races could compare with the riotous effort we had at Park House.

Chapter Seven

During the term-time, Lord Althorp was often away, although he managed to organize his schedule to ensure he was at home most of the time during his half of the school holidays with the children. During his absences it was not possible for me to go out in the evenings. He was well aware how lonely life could be as the house was quite isolated. He was also anxious that I should be content and happy and that it was necessary for me to sometimes see my own friends, to have the company of people of my own age. I had full use of the car on my days off and my free weekends. My petrol was also paid for, but there were still long periods when I was not able to leave Park House.

Lord Althorp told me that I was allowed to have friends to visit whenever I wished, as long as it did not interfere with my duties. I was pleased with this concession and made sure I did not abuse the freedom. Most of my friends lived in Norwich, so it was quite a long drive for an evening out. Nevertheless, several did make the journey on different occasions. I was never quite sure if they took the trouble to drive so far just to see me, or whether curiosity about my job and home were their motivation. If Sarah was at home and Lord Althorp away, she would join us for dinner and we would eat in the dining room. It would be pointless for me to pretend that I did not revel in the opportunity to act in a blasé fashion about my situation and to bask in the astonishment portrayed by my visitors, when they found themselves being entertained in such an unusual setting and waited on by a butler. Betts was less than pleased at yet another infringement on what he considered to be the correct code of behaviour between 'upstairs and downstairs'.

Suitably impressed, friends would leave for the journey home, their opinions on my decision to take a nanny's job completely reversed in the space of a few hours. However, I made sure I did not upset the apple cart completely, and should I have visitors when Sarah was not at Park House, I did not place Betts in the invidious position of having to wait on 'mere commoners' – that would have been too much to ask of him and I would not want to be treated in such a manner. On those occasions I would bring the table in the nursery near to the fire and, with candles burning and curtains drawn, the setting could not have been more homely and was one that was easily mirrored in countless houses and flats. I will give my friends their due, whenever I invited them over, they forbore to ask whether Sarah would join us or not, so perhaps, after all, it was me they came to see! If we ate in the dining room, the cook would prepare our food as normal, but if we were alone upstairs, I chose to cook our dinner as if we were in my own home. Indeed I felt so at ease, I did consider Park House to be my home for the length of time I worked there. When my job was finished there, Lord Althorp invited me to return whenever I wished and with whom I wished. Indeed, a year after I left I returned with a friend on another glorious summer's day. All the children were there and we joined them in the pool and had a wonderful afternoon, swimming and talking, catching up on all the news.

As my first summer holidays with the children drew closer, Diana, who had grown increasingly relaxed with me, and to whom I frequently wrote, recounting incidents and news from home, including the visits from my friends, was very keen to know if I had a 'boyfriend'. Sister Sarah had still to reach this elite league as far as Diana was concerned and Sarah was giving away no secrets. As I was a few years older, it was quite possible that I could contribute to the gaps in Diana's knowledge of 'adulthood'. Diana bombarded me with questions about my friends, had I ever been in love, what was it like, what had happened, why did it end, would I ever marry, was I afraid I would not? 'You're getting old'; that put me in my place. At twenty-one, I did not feel old, but Diana's mother had been married at eighteen and at the age of ten, to Diana I must have seemed old. I had just escaped from one engagement and felt I had years ahead before I needed to commit myself. I always answered such questions from Diana in a general manner, as honestly as I could without being too personal. I felt her questions deserved a straight answer, but that there was no need, at her age, to expound on the subject. During the course of the summer Diana met one or two of my friends, already older than myself. To her they appeared positively ancient and she expelled from her mind any ideas of romance for me.

Eight years later when I eventually married all the children wrote to me to offer their congratulations.

During the course of that summer term, the children busy with school and I with my work, the wheels of the law were grinding relentlessly on behind the scenes in preparation for the court case due to start at the beginning of July – luckily before the children finished school. In June, the solicitors paid another visit to Park House. Later that evening when Charles was in bed, Lord Althorp called me to his study. Even more embarrassed than when he had initially told me what was going to take place, he said a statement had been received from the children's mother, most of it relating to me. He was genuinely upset. It was extremely detrimental and he, thinking I would need to be placated, implored me to understand that he did not agree with anything that was stated, to understand that it was written by a mother who was fighting for her children.

He asked me not to take it personally or too much to heart, but to comprehend under what circumstances it had been written. That said, it would, however, be necessary for me to consider its content for a few days and then together we would write a reply. He proceeded to read the statement to me, constantly breaking the dialogue as he tried to excuse his ex-wife's comments. I was rather taken aback at the attack on me. At every level my competence was called into question and thus my ability to care properly for the children. Although I made allowances in that she had no alternative if she were to win the case – I was considered one of the major links that needed to be broken – I, nevertheless, was not willing to let the remarks pass without written comment. When Lord Althorp had completed the reading, I asked to be allowed to sit quietly and read it myself in order to memorize as much as possible. Afterwards, I agreed with his suggestion that I would think about it for a few days and then together we would compile a reply.

I left the study with a mixture of feelings racing through my mind. I felt wronged, used and misquoted, but intertwined with these emotions I felt sadness and compassion for a woman whose only natural wish was to gain custody of her children. It was true she had left them, but I always firmly believed – and still do – that there are usually two sides to every story and as her exit from Park House had occurred before my occupation, I was not keen to make any judgements. I could understand her position. I had come into the children's lives and they were happy. I was not trying to replace a mother, but there was no longer a succession of au pairs and nannies forever coming and going. Even after such a short time in the job, it was obvious I had gained the children's affection and there seemed to be every likelihood that I would stay the course.

I had simply accepted a job. If I had not been chosen someone else would have been. Would they then have been confronted with the situation that now faced me? I believe so. I do not believe that it was a personal attack, I just happened to be the person there when the custody re-application was filed. I had had no idea that I would be involved in this kind of a case, and I was extremely emotionally upset to read such a statement concerning myself. To sleep that night would be impossible. I had so many thoughts in my head and I could not wait to transfer them to paper. I did not intend to mull it over for a few days; now, while it was so fresh in my mind, was the time to write the reply. I knew that until I did that I would not be able to concentrate on anything else. In less than twelve hours I would have Charles up to get ready for school, and I did not wish to appear distant and distracted. I did not want him, even indirectly, to be affected by this. All was quiet when I returned upstairs. I looked in on Charles who was sound asleep in his bed. How innocent and angelic children look when they have drifted into the Land of Nod. The look of peace on his face made me even more determined that I would do everything in my power to ensure that the settled existence we had established would not be disrupted. After all, although the custody of the children was with the father, all the holidays were split equally and I could not see that there was much to be gained by opening up all the old wounds.

I pulled my chair closer to the electric fire. In the winter with an open fire blazing and the children in bed, I loved to sit and read and write letters, essays, poetry. The power of a pen in my hand always relaxed me and words flowed so freely. Now, on a June evening, still daylight outside, there was no need for a real fire and an electric heater had been temporarily installed in its place. Warm as the evening was, I felt chilled and switched it on. Upset, shock and disbelief had affected me. I took pen and paper and started to write – how different from my usual ramblings – now I was in earnest. Emotion and adrenalin were my aids as I scribbled page after page in answer to the condemnations and accusations levelled against me. Daylight gave way to dusk, then darkness and still I wrote, oblivious of time, conscious only of the necessity to pour all the thoughts from my head on to the paper and thus exonerate and distance myself from such unpleasantness. Finally I finished, having given my response, point for point. The writing was fluid but a mass of scribble – my fast type, I called it – and it needed only for me to copy it into a legible hand. This I did with scarcely an alteration.

By the time it was finished, the short hours of darkness had passed to reveal a brilliant sunrise and the start of another day. Exhausted, but exhilarated that my task was complete, I went to bed to rest for two hours. I was far too tired to sleep and my mind was so active, but eventually I dozed off, only to be woken by Charles telling me I was late. For an hour I put everything from my mind as we rushed about to get ready for school. On my return from Silfield, I took my statement and searched out Lord Althorp in his study. I told him what I had done, why I had to write immediately, and handed him the papers. He made no comment except to thank me and express appreciation that the distasteful task had now been completed, instead of remaining a burden to overshadow the next few days.

I took Peppermint for a long ride through the woods and down to Wolferton, passing all the rhododendron bushes now, in June, in their full glory, a real picture of colour and an attraction for many visitors to the royal estate. The beauty of my surroundings calmed me and I returned feeling relaxed and determined that again I would dismiss the court case until I received notice to attend.

All too quickly the time passed and suddenly the beginning of July had arrived. Luckily, except for Charles at his day school, all the children were still away. As the date for the case drew nearer, there was very little else talked of in the house, for all the staff had been interviewed by the solicitors to bear witness on Lord Althorp's behalf as to the happiness and well-being of the children, although not all would be asked to attend the court. The staff were pleased to do this to help their employer as they genuinely did believe the children were better off at Park House and agreed there should not be further disruption in the home. Even so, it was an uneasy period as none of us had been involved in such a case before. I managed to keep this sense of unrest away from Charles and everyone made sure that nothing was discussed in his presence. When he came home from school we swam in the pool if the weather was fine or played indoors in the nursery wing where we were never disturbed. It was not difficult for me to dismiss the forthcoming hearing from my mind, unless I was in the company of the other staff. I had no preconceived idea of what would happen. My only experience of court cases was Perry Mason on TV and as they were always murder trials I did not imagine there would be any similarity.

Finally the date of the hearing arrived. The previous day a sombre Lord Althorp left for London. Before he left he again asked me to the study. He had a good idea of the pressures that would have to be endured during the following days. He really knew very little about me and must have wondered how I would stand up under the experienced, rapid, quick-fire questioning of his ex-wife's counsel. In my naïvety – I exemplified perfectly the saying 'ignorance is bliss' – I assumed I would just be asked questions and all I had to do was to answer them straightforwardly and with truth. I was totally unaware how skilfully manipulative the men of law can be and that their aptitude with words can make right seem wrong and vice-versa. I innocently thought that as there were no problems with the children at Park House, regardless of what might have been said, this would be proved so and everything would stay the same. I just saw the whole issue as an expensive, pointless exercise. When Lord Althorp spoke to me in the study he explained that I would be asked questions that arose from my statements and would have to answer questions made by the opposition. I really saw no problem in any of this and assured him I would be all right. He told me to take my time in my replies and not allow myself to get hassled. He was trying to prepare me for what lay ahead in as accurate a way as possible without causing me alarm. I told him not to worry, I was sure everything would be fine.

The case was expected to, and did, last for five days. As it progressed we would be told when we would be needed and then the Smiths and I would travel to London by train. The butler and his wife were not involved. They had been with the family for too short a period for their judgement to bear any relevance, and they had very little to do with the children. Naturally I had told my parents what was going to happen. They had made very little comment, but they were more aware of the implications and stress involved and told me later that they thought of nothing else but of how I would manage the day that I was in court.

Twenty-two years ago, when I was twenty-one, divorce and high-powered court cases involving the top QCs in the country were not something that my family, friends or indeed acquaintances had ever had any dealings with. Divorce was not as common as it is today. Expensive and apparently nearly always acrimonious, it was widely regarded as an indulgence of the so called 'higher echelons of society' and something for us to read about in the gossip columns of the daily tabloids. Whether right or wrong, most of our contemporaries had to work at their marriages and make the best of them. At that time, I knew of only one person, a few years older than myself, who was divorced. She was regarded with a mixture of awe, that she had acquired this unusual status, and of pity that she had failed in her marriage. It can be seen how very little prepared I was for what lay ahead of me.

Left behind at Park House after Lord Althorp's departure, we waited eagerly for news of how the case was proceeding. Although we all went about our duties as normal it was impossible to think of anything other than what was happening in London. Every evening he phoned, but it was not possible to say in whose favour the case lay. On the evening of the third day when Lord Althorp phoned, he told us we would be needed in court the following day and to take the early morning train from Kings Lynn station to London and then a taxi to the Queen's Buildings. He spoke first to the Smiths and then to me. He told me that the children's mother was putting a great deal of emphasis on my unsuitability to care for the children. No experience, no relevant qualifications, scarcely older than Sarah, acted more as a contemporary, not as a figure of authority. The mother claimed that Diana's riding accident during the Easter holiday was due solely to my irresponsibility.

I was honestly not concerned by these statements. I realized the mother's surest way to get the custody order in her favour was to prove that Lord Althorp did not employ competent staff to care for the children and subsequently the attack would be directed at me. She was hardly likely to acknowledge any positive points about me, for then there would be no case. I just considered it was up to me to tell them the truth and to show there was no substance in her accusations. Lord Althorp asked that I should dress in something quiet and unassuming as even my mode of dress had been criticized as unsuitable for a 'nanny'. (I usually wore practical clothes such as jeans and sweaters.) He told us that we would be met when we arrived at the court, but that he himself would be inside court. He wished me luck.

Early the next morning, Smith drove us to Kings Lynn station. Arrangements had been made for Charles to stay with friends as we were not sure at what time we would return. I read for most of the journey, whilst the Smiths reminisced on the original divorce case. Mr Smith's best dark suit had been given an airing to dispel any hint of mothballs. Mrs Smith, her wavy, grey hair newly set, was smart in a light summer suit, while I was dressed in what I hoped would be regarded as decorous fashion, in a blouse, skirt and a light jacket. We spent the greater part of the journey in silence, each wrapped up in our own thoughts. On arrival in London we took a taxi as we had been instructed. No city on a summer's day is very pleasant. So much preferable to be in the country. London on this particular July day was already very warm. An unusually clear, blue sky promised more heat as the day wore on. Ten years later I would be in London again on a hot July day, for the marriage of Diana to Charles, the Prince of Wales. Never could I have imagined that the young girl whom I was going to help fight for in court, would, ten years later almost to the day, become a Princess – her childhood nickname of 'Duchess' (affectionately so called by her step-father), be usurped by an even grander title.

We entered the imposing building and made enquiries as to which room the hearing was to take place. Men and women in dark suits, some with bulging briefcases, others, their heads immersed in files, walked with an air of purpose in the direction of their destinations. Following the instructions we had been given, we found ourselves outside the allotted room. A man came forward to meet us, carrying the requisite file, to confirm who we were. The register marked, we were asked to sit on some wooden chairs outside the courtroom and wait until we were called. Even this came as a surprise to me, as I had assumed that we could sit in and listen, then be called to the stand – that's how it was on the television! We did not have long to wait until Mr Smith was asked to enter and shortly after that his wife went in and I was left on my own. As there was not much time between the two Smiths, I expected that within minutes I too would be inside. This was not to be. I waited and waited, expecting the door to open at any moment and to be ushered into court. Time passed by so slowly and still no one appeared. I had no idea what was taking place behind the closed doors or how much longer I would have to wait to be called.

There was an adjournment for lunch, but I saw no one as we were not able to mix. I sat and read my book. I was not feeling in the least bit hungry and just wanted the afternoon session to start. I began to wonder if I would be ready to go home with the Smiths or if I would have to stay overnight in London. We had already discussed this possibility and it had been planned that Mrs Smith would stay in the house and look after Charles. Although friends had collected him from school, we had not arranged for him to sleep away as it was better that he should be in his own home. When the break had been made for lunch, the usher had informed me that in all probability I would be called as soon as court resumed for the afternoon.

I was asked to take the stand. I entered the court. In front of me, at the far end of the room, sat the judge. I walked down the centre aisle as directed, to the stand. This was a raised wooden dais, rather like a pulpit, which was at the front of the room to the right. On either side of the aisle sat each aggrieved party with their lawyers and secretaries and the witnesses who had already stated their case. In one of the front seats sat the children's mother and across the aisle sat their father, my employer. I took my place and a man walked towards me with a Bible for me to swear the oath. So far, so good, not dissimilar to what I had seen on *Perry Mason*. A glass of water was provided. Afterwards I wondered when I was supposed to get a chance to drink it. Even under the intensive questioning that followed, as my mouth became drier and drier, while I endeavoured to ensure that my answers were completely concise and accurate and could not be misconstrued, I could not imagine pausing to take a sip of water as that would have destroyed the continuity of my concentration. The judge spoke kindly to me and told me that I was allowed to sit if I wished. I declined the offer, feeling that I could retain better control of the situation if I stood. By this time it was so warm in the room that the judge gave permission for the men to remove their jackets and to be in their shirtsleeves.

The questioning began. Lord Althorp's QC led me through a series of questions relating to comments made in my statements to get my confirmation and to highlight the relevant points that would strengthen his client's case. There was no problem with any of this as we were both on the same side, so there was nothing hostile about his questions. Then it was the turn of the other side. Questions were fired at me. I was hardly allowed to finish the answer to one before attacked by another and before I could give the complete, balanced answer a further one would be barked. The judge was always sympathetic when I insisted on answering an earlier question in full. My brain immediately went into overdrive; it was vital to retain my concentration and keep my mind razor sharp. Here was an adversary determined to win his client's case by undermining the girl who stood in the witness box. I refused to be drawn along at the speed forced by the man who questioned me. I answered deliberately and with a clear head, careful not to say anything that could be turned against me.

I could remember exactly what I had written in both statements. This was not difficult as it was the truth. Sentences were thrown at me that had been twisted giving an incorrect meaning. I now gave an accurate translation. I answered with clarity, looking straight into the eyes of the lawyer. My head was held high to retain my self-esteem and bolster my confidence, I took advantage of my raised platform to look with assurance at those around me. Gradually though my mouth became dry, the room got hotter and hotter, the pressure grew in my head, the questions went on interminably, the faces of the people below swarmed together, no longer definable and my every nerve focused on this man, determined he would not beat me or get the better of me.

A momentary pause, and for that second just one face only became clear, that of the children's mother. She sat impassive,

94

listening to my testimony, weighing up the damage my words would do to her case and at that moment my voice wavered, I could hear it nearly break as I answered the next harshly rasped question. My eyes filled with tears, but I did not cry. I reached out a hand and held on to the stand for a moment just to steady myself. The judge interrupted and asked if I wished for water or wanted to stop for a few minutes. I answered in the negative, but used the moment's respite to take a few deep breaths, moistened my mouth with my tongue and took control of my emotions again. It was the sight of the mother which had thrown me for that instant. Here was I, a girl with my life ahead of me, innocently accepting a nanny's job by way of a change from my usual career moves. The last thing I had expected was that I would be in a court fighting to help the father to keep his children. I had no argument against their mother. What could be more natural than that a mother should wish for custody of her own children? A sudden sadness swept over me that two people who had loved, had four living children, should end up in court fighting with such bitterness, and that I should be one of the main people involved in this battle. Both parents were entitled to their children, but naturally my loyalties lay with their father and it was necessary for me to defend my character and capabilities.

The words 'and finally, one last question' brought me up with a sudden jerk. My whole being, centred as it was on this one man, had moved on to another plane. I could scarcely believe that the drama, which for weeks had been building up in my mind, was about to end. An answer and it was over. I was thanked by the judge and told I could leave the stand.

My legs that had supported me so well throughout had suddenly turned to jelly and I wondered if they would be capable of propelling me towards my seat. I knew where that was, for Lord Althorp had stood up as I walked by to point to a seat behind him and to mouth 'well done'. I moved as if in a trance past two people in my row – perhaps they were the Smiths, but that could not be, they had been freed at lunchtime and in all probability were already home – and sank gratefully into my chair.

Now it was over, the adrenalin and inner strength that always comes into play when the going gets tough, had deserted me. The hearing was adjourned for the day. People I did not know turned to congratulate me. Lord Althorp and his QC told me how impressed they were – by what? I hardly heard their words, as I watched the children's mother walk hurriedly, surrounded on all sides, yet alone, from the room. I had done nothing special, only told what was right and the truth. This was all outside of my league and really I wanted nothing to do with it. I wanted no share of the despair of a mother or the jubilation of a father, even though in my view it was his just desert. I just wanted my job, honestly and without hassle. It was explained to me by Lord Althorp's QC that my testimony almost certainly meant that the father would win. It transpired that during my long wait outside the closed doors, the mother had been called to the stand and my second statement read, paragraph by paragraph, while she was asked to comment on it. This had won the day. I felt no sense of victory. I was an innocent pawn in this distasteful game. I wanted only to distance myself, to get outside again into an ordinary world and back home to Sandringham.

I had time before my train, so I stopped off in Oxford Street and, walking into the first shop I saw, bought a light summer dress. Pushing my court clothes into the bag, as if the very action would obliterate all that had happened that day, I walked out into the late afternoon sunshine, determined to get back to Park House, put the whole sorry business behind me. The future, as far as the rest of my contract was concerned, now seemed assured.

The next day the case closed and, as predicted, Lord Althorp retained custody of the children. It is necessary to mention that, during the euphoria that must have enveloped him as he realized he was going to win, Lord Althorp remembered that I too had parents who must have been very anxious for me. Excusing himself from his friends, he telephoned my father to tell him how well I had stood my ground and how proud he was of me. Such thoughtfulness was so very typical of Lord Althorp and is a trait that he passed on to all his children. In the meantime, I caught the train to Kings Lynn where Smith waited to drive me to Park House, to prepare and look forward to the summer holidays with the children.

Chapter Eight

I had a few days alone with Charles at Park House before the summer holidays were due to begin although he was still at school during the day. I was grateful for this respite after the pressures of the previous week. Charles and I were often alone, but I loved the gentle drifting of endless days set in a place seemingly untouched by the real world. I was surprised at how quickly the tranquillity enveloped me and helped me dismiss the disturbances and discomfort that the trial had brought into all of our lives.

Diana was the first of the children to break up for the holiday. The days before we were to be joined by the other children would enable me to see if Diana had any inkling of what had happened while she was away at school, and if she had, to help settle her mind. I had nothing to fear. Whatever feelings the parents had towards each other, they made sure the children were not affected. For any events that were held at the school, arrangements were made that either one or the other parent attended, never both, so Diana was not conscious of an atmosphere between them. Diana was always equally pleased to see either parent. Both parents attended only her confirmation when she was at West Heath – such an important occasion – until her wedding of course, but that was a long time in the future.

Now I welcomed Diana home, waiting for signs of unease. But so far as I know none of the children ever realized that the retrial had happened. Happy to be back at the place she loved the best, with weeks of glorious holiday ahead of her, Diana was on top form. She had completed her first year at Riddlesworth and had done it in style. Excitedly she told me she had won the 'Legatt Cup' for helpfulness, for volunteering to do things around the school. This did not surprise me at all; Diana always liked to feel that she was being useful. I was very pleased and her father was so proud of his daughter. She had proved to be popular with the staff, she was eager to please and well-mannered. Always co-operative, she carried out appointed tasks with willingness. Her report on her conduct was glowing and she deserved her reward.

Certainly it was true that Diana was lucky she had not gone as a complete stranger to Riddlesworth, but it had still been a very big step for her to take after the little day school of Silfield. The friends who had advised Lord Althorp on this wise move to help fill in the long hours of freedom that attendance at a day school gives – Lady Wake-Walker, Diana's aunt, and her godmother, Sarah Pratt – both had daughters there, and of course Alexandra Loyd had started at the same time. From when I first knew Diana, I was impressed how admirably she always tackled change in her life. From having a mother at home to no mother, from day school to boarding school, and eventually from being a girl about town to becoming a Princess. The sheer determination and strong will she displayed from early childhood never left her.

Diana was a competent, capable, adaptable little girl. After the initial, and to be expected, homesickness, she had settled well at Riddlesworth. The school advocated that a boarding school should provide a stable, family atmosphere to help children develop naturally and happily and to provide security; as much as possible, a home from home. The headmistress, Miss Ridsdale (or Riddy as Diana and the other girls nicknamed her), recognized the individual qualities of each of her pupils. The qualities that Diana possessed, her practicality and kind-heartedness were soon acknowledged. She wisely gave Diana every opportunity to put these to use, thus building up her confidence.

At the start of the holidays, with Diana home, we switched from term-time routine to holiday routine with no effort. I always found it remarkable how efficiently and smoothly life at Park House rolled on, considering there was no mother at hand and Lord Althorp was often away. I was pleased to have Diana to myself for a few days. She had arrived back from school laden with her belongings, trunk, tuck-box and of course, Peanuts. In the year that Diana had been at school, she had grown quite considerably, so some of her school clothes, if they could not be lengthened, would have to be replaced. Diana's mother always attended to this, buying from Harrods, the shop that stocked the school uniform. Like many mothers, she also preferred to choose most of Diana's casual clothes too and these would be sent back with her when the holiday time with her mother was complete.

As I had at the start of the Easter holidays, I now left Diana to settle in and get herself organized. This did not take long and with Charles still at school, she seemed as pleased to have my company to herself, as I was pleased to be with her. She was surprised how quickly our puppies had grown and they now accompanied us when we went for walks. When they came, I took just Suski along with us too, hoping they would benefit from the example of her good behaviour. Amina certainly did not need any encouragement from the springer spaniel, Jill, to disappear into the undergrowth. My efforts were focused on having her concentration so she remained with me. Suski was intended to be the good influence on her rather erratic behaviour.

Diana had matured considerably between Easter and summer. True, we knew each other better and were therefore more at ease together. The success of winning a prize had given her added confidence. The pleasure expressed by her father, the staff, Charles and myself at seeing her home, must also have contributed to her sense of feeling wanted. She cared greatly for her young brother with a self-imposed sense of responsibility towards him imbued in her since the early departure of her mother from the family home. This did not prevent her from experiencing and revelling in a sense of superiority over him, now that she had finished one year of boarding school, placing her in the same category as her sisters, while Charles was still at day school.

During those first days of Diana's holiday, we walked the dogs twice a day. Naturally we talked when we were together in the house, but then we would both be occupied with other things. When we walked together, we could give each other our full attention. At first we talked about school. Silfield had been a wonderful stepping stone from Ally – the governess who had taught at Park House, but could no longer find the heart to remain once the children's mother had left – to Riddlesworth, but it could not compete with Diana's new school, with its extensive timetable, and she was full of enthusiasm to relate to me all her new options.

Diana told me that Scottish dancing and natural dance movement were all part of the curriculum, but she was allowed ballet lessons as well. Another extra class was riding and I joked with

Diana that I was surprised she had not put her name down for that as well as the ballet. She did not realize immediately that I was only teasing her after the experience of her fall during the Easter holidays, and earnestly explained to me that as the leg requirements of the two were so different – one needed a straight leg, while the other bent – it was not sensible to try to do both.

From those early schooldays, through her teenage years and into adulthood, Diana had maintained her love for dance and singing. She wrote to me eighteen months before she married and told me then that the love of her life was to dance and sing. Critical of herself, she said she had an 'awful voice' and compared herself, quite without justification, to 'an elephant when dancing – so no one watches me'. This modesty totally belies the truth about her competence, which has since been shown on stage – with Wayne Sleep, for example.

I laughed with Diana and said I was sure the leg positions had nothing to do with her reluctance to ride. Diana, a real tease herself, could stand being teased and took my jests in good heart. I reiterated that there was no need for her to ride, she was involved in plenty of other sport, but why didn't she admit the fall had not helped her enthusiasm? Quite rightly, she put me in my place by reminding me that she had also fallen while skiing and that had not affected her fondness of that sport. It never hindered her future participation; indeed, when she had left finishing school in Switzerland, she wrote and told me how she had 'hated it, except for the skiing'.

So our wanderings were filled with good-natured banter which proved what an easy relationship we were beginning to establish. When we walked, we often met Ally, whose exit had hastened the children's introduction to school life. She had retained a diplomatic friendship with both parents. When Diana introduced me to her, I was not surprised that she had displayed such diplomacy. She was a dignified, refined lady, eloquent and courteous with, I would imagine, a very strict code of behaviour which was expounded upon in the nursery classroom with gentle, quiet authority. She too had a keeshond, and now that she was retired, she was often in the woods and if we were going in the same direction, we would walk together. Diana never forgot her early influence, nor the kindness of her old governess. She invited her to her wedding, but sadly Ally died a month earlier.

When we walked with just the pups and Suski, we had more chance to see the wildlife. We both loved the gentle fallow deer, they looked so beautiful. Far from tame, they would disappear into the depths of the woods as soon as they spotted us. However quiet we were, we could not persuade them we meant no harm. Sometimes a stag was with them, antlers held high. He looked so proud and noble, in his own way as magnificent as the larger members of his family that are to be found in Scotland. Diana loved the deer as she loved all animals. I am sure that one of the reasons she so enjoyed the story of Hiawatha was because she felt she could relate to the affinity he had with all the creatures. I could never believe she would willingly be enticed to go stag hunting in the early days of her marriage. I wondered then if she remembered the deer that had so often shadowed us on our walks. She abhorred killing and any unnecessary infliction of pain on defenceless animals merely for human pleasure: not an easy belief to hold in the circles in which she later had to move.

Talk of school antics was replaced by talk of plans for the long summer holidays. We had had a few days on our own and in two days' time Charles would break up, while Sarah should arrive that day, to be followed the next week by Jane who was to spend the first few days of her holiday with her mother. When Jane did come to Sandringham I found her so good-natured and thoughtful. She always fitted in, no dramas, and she had a relaxing effect on her father. I considered Sarah to be thoughtful and giving one moment and then entirely self-centred another. Both girls had tremendous characters; one was just more aware of Sarah as she was so volatile. I used to have to warn her, 'Now, don't encourage Diana, don't lead her on.' I never had to speak to Jane like that.

Beside the annual flower show and the Kings Lynn Festival, we planned to spend days on the beach, play tennis and of course make full use of the pool. There were always visitors and friends to look forward to as well. With Sarah's imminent arrival on her mind, Diana told me that Sarah had written to her and said how strict the headmistress was at West Heath and how girls would be expelled if they were caught smoking or drinking. I told Diana I thoroughly agreed with this rule and that both were habits to be avoided even when she was of legal age. My advice was not needed. Diana, interested as she was in sports and with a wish to be healthy, was never tempted to smoke or drink. She did have a sweet tooth and chocolates were her greatest temptation. Cook, aware of this, always supplied a wonderful choice of desserts when Diana was at home, which Diana would eat with gusto and then complain that she was fat. I assured her it was only puppy fat which would disappear as she grew older. But it was not until her marriage to Prince Charles that Diana really slimmed.

I suggested to Diana that as we had so much time in the school holidays, perhaps we would get a chance to do some of our own cooking especially if her father was away and cook had time off. We had enjoyed our experiment of baking bread in the previous holiday and now we could go one step further. Our culinary skills did leave a certain amount to be desired. Baked beans on toast or boiled egg became Diana's fortes. Later when Diana had escaped from the finishing school she so disliked, she told me that her mother had sent her on a twelve-week cookery course which she found 'great fun'. Perhaps her attempts at Park House provided her with good grounding; in any case she left the course feeling 'fully domesticated, just what my mother set out to do'. The final feather in her domestic cap was her experience with children. She confided to me that the 'first test of my maternal instincts was a complete failure'. That episode did not deter her and, when she moved to work for another family, 'I loved it'. This, of course, was all in the future, but it is interesting to remember Diana as a child, what we did together and what we talked about and thus relate it to her later life.

We returned from our afternoon walk to find that Sarah had arrived. As we neared the house, we saw the Simca standing by the front door, boot open as Smith, helped by Sarah, unloaded her belongings. He had been to Kings Lynn station to collect her and looked in need of a cup of tea to help him recover from the chatter and exuberance of the homeward journey. Diana rushed ahead of me to meet her sister, the understated response given by Sarah skilfully covering her pleasure of seeing her young sister. I told her how good it was to see her back and, greetings over, together the two girls disappeared through the front door. Smith drove off in the car and I wandered round to the back of the house to put the dogs away in the kennels. I knew I had some time on my own while Diana watched and chatted to Sarah as she unpacked her cases.

An hour later, I left to drive to Silfield to collect Charles. He too was looking forward to the long holidays and regarded it as grossly unfair that he still had two more days at school while his sisters had already broken up. I told him not to worry and that when he started at his prep school, he would have equally long holidays. This was not much of a consolation to him. Boarding school was an unknown quantity and he more readily accepted the shorter holidays at his day school. On our return to the house, Charles went at once to see his sister but apart from the natural affection between older sister and young brother their age difference meant they had little in common. Jane, although just two years younger than Sarah, had more of an affinity with Charles, their natures were similar, both gentle and more serious minded.

Sarah had arrived back in Norfolk ahead of her friends. I had decided to take the next day as my day off as it was my last chance before Charles broke up and there would be no more breaks until the children went to stay with their mother, four weeks later. Charles had been invited to a friend's house for tea after school and I told Lord Althorp that if Smith would collect him, I would make sure I was back by the time they returned. Unless I was going away for a weekend or had something specific planned which entailed a full day away, I always saw Charles off to school and met him on his return. My life at Park House could scarcely be constituted as 'work', the most important part of my job was that I was there and helped to make a good, secure, happy home. Sometimes on my day off my mother or father would come to Park House to spend time with me and we would go out for lunch in one of the old pubs that abounded in the nearby villages. Lord Althorp always made my parents very welcome as he did my friends. On one of my father's visits, he brought my Canadian uncle and aunt with him. Like many visitors from the New World, my aunt was 'doing England' in five days, while my uncle, who did not share the same ambition, was content to spend his time playing golf. They did however put one day aside – which made 'doing England' even more of a feat – to visit their niece. My aunt, a through and through royalist, was thrilled to have the opportunity to see the Queen's winter home. Years later though, it is with the story of her hour-long visit to Park House, childhood home of the Princess of Wales, that she has regaled her friends – she never would have imagined it!

On my last day off, I suggested to Sarah and Diana that they might like to come to visit my parents with me and we would stop somewhere on the way for lunch. I knew Sarah was at a loose end until her friends arrived home from school and it would make a break for us to go out together. Both Sarah and Diana readily agreed with my idea. As soon as Charles had left for school, Diana said she would see to her guinea-pig and spend some time with Mrs Smith telling her what clothes in the trunk were no longer of any use to her, while Sarah and I went for a short ride across the park. Sarah was keen to ride Peppermint again after several weeks away, and I took Romany. It was at times such as this that I missed my own horse, but I rarely rode in the holidays as I was too busy with all the children at home, so occasionally, as on that particular morning, Romany was fine, even though a bit small.

We planned to be away from Park House by 11 a.m. and managed to leave on time. Due to her seniority, Sarah was elected to sit in the front with me, while Diana, complaining, had to accept a back seat, not something she was ever keen to do either in practice or metaphorically. She said it was not fair and she would feel sick, only to be told by her sister to be quiet. I added that she had no choice as she knew her father always said the youngest children had to sit in the back of the car. Diana, accepting defeat, acquiesced and accepted her position under sufferance.

We stopped for a light lunch in a small café near Norwich. I knew my mother would have prepared sandwiches, cake and trifles for an early afternoon tea so there was no need to eat a large meal. Sarah wanted to stop in Norwich so she could call at a saddlers. She needed more saddle soap and leather dressing as she hoped to persuade Diana, playing on her sister's love of keeping everything clean, to extend her talents to encompass tack. There was one on the outskirts of the city, which meant we did not have to drive into the centre. I was grateful, as I doubted whether we would ever arrive at my parents' house if we got involved with shops.

As we drove through the suburbs of Norwich I showed them

where I used to live in a three-bedroom rented terraced house, which I had shared with two other girls when I had worked in Norwich. Diana was interested to know who did all the housework and whether we had taken it in turns. I said we were meant to but it did not always work out that way. They thought it was a good idea to share, although Diana said she would hate to be with untidy people. As I looked at the house, I could not help but think what a far cry it was from my home at Sandringham. I had been happy there, independent and carefree, I had enjoyed a good working – I worked for an employment agency – and social life. Positioned in a popular part of the city, its narrow, steep street lined either side with mean-looking terraced houses it was not the sort of home in which the girls were ever likely to live. Diana told me that their father had a terraced house in London where we later stayed during our visits to the capital. Then I realized what a loose comparison Diana had been kind enough to make. There is a considerable difference between a little terraced home shared by three young girls earning their first wages, and an elegant, three-storey house in one of the most exclusive parts of London.

During the last part of the journey from Norwich to Flegg-burgh, I pointed out landmarks connected with my own childhood. As we passed through Thorpe on the eastern side of Norwich, I showed them the school I had attended from when I was ten years old – Thorpe House School, a lovely old school, approached by a long drive skirted either side with woods which shielded it from the road. Diana asked if it took boarders, and I explained it was only a day school except for a handful of girls who had boarded elsewhere in the city. Sometimes, if I was really lucky, my parents would take me by car, but usually I went by bus, leaving home at 7.30 a.m. and arriving home at 5.30 p.m. There was no special school bus so we had to rely on public transport which did not take the direct route for the fifteen miles to Thorpe; instead it was a tortuous journey that wended its way through all the little villages. At the thought of such a trip every day, Diana felt that there were some advantages to boarding school life.

We travelled on the road across the marshes from Acle to Fleggburgh. I told the girls how I used to ride with a friend on the marshes looking for coypu runs into the dykes, then we informed the coypu control who would come and destroy them. 'How cruel,' said Diana. 'Why should they do that?' I told her it was because they did so much damage to the waterways. When Diana asked what they looked like, I described them as rodents that originally came from South America and looked like very large rats. They come from the same family. Sarah, unable to let an opportunity to tease Diana slip by, added that they were not dissimilar to a very large version of Peanuts, all part of the same animal group – vermin. 'Leave it, Diana, leave it,' I said. 'She's only teasing you.' I could sense Diana's hackles rise at such an unsavoury comparison to her beloved pet. I really did not want us to arrive at my parents' home in the middle of a heated debate. To rapidly change the subject and calm the waters, I told them how my brother John and I used to love to come with friends to fish in part of an area of the marshes called the 'Muck Fleet'. This surprising name did the trick, quelled the rodent uprising, as they laughed at such an unusual name. 'Why was it called that, did it smell?' wondered Diana. I assured her there was no smell, but neither did I know how the name had originated. I said John and I used to like to go off on our bikes to explore. I loved the wide open spaces of the marshes while he preferred the common where we picked blackberries in the autumn amongst the hedgerows. I explained that as it was land owned by the church, people were allowed to graze their animals during the summer months. I described the lovely little cottages with their thatched roofs that could only be reached at that time by foot or bicycle. Diana wanted to know if we would get a chance to walk around it and out to the open Norfolk Broads area that lay beyond, but I said I doubted we would have time on this visit. In fact, we never did.

The journey passed so quickly, made all the more pleasurable by such childhood stories, exploits with slight variations, that are shared by so many children who spend their early years in the countryside, which, with my eager audience, had been a joy to recount. On arrival at my parents' home, introductions over, we sat in the lounge and talked. As I had prophesied, my mother had laid the coffee table and trolley with goodies, all home cooked, drawing on her years of experience in producing food that she knew would be appreciated by youngsters. The selection of sand-wiches included ones filled with peanut butter. 'We were talking about Peanuts on the way here,' said Sarah, with a sly, sideways glance at Diana. I shot Sarah a warning look that I hoped implied 'Don't you dare'. There was no need for my concern. While Sarah was completely at ease, Diana was far too overcome with her normal shyness to attempt to answer back, even had she heard her sister's comment. It made no difference where we were, only on home ground did Diana become confident. My mother was homely and natural, the years of teaching before her marriage providing her with more than enough experience to cope with a young girl overcome with shyness. In such a setting, it was not long before Diana began to relax and what my mother's manner did not achieve, her lovely cakes soon did as Diana eagerly accepted the offerings which my mother was only too happy to keep putting her way. She was of the school which strongly believes that 'it's lovely to see children with a healthy appetite'. In her eyes, fads, such as diets, were a complete nonsense. 'Just help yourself, dear,' she said to Diana, who politely waited to be invited to take another tasty biscuit or bun. Diana, gaining in confidence, glanced shyly at my mother with eyes just slightly raised, and started to obey her instruction.

My father, busy in the shop, popped in now and again for a quick chat, his easy-going, open manner making both girls feel at home. By this time Diana had ceased to study the lounge carpet. Though still quite quiet, she politely answered my father and managed to look up at whomever she spoke to. Sarah made up for her sister's reserve, laughing and joking and a lively conversation flowed naturally. On form, Sarah always left a feeling of warmth behind her. The vibrant, outgoing disposition which she possessed attracted people towards her. My parents remembered her visit, long after that of her little sister.

Making our farewells, we started for home. I wanted to make sure I was back for Charles's return at 6 p.m. As soon as we were in the car, Diana started to chatter away nineteen to the dozen. She had heard her sister's comment about the sandwich filling. 'Honestly, you are *mean*, Sarah,' but I hushed her and said it was just a joke. I was always so sorry that so many people did not see this bright, chatty side of Diana, but guessed it was just a matter of time and that as she grew older and more confident, she would do herself as much justice in company as she did in private. The journey home was uneventful. Charles was to finish school the next day and we decided that we would all go to the station to meet Jane when she arrived at the weekend. Diana advocated that we should also take Gitsie and Amina with us as Jane had not met them. I said that with all of us and the luggage there would not be room and she would see them soon enough at Park House.

Charles finished school, his report was good as had been expected. He was an easy affable pupil who coped well with his lessons and caused no concern to his parents. As planned we met Jane at the station and with everyone then collected at Park House we felt that the holidays had started in earnest. Jane's arrival caused hardly a stir, and she fitted in as if she had never been away, although her room gave lie to this because it never quite achieved the same lived-in feel as did Sarah's room. Certainly it was a great deal tidier. Sarah and Jane, both pupils at West Heath, did not have much in common. Sarah, equally capable, often seemed to throw opportunities away because of her cavalier approach and left school after O levels. Jane, much more serious, completed school in a more conventional manner, getting her A levels. They both enjoyed swimming and tennis, but because Jane spent most of her free time with her mother she had not maintained the same number of friends in the area as Sarah, so during her visits to Park House nearly all of her time was spent with her brother and sister and both Diana and Charles loved the time she gave to them. However, neither Sarah nor Jane could resist the opportunity of good-naturedly teasing Diana. There was a great deal of banter which Diana brought upon herself. Her main interest lay in whether her sisters met any boys when they were allowed out from school. She was never able to extract an acceptable answer from them on this subject. Instead they would turn the tables on to her and tease her about any she found attractive. Diana, still so young, had at that time very little chance of meeting boys, her step-brother and Prince Andrew being just two of a small selection. When the royal family had stayed at Sandringham the previous winter, after attending the Sunday morning church service Diana had made the mistake of announcing that she thought Prince Andrew was very good looking. Her sisters had not allowed her to forget this admission and used it as ammunition against her when her questions to them became too personal. It was just good-natured talk, but whenever they accused her of having a 'crush' on Prince Andrew Diana would turn a brilliant red and hotly deny it.

Possibly because their own mother was so young when she married, it was always assumed that the girls would marry early. So when they teased Diana, she always retaliated by betting which sister would marry first, always supposing that 'anyone would want to marry them'. As Sarah was the eldest it was taken for granted that she would be the first to marry. It was, however, Jane who married Sir Robert Fellowes, now the Queen's private secretary, who helped Diana fulfil her ambition to be a bridesmaid again. She had loved being one once before when she was much younger. Diana described it to me as one of her 'happiest days for a very long time' and 'very emotional'. Later, when I told her I was to get married, she wrote and said that 'if Jane and Robert's marriage was anything to go by, the whole thing should be blissful'. Their marriage reconfirmed in Diana's mind the belief she held from childhood, that two people who loved each other should maintain a happy marriage, a partnership and a unity made even more fulfilling by having children. This is a belief she still upheld when years later I took my son, then four years old, to the birthday party of Jane's first daughter, Laura, at their grace and favour home in Kensington Palace.

As Diana was often teased about Prince Andrew, it was quite ironic that a few years later Sarah was the first sister to go out with one of the royal princes. Diana had written to me and told me that they had been busy trying to marry Sarah off, it was even considered at one stage in 1977 that Prince Charles might be a contender, but 'that died a death'. Not long after this event, I met Diana and Sarah in London for lunch, when we joked about the whole episode. There had been enough pictures of Prince Charles and Sarah together in the papers to make her instantly recognizable and Sarah quite enjoyed the attention she had focused on her in the restaurant, while Diana also basked in the interest, the crippling shyness of her childhood already having become less acute. In truth, we all found it harmlessly amusing. The reality was that Sarah shared with Diana the same views about the necessity to really love the person you wanted to marry, and, much as she enjoyed the company of Prince Charles and shared many of his interests, music, horses and skiing included, she certainly did not love him and made sure the media were aware of this in her blunt, outspoken fashion. Sarah stressed the relationship was platonic. 'I am not in love with him and I wouldn't marry anyone I didn't love, whether he was a dustman or the King of England.' Thus Sarah broke the unwritten law of never speaking to the press and brought about an end to her relationship with Charles, although he, admiring her frankness and honesty, remained on friendly terms with Sarah even after her marriage in 1980 to Neil McCorquodale – by coincidence another member of Barbara Cartland's family. Sarah never entertained the idea that their relationship would become permanent, however much the press might speculate – a hobby they had pursued for many years whenever Prince Charles appeared publically with a different girl. Sarah, much more extrovert and worldly than Diana, was more aware of the implications of a royal marriage, conscious that it spelt an end to all privacy both in past and future life. She never intended to put herself in a situation where her every move would be analysed and discussed throughout the world. Jane and Sarah both have sustained stable marriages, which unfortunately their young sister, whose only ambition from childhood was for such a marriage, has failed to do. The collapse of her marriage added extra strain amongst the sisters with Jane being in the most invidious position, her loyalties torn between her husband and his Palace duties and her sister, Diana. A most unfortunate set of circumstances. After the mistakes made by their parents, all the girls wanted to be as sure as possible that they would not follow in their footsteps. Diana, ironically, fell in love with one of the only men in the country from whom separation and divorce would have been considered impossible. In her wildest dreams she could not have anticipated that her chosen love would come with such a guarantee. How ironic that even that failed to prevent the collapse of Diana's hopes and dreams, and proved that guarantees are not necessarily unassailable.

Prior to Diana's wedding, when she expressed her doubts to her sisters as to whether Charles did really love her, that all-important factor in her eyes, they, both secure in their marriages, assured her it was pre-wedding nerves and Sarah, long since forgetting why she had not been interested in marriage to Prince Charles, even had it ever been a possibility, teased Diana as she had always done, this time by telling her it was too late to do anything now, her face was on all the teacloths and not to worry.

Advice that, by the evening before her wedding day, Diana, staying at Clarence House with her sister Jane, had accepted. Jane wrote to me afterwards that they were so excited and there was so much noise they 'did not sleep a wink that night'.

I did not allow teasing to go on for too long at home, as Diana against her two quick-tongued older sisters made for a rather unfair competition. It was necessary for both Diana and Charles to learn to stand on their own two feet as there would be times at school when they would need to stand up for themselves and would not be able to rely on an adult to help them. They needed to learn how to cope without being hurt. I knew how incredibly cruel children can be to each other, particularly if they discover a weakness in one of their contemporaries. Charles did not leave himself open to being teased by his sisters in the same way that Diana did, neither did it concern him, he just let it pass over his head. I never allowed Sarah to tease Diana to the stage where she got upset.

Sarah, Jane and Charles all did credit to themselves academically at school, so with the end-of-term discussion about the reports, I was so pleased for Diana that she had won the Legatt Cup, to put her on a kind of equal footing with her brother and sisters. When we were on our own, Diana discussed tests and exams with me and said how much she dreaded them and she wondered if she would ever be able to manage to pass them. Was it, she worried, necessary to have exams to work with children? I told her it was not, but that there were courses she could join to give her a suitable qualification and that such courses were not dependent on academic success. I told her, as I had done before, that the most important thing was that she made an effort, and this is obviously what she had done, which is why she had been rewarded with the cup. I added, to boost her confidence, that it takes all sorts of people to make a world and how hopeless it would be if everyone was good at the same thing. Platitudes may be repeated on countless occasions, but can still bring consolation. Practical aptitude is as important as academic aptitude and it was rare to find people who excelled in both. I told Diana about one of my friends, who was good at his work, but found it impossible to put his knowledge on to paper for his exams and never managed to pass any except biology. This, however, had not prevented him from obtaining a good job where his qualities and capabilities were recognized. I stressed to Diana that if she believed in herself, others would believe in her and she would do well. On no account was she to consider herself not as good as her contemporaries, just because she found tests and exams difficult and nerve-racking.

Diana was interested to know how I had managed at school. I told her that in practical subjects and sport, except for tennis, I was not much good, but that I did all right in exams. I hastened to add that did not mean I enjoyed them, I merely regarded them as a change from lessons. I explained that as I had been at day school, it was necessary for me to do my homework in the evenings. As the exams drew near, there was no homework as we were meant to spend the time on revision. I told Diana how strict my parents were about my revision and that immediately our evening meal was finished I had to go to my bedroom to work. But there, instead of poring over my books, I would get out my atlas and plan my journeys across Europe and then the rest of the world. Usually my travels were going to be on horseback. That, I explained to Diana, was the nearest I ever got to geography revision and really it did not cover the syllabus. I said I always did well in subjects that for me required no revision, such as English language, French and maths, but in others I just scraped by, although I did make an effort for the state exams. As I pointed out to Diana, I accepted I was not much good at practical things so it was necessary for me to do well in something. We laughed and agreed I was not really domesticated as Diana was always helping me to do the jobs in the house that I found so tedious and in which she took such pride. I then suggested we put all thoughts of school behind us for a few weeks and concentrate on the pleasures of the holidays.

Chapter Nine

All year round, visitors were attracted to the Sandringham estate. During the summer, except when any of the royal family were in residence, the house was open to the public. That, with its well-cared-for grounds, the nearby church and the estate itself, with large areas left free for tourists to explore, made an enjoyable day's outing. Even when the grounds were closed to the public, many still made the trip, especially at weekends, to take advantage of the lovely walks and see for themselves the beauty of this special part of Norfolk. The Queen's stables were in the same vicinity and at nearby West Newton were the dog kennels where her gun dogs were bred and trained. Regardless of the time of year, a fine day would ensure that the wide, green verges on either side of the road would provide a temporary camping ground for the day trippers, lucky enough to have the opportunity to glimpse this part of royal England.

They came well-equipped with picnic table and chairs, gas burners to brew up a nice cup of tea, which no self-respecting Englishman can do without, and Tupperware containers full of sandwiches, salad and other picnic foods. After a relaxing meal, some would choose to set off on a walk, their dogs leaping about with ill-concealed excitement in anticipation of all the new smells they would encounter and, if they were really lucky, they might even come across a rabbit or two. A good walk to settle the lunch, take in their surroundings and by the time they returned, meal digested, they could start on the picnic tea. Others lay back in their deckchairs and sun loungers, took up the newspaper and prepared to relax amongst the peace and beauty, while their disgruntled dogs, hooked by their leads on to car bumpers or to the leg of the chair, could only look on with envy at those with more considerate masters and who were fortunate enough to be allowed to set off into the unknown. The only hope for those held captive was that there would still be some rabbits left by the time their owners had completed the after-lunch snooze.

Although large tracts of the estate were open for exploration by the visitors, there was much that remained private and was used only by the local people. I preferred Sandringham out of season when it was much quieter and we rarely saw any traffic. I acknowledged how pleasant it was for those who lived in towns to have the opportunity to benefit from the relative proximity of this countryside. During the times when there was a large invasion of tourists, in the school summer holidays, we rarely went outside the gates of Park House; instead we spent our time in the grounds of the house or in the parkland area hidden from the road by thick shrubs and trees and if that were to prove an insufficient barrier, this screen of foliage contained a wrought-iron fence that surrounded the entire area. Still, it would not have been difficult for visitors to venture further, the place was by no means impregnable, but already they had so much space where they were legally entitled to wander that courteous and well-mannered, appreciative of their surrounds, most observed the 'No Entry' and 'Private' signs.

Sundays were, without doubt, the busiest day for the grass verges. It was not unusual, especially if the weather was good, to find every inch covered with cars lined side by side, with just enough space between to allow for the picnic. Thankfully, the people who came to share our beautiful estate, came for the peace and tranquillity, so there were no offensive radios or ghetto blasters screaming out, shattering the silence and obliterating the birdsong. There was thoughtfulness and respect paid towards fellow travellers.

On one of the first Sundays during the summer holidays, Sarah, at a loose end, suggested that we go for a ride. Jane was with Charles and Diana, so there was no reason why I could not be free for an hour. We set off, after I had reminded Diana and Charles that they were not allowed to swim until my return. This was one of my major rules: the children were never allowed in the pool unless they were under supervision. They never questioned or disobeyed me once, realizing the seriousness of the consequences should there be an accident. I was especially nervous about Diana diving, in case she miscalculated the depth and hit her head on the bottom.

Sarah and I rode across the park. It was a glorious day and although still quite early, visitors had already begun to arrive. We could hear the cars in the distance and determined to make the most of the weather that for once had shown consideration towards those free from work. We left the park at the far end and decided to ride home via West Newton and the verges by the roadside. As we rode towards the Loyds' house we looked across the fields and could see in the distance moving coloured dots – the cars driving along the straight road that led from the Kings Lynn–Fakenham road down to the estate. It was certainly going to be very busy later that day. We had a few canters as we crossed the park and now rode our horses quietly in a walk towards home. We passed the turn-off that led to the Queen's stables and neared the Norwich gates, the main entrance to Sandringham House. Across the gravel drive and on to the verge again. I was in mid-sentence and suddenly Sarah disappeared, not quite in a cloud of dust, but certainly with a thunder of hooves, as without warning she galloped off towards home, Peppermint rapidly gaining speed, realizing she was to be allowed to break the hallowed rule that the homeward stretch is to be ridden at a walk to allow the horse to relax and cool down. My horse, borrowed from a friend for the summer, not to be outdone and sensing no resistance from me – for who can resist a gallop with such good going underfoot and the challenge of a race to boot – picked up the gauntlet, 'Race you', slung at me by Sarah as she took off and accelerated from 0 m.p.h. to a speed that would do justice to a racing car.

I really knew it was not the correct way to conduct myself. It would have been more responsible if I had refused to follow Sarah's example and, instead, set one of my own by arriving home in an orderly manner. For some subconscious, inexplicable reason, the impulsive side of my nature came to the fore reminding me I was still young and now and again common sense was pushed into second place. So rarely did this happen, I cannot remember another example but that is what happened on that Sunday. I loved the excitement of the chase, everything passing in a blur, wind in my face, it was just so exhilarating. My horse, slightly faster, soon made up the ground and drew level with Sarah. The visitors, their cars just parked, looked up startled as we careered past, interrupting them for a moment from the concentration and progress involved in setting up temporary home while they soaked up the peace around them. The last thing they had expected was to see two girls on horseback charging past at a quite unacceptable pace, disturbing the silence they had so recently discovered.

Quickly we passed them, the sound of their yapping dogs still reverberating in our ears as we left the verge and crossed the green near the entrance to the church. I shouted to Sarah that we should stop. Side by side, a perfect combination, we jumped the wooden bench seat – luckily vacant at this early hour, no one yet returned from their walks and needful of a rest – and pulled up at the entrance to Park House. One rule we certainly would not break was to travel down the drive at anything other than a walk. It was far too dangerous and we were definitely not that irresponsible. We agreed the race was a draw, walked the horses around for a few moments to cool them, before we turned them out to graze, laughing as we recalled the astonished look on the tourists' faces as we had raced past.

Later, by the pool with Charles and Diana, Smith came to speak to me. Sarah and I had been so involved with our race, that we were oblivious to any of the cars that had driven by. It transpired that Smith passed us in the jeep and had been appalled at our 'thoughtless, irresponsible behaviour'. He accused us of showing contempt for those who just wanted a quiet day out in an area that we took for granted. I was rather taken aback by this onslaught. Contempt had been the last thing on our minds, it was just good fun that had not harmed anyone. Even as Smith spoke to me, I knew that I would not be the only recipient of his sharp tongue. He would have no hesitation to speak to Sarah in the same fashion even if she was his employer's daughter. He knew he was on safe ground with Lord Althorp, who would also have disapproved of our race.

Diana, seeing the discomfort on my face as it became apparent that Smith was rebuking me, ceased her swimming to wander casually by, but within earshot, for the chance to hear someone else being reprimanded for a misdemeanour that she could so easily relate to as it so exactly personified her idea of fun, was too good an opportunity to miss. Smith reminded me of what I knew already, that Lord Althorp would not have been impressed. I silently agreed that in hindsight it had been a stupid way to act and

116

Lord Althorp would definitely not have approved. I was concerned that Smith would try and 'bring me down a peg or two' – the terminology he now and again used when he spoke about me – in his employer's eyes by recounting the affair to him, but although Smith and I did not always see eye to eye due to different schools, different generations, he would not knowingly make trouble for me, just leave me to worry for a time as to whether he would speak out or not.

Smith left and Diana came to sit with me. 'Oh dear,' I said. 'I hope there is not going to be any aggravation. I guess it was a silly thing to do.' Diana, knowing Smith better than I – he had protected her in the same way several times, by keeping his own counsel – assured me, 'Smith won't tell Daddy, he just enjoyed telling you off, don't worry.' Sarah had already left to visit her friend Isabel but I knew she would not be at all perturbed either by the rebuke that Smith would hand out to her, or as to whether her father was told or not. She could just laugh and know nothing more would be said as long as she promised it would not be repeated. Thereby lay the glaringly obvious divide between us. Although I shared the same life and was treated with respect and in some ways on equal terms, I was an employee and had to be answerable to Lord Althorp. Quite rightly; he did pay my wages! There was certainly no danger of any repetition, I had no intention of doing anything to displease Lord Althorp.

Jane would stay until the end of the Kings Lynn Festival and would then depart to her mother's home so I wanted to ensure that we had as many enjoyable outings as was feasible to fit in during the time she was with us. At weekends it was better to stay within the confines of our grounds; however, it was much quieter on weekdays so we determined that the first fine day we would visit Brancaster Beach where the family had a beach hut and have a real day out by the sea.

I put the visitor-scaring escapade firmly behind me. Diana had, quite correctly, assessed that Smith would not cause any trouble so it was best forgotten. I checked the weather forecast and the tides and we set our sights on the Tuesday, which was also convenient for the friends who would come with us. To have a good party and make the trip worthwhile, I said to the children that they could each invite a friend. There would not be much room in the jeep but we would manage for the short journey. It was to be our first visit of the year, for although only fifteen miles away, the combination of the organization to get there and the many pleasures afforded at home, meant that full advantage was not taken of the beach hut. There had been strong winds and storms in the spring and as it was a very exposed stretch of coast, it would be interesting to see how much, if any, of the hut was still visible or if it would be entirely covered by sand.

We decided to take the jeep, for besides ourselves, friends, the two puppies and the food, we also thought we ought to take spades, in case there was digging to be done. The other reason for taking the jeep was that the access to the hut was down an unmade track, not very accessible at the best of times and after the storms we were unsure just how passable it would prove to be. The arrangements were made and everyone was very enthusiastic. Cook prepared a fantastic hamper, she could not have the children's friends going back to their respective homes complaining about the food. Quite rightly, she took great pride in her catering abilities, be it for a dinner party, or, as in this instance, a picnic for children to take on the beach. We had chicken, pâté, cheese, a selection of sandwiches, yoghurts, cake, crisps and soft drinks. I thought there was enough food for an army, but the cook, more experienced in such matters than I, had correctly assessed the appetites of healthy children especially when they have been sharpened by the strong sea air.

Somehow, we all managed to pile into the jeep. The weather, which had been dull for most of the summer, had again managed to surpass expectations – as it generally did on days when it really mattered – it was warm, bright and sunny with no sign of any dark clouds threatening on the horizon. We set off in high spirits. The journey from Sandringham to Brancaster passes through mostly open countryside. Fields that have had their hedges removed, destroying the homes of wildlife for the sake of a few more acres of grain to add to the already considerable mountain, created acre upon acre of corn that waved golden in the sun on this lovely English summer day. It stretched as far as the eye could see, presenting quite a formidable task for the combines that would soon transform this sea of yellow into neat bales, leaving the land to return to its natural soil brown. Diana and Alexandra thought

118

how cruel it was that birds and animals should lose their natural habitat just for the sake of man's greed. I explained, too, that by removing the hedges all the natural windbreaks had been destroyed. As the land was so unprotected and the winds so fierce, much of the topsoil had been lost. Diana thought that it 'served them right for being so greedy'.

From the village of Docking it was just another four miles to the coast. The road skirted on either side by the endless fields that reached towards the sea. Norfolk calls its people back more than any other county in England, and it is because of the wide, open spaces and a sky that seems to go on for ever. Even the light is different and the wild North Norfolk coastline, so unspoilt as much of it belongs to the British Heritage and National Trust, has always been home for many artists and writers. Still a few miles from the sea, but the unmistakable tang of salt is in the air. The hauntingly eerie screech of the seagulls as they wheeled overhead could easily be distinguished, even above all the noise that emanated from the jeep. It was still too early yet for the birds to move further inland in search of the plough. Well before we were within earshot of the sea, it was possible to imagine we could hear the crash of waves on the beach. 'Not much further now,' cried the children. Diana, who liked to show off in front of friends, contradicted the general opinion expressed and pointed out that we still had to pass through the village of Brancaster. Sarah told her to stop being such a big-head and I told them all to be quiet and use their energies on guessing whether the tide was in or out.

We drove into Brancaster. Some of the old inhabitants still remained, whose families had lived there for generations, reaping their livelihood from the harvest of the sea and the land. As is so often the case though, the younger generation move away, looking for more excitement and better work opportunities in the cities and towns, and eventually their homes are put up for sale. Ironically, as country people move to the towns, high-flying executives or people who are just weary of city life decide to opt out and move to the country. Attracted by the unspoilt solitude of the protected North Norfolk coast and the lovely grey, flint cottages, they buy them and renovate them for their retreats or weekend homes. The money they can afford to pay far exceeds that which is available to any young local couple who might be tempted to move back to their area. Thus many of the villages become partly dormant with properties on the market at highly inflated prices. Brancaster was not as badly affected as some villages and still retains a nucleus of village life. In many ways it is sad to see the demise of the local population, but good to see homes that otherwise might have fallen into disrepair due to shortage of funds being lovingly restored, and much creative talent introduced into the region.

We turned off the main street on to the road that leads to the beach. It is flanked on either side by dykes lined with tall, swaying reeds and bulrushes. At the end of the road was the golf club. Here we said goodbye to tarmac as we swung right on to the access road to the beach hut. I immediately understood why Smith had recommended that we took the jeep. It was obvious that the Simca, even had there been room for all of us, would not have survived the journey across this rutted track. Sarah told me that normally here they let the dogs out as there was no danger from traffic, and let them chase after us. I readily agreed to this suggestion, as the dogs, sensing a new adventure, had started to leap about and added their excited barking to the already high volume of noise in the jeep. Stopping, I opened the door and they jumped out. Amina, sensing that rabbits abounded in the sand dunes, was off like a flash of lightning. Gitsie, much more reticent, looked at me with a quizzical frown on her face as she wondered what was going to happen. I glanced in my rear-view mirror as I drove slowly off and saw her chasing behind the jeep, determined not to let me out of her sight even though I seemed intent on deserting her! Amina, the sound of the jeep interrupting her furrowing in the dunes, joined in the chase. It was fairly unimportant to her whether the object of the hunt had legs or wheels!

I had checked the tides earlier in the local paper. Now, for the last few minutes of the journey, I had the children guessing if the sea was in or out. Hidden by the sand dunes, it was pure guesswork. The 'ins' won. Had the tide been out I would have chosen another day for our excursion to the beach. When it is out at Brancaster, it goes nearly to the horizon and there is no chance of swimming except in any pools that might remain. Halfway between shoreline and the horizon, lay an old shipwreck. Many people over the years had inadvertently risked their lives by walking out to explore the old wreck. Like a mirage in the desert, it was much further away than it appeared but worse than that, it presented danger. When the tide does turn on that part of the coast, it races in so fast, the speed is difficult to believe and to beat. Eventually, after some fatalities, the wreck was blown up to eradicate any further risks of death. However, when we used to go to the beach, the wreck was still there, a great, ugly, misshapen brown bulk on an otherwise golden expanse of sand. I gave the children very strict instructions that on no account were they to even consider and be tempted to explore the wreck, and spared no words in explaining what would befall them, both from the elements of nature and from myself, should they dare to ignore my warning. There was no need to do so for the beach and sand dunes lent themselves to so many activities.

Sarah and Jane, who could remember more clearly than the younger children the exact location of the hut, announced in unison that we had reached our destination. I stopped the jeep and we all piled out. Diana and Charles raced ahead to see what, if any, damage had been caused to the beach hut. During the journey speculation as to its condition had varied from 'There won't be anything wrong with it' from optimistic Jane, to 'I'm sure it will be completely ruined' from dramatic Diana. I shouted after the children to come back and help carry some of the gear. We seemed to have brought a tremendous amount for one day's outing. The other children politely helped with bags, while Sarah and Isabel took the all-important picnic hamper. Diana came rushing back to tell me, 'We definitely need the spades, you can hardly *see* the hut.' 'Great,' I thought to myself. 'We're going to have to spend the whole day digging.' I had told Lord Althorp we would sort out, as far as we were able, any damage that might have occurred. I handed the spades to the children and collecting my own bag, clambered over the dunes to inspect the damage. I heard Sarah's voice. 'Honestly, Diana, you do exaggerate.' Sure enough, visions of a day's heavy work disappeared in a flash to be replaced by one of relaxation in the dunes, as the majority of the hut came into view. Certainly some digging would be necessary, but not the Herculean job that Diana had implied.

The spring storms had made a valiant effort to engulf the hut but had failed. Jane told me that steps led to the entrance, but these had been completely covered and it was now possible to walk

121

straight in. I instructed the boys to start clearing the sand away. Jane searched inside for a container to put water in for the dogs who had collapsed exhausted in the sand after their exertions, Amina adding to the organized chaos by wagging her tail and sending up a cloud of sand that threatened to add a unique grit flavour to the contents of the hamper which had been prematurely opened by Diana in her search for some biscuits, as Alexandra was apparently hungry! I told Diana to shut the lid on the basket and that they could sweep away the sand that had blown under the door, covering the floor with a thin yellow film. The tasks were tackled willingly. I told the children that if everyone helped we could all be free sooner to make the most of the day. Sarah and Isabel, after they had carried the bags inside, thought their share of the work was done and spread out one of the blankets. They sat in deep conversation, I can only imagine discussing the heavy implications and responsibilities of being a teenager!

Soon all was restored to what I was assured was normal. At least the beach hut had withstood the battering of the winds, not a mean feat considering the ferocity of the weather in such an exposed area. We all changed into our swimming costumes and walked down to the sea, the children charging ahead, leaping from the top of the dunes and rolling the rest of the way down. Diana, landing ahead of the others, issued the challenge, 'You can't beat me', jumped up and was away, her feet seeming to barely touch the sand as she flew towards the sea, her hair streaming out behind her. The others, conscious of her unfair advantage with the headstart, chose to disregard her and left her to run alone as they went at their own pace to the water's edge, arriving in time to laugh at Diana who had rushed in with total disregard to the temperature, which even on this summer's day could only be called freezing. Gasping for breath, she shouted out for the other children to join her. 'It's lovely' – a comment that most chose to disbelieve. I certainly did. I gingerly allowed the waves to lap around my ankles for a few minutes before settling on the sand to watch the antics of the children. The three eldest girls ran in laughing and shrieking out at the sudden drop in temperature, while the boys were more cautious and played for a time on the edge until they got used to the water. The dogs, too, decided the sea was not for them. Gitsie flopped down beside me while Amina could not let the opportunity of investigating all these new smells pass her by. Sarah had brought a ball down to the beach and they all played piggy-in-the-middle in the sea. The game was accompanied by much splashing and great hilarity.

Even with all the activity, there was no disputing the fact that the sea was cold and it was impossible to stay in there for long. Sarah and Isabel wandered up the beach back to the hut, saying they would get the lunch organized. Jane and I briskly rubbed down the younger children, with towels already sticky with sand – an impossible task to prevent the sand from getting everywhere however much care is taken – and then supervised the building of sandcastles, Charles and John using their buckets to design one full of towers. Diana sent Alexandra off to collect stones to decorate the mound that she piled up with her hands and with her spade carved out a moat to surround the so-called castle which Charles derisively ridiculed as looking nothing like a castle. It was so unlike Charles to criticize anyone that his comments must have been made for the benefit of his friend. Diana, rather taken aback at this unusual attack from her brother, none the less jumped rapidly to the defence of her structure. Never at a loss for words when she was with people she knew, she announced that it was meant to be a ruined castle and, she claimed triumphantly, 'Yours will be too when the tide comes in.' It was decided to call a truce and Charles agreed a moat was a good idea. One was added in readiness for the next incoming tide, which in the darkness of night would silently surround the sand buildings, filling the moats and crushing the castles with its watery fingers as it crept rapidly across the sand to the dunes, only to be repelled by an invisible force, more successful than Canute, and sent on its way back to the far horizon.

I began to tell them the story of King Canute, but they both already knew the story from school. Diana, sandcastle forgotten as her imagination set her off on another track, rushed to the edge of the sea and theatrically striking a pose, arm raised, pointing seaward, proclaimed, 'I command you to turn back.' The waves receded. 'See, it worked,' she shouted. 'No, it did not,' replied Charles. 'The sea is going out anyway, it had nothing to do with you.' I decided now was the time to eat and as everyone was starving, I had no difficulty in persuading them to leave their building projects and come for lunch.

Cook's wonderful picnic had been set out by the older girls in a display on the table that was stored in the hut for use on such occasions. We all helped ourselves and then with our plates loaded sat on the blankets in the shelter of the dunes. The beach huts were well spaced apart, so even at a weekend there would be privacy, but on this Tuesday there was no one else about. It was a lovely feeling to have so much beach and space to ourselves. The food disappeared quickly as everyone was so hungry. Sarah and Isabel had organized the lunch so, amidst moans and groans from Charles and Diana, I said that we would clear away. The older girls asked about the time we planned to leave, then, collecting their bags, set off down the beach to find somewhere secluded and quiet to sunbathe, saying the youngsters made too much noise. We quickly packed the empty plates and the few leftovers into the hamper – the cook's quantity control had been excellent and very little food remained. I told them I intended to sit and read for half an hour, then we could all go for a walk. The boys immediately invented a game of their own in the sand dunes around me. The amount of noise involved indicated it had something to do with warfare and I was quite envious of Sarah and Isabel who had been able to escape. Diana was not keen to sit and rest so Jane volunteered to walk down to the sea shore with the girls as they wanted to put the finishing touches to their sandcastle. By this time the tide was running out at quite a rate and I warned them that on no account were they to go in the sea. Quite apart from the fact they had just finished lunch, I considered its tide unsafe. The expected grumble from Diana did not materialize; even she had found the sea cold and was not anxious to brave it again.

It was so relaxing to lie back on the blanket – I did not read very much – to feel the sun warm on my face, caressed gently by the breeze and to hear the never-ending roar of the sea as background music. The combination of the three, sun, wind and sea created a very soothing effect and it was only the shouts of the boys that prevented me from drifting off to sleep. Thirty minutes later, I called them to join me and the three of us walked down to meet Jane, Diana and Alexandra. I complimented them on their efforts with the sandcastle and said how impressive it looked with the pebble adornments. The walk along the beach was so pleasant, the children rushing in and out of the edge of the waves, chased by the dogs. When they tired of that game I suggested that we looked for shells and see who could find the most unusual and the best conch-type shell. There was a large variety of shells and colours, but naturally views on what was considered unusual differed. I said if we all chose our favourite then we would ask Sarah to judge when we met her later. Alexandra was the first to find a conch shell which increased the alacrity of Diana's search until she too was successful, followed quickly by the rest of us. I instructed them to hold them to their ears and to tell me what they could hear. Diana thought I was going to play a joke on them and I had to convince her that there was nothing in the shell that would suddenly leap out at her. Satisfied that it was not a trick, she too raised her shell and they could all hear the sound of the sea roaring as if on some distant shore. I told them always to keep the shell with them and wherever they were, however far from the sea, they needed just to listen and the sound of the sea would be with them.

We walked on and Jane asked me if I had spent much time on the beach when I was young. I told her how much I loved the sea right from the time when I was a child. I described the times I used to ride on the beach at night if there was a full moon and the light shone on the waves as they broke, turning them into silver. Diana asked if I was scared to ride at night on the beach, but I assured her no, that we just galloped along by the edge of the sea, splashing through the pools of water left behind as the tide went out. There was never anyone about and who could catch us anyway? Diana wanted to know, as we had lived only a few miles from the sea, if our parents had often taken us to the beach. I explained that my father had had to work nearly all the time but that if there was any free time and the weather was good we would make an outing to nearby Winterton or Horsey, which I loved as there were always pools which were safe to play in and much warmer than the sea. Diana wanted to know if we went alone or with friends and I told her it was nearly always just the four of us as I had my brother to play with and he was my best friend, to which Diana replied that Charles was certainly not her best friend. I said it was different, because John and I were twins while she was three years older than Charles. He counteracted this remark by stating that neither was Diana *his* best friend. 'She's all right' was as much as he was prepared to commit himself. To put an end to a situation that promised to become argumentative, I recounted to them the story of the time my brother and I had wandered off and got completely lost. We always sat in the sand dunes and when we tried to find where our parents were we discovered that all sand dunes look the same. Luckily, an elderly couple walking their dog along the beach realized we were lost and helped us to look for our parents. Diana, avid reader of adventure stories and mysteries, wondered if we were worried that we might be kidnapped. I assured her that in the days when we were children, everywhere was really safe. I added that to avoid a repeat, on future visits my parents put up a Union Jack flag on the highest sand dune so we could always find our way back.

By this time we had reached the beach hut again and there was just fifteen minutes before Sarah and Isabel would join us and then it would be time to leave. 'Must we really go so soon?' asked Diana, who always tended to question decisions more if she was in company with a friend. I replied 'Yes', and advised her not to waste time arguing about a foregone conclusion, but to make the most of those minutes. She and Alexandra promptly joined Charles and John for the last jumping competition in the dunes, while Jane and I collected all the bags and rolled up towels covered in sand that refused to be shaken off. Sarah and Isabel appeared right on time and were immediately propositioned as sea-shell judges, announcing Alexandra as winner, a result readily accepted as she had found her shell first. I locked the hut, distributed belongings to be carried to the jeep and our tired and somewhat subdued party headed for home. It was the right time to leave, for the sun had lost its strength and we were chilled by the breeze that now blew from the sea. The day had been a great success, but we now all looked forward to arriving home and to hot baths. 'Empty your shoes before you get in,' I had warned everyone, but it did not do much good. A trail of sand was left in the kitchen where we took the hamper, a trail of sand marked our footsteps along the corridor and completed its journey in the bathroom. A great carefree day, just a pity about the stubborn tendency of sand!

We spent the next two days quietly at Park House until the end of the week, when, with the Kings Lynn Festival due to start shortly, Sarah decided she simply had no clothes to wear and asked me if I would go into Kings Lynn with her to choose one or two outfits. I readily agreed and asked Diana if she would like to come with us, for, although her mother bought most of her clothes, she still enjoyed an outing like this with Sarah and me. Jane, who spent much more time in London, said it was not necessary for her to come and instead offered to stay with Charles who was grateful that he had escaped from what threatened to be a boring afternoon for him. We took Amina with us to humour Diana who felt it would be a good experience for her to visit a town. I said that if we took her it meant we would not be able to have tea and cakes which I knew was the best part of the afternoon as far as Diana was concerned. Not to be deprived of this treat, she said that she would put Amina back in the car when the shopping was finished. I gave in and as soon as lunch was finished we left.

There was never a problem parking in the town. In the middle was a large square so although it was the end of the week and the town was busy with shoppers, there was still plenty of room. In Diana's eyes three shops held top priority. Failure to visit these made the trip to town futile. These hallowed premises were a chemist shop, a bookshop and newsagency where she could buy her comics and any new crayons and other items for her pencil case and, on the outskirts of town, the pet shop. I promised we would visit the latter if we had time, although I have no idea why Diana was always so insistent to go there as she knew she had no hope of persuading me that some poor caged creature would not be able to survive unless she rescued it! It has to be said she had much more success if she managed to cajole her father into a visit. I told Diana the main point of this visit was for Sarah to buy clothes. Thus appeased, we entered our favourite clothes shop, a small boutique with sensibly priced smart, casual clothes. A few were chosen for trial and Sarah disappeared into the cubicle, separated from us by only a curtain so we were able to continue our conversation while she tried on the clothes. Amina sat quietly by my side, while Diana flicked through the items on the rails and stands, asking my opinion on whether this or that would suit her. However, her interest in fashion was far from developed at that age. It was all rather hypothetical as they were not children's clothes, but it did indicate the colours that appealed to Diana, vivid and clean. Amina started to shuffle around but I paid no attention, busy both talking to Diana and offering my views on any clothes that Sarah tried on.

Suddenly I looked down to reprimand Amina and tell her to sit still and noticed a wet stain spreading over the plain, pale carpet without any pattern to help disguise it. I knew, with certainty, that there had not been a sudden leak from any underground drain and that Amina was the culprit. To make our escape with as much decorum as possible was now the main item on the agenda, I called Diana over and in a whisper told her what had happened and asked her to stand on the offending spot. When she looked as though she was about to go into convulsions, I implored her to be quiet and stay still. 'Can we go to the pet shop?' she asked. I realized I was being blackmailed but under the circumstances felt I had little choice but to comply. Now was not the time to get into a debate with Diana about the advantages of helping your fellow man! I told Sarah it was time to leave – urgently. I already stood in the middle of the room to prevent Amina rubbing against the clothes. Diana, too, was now positioned similarly and looked rather conspicuous, like a statue, unmoving. I could have explained to the shop assistants what had happened, but I was so embarrassed my only thought was to leave. Thankfully, Sarah had chosen her clothes, I took them from her, paid the bill while she got dressed and we all made a hasty exit, Diana and Sarah finding my embarrassment highly amusing. Once on the pavement, I joined in with their laughter as we could imagine that by now the poor assistant would have realized what had happened and even at that moment be busy with warm water and disinfectant to repair the damage and remove the offending stain.

Amina, in disgrace, was bundled into the car, and we quickly went to the chemist and newsagency then made our way to our favourite coffee shop. Over major decisions between meringues and chocolate éclairs, we discussed our purchases and I agreed that Diana did deserve a visit to the pet shop as she had managed to suppress her giggles for such a commendable time! Small items were bought for all the animals, chew bones for the dogs, a ball with a bell in it for the cat, although I doubted whether it would prove to be a big enough diversion from the pleasure of mice hunting, and some special food for Peanuts as a treat. I and the pocket money exhausted, we returned to Park House, everyone pleased with their purchases and I vowed Amina would not visit town again until she had learnt some manners.

The end of July drew near and with it the main local event of the summer, the Sandringham Flower Show held in the park. This show still takes place every summer, but now it is a much larger concern and attracts visitors from far and wide. When I lived at Sandringham, it was very much a show for the locals and those who lived in the surrounding communities. All were encouraged to participate in one of the classes. Diana, Charles and I watched in excitement as the three main marquees were put up. We were not alone for long and were soon joined by children from the village while the older folk wandered down and gave advice, unheeded, on the best way to erect a tent. Prolific guidance distributed, they then turned their attentions to the discussion of the best produce to offer for exhibition and, more to the point, judging. One expressed fears that a certain marrow which had held such promise was not going to make the grade, while someone else's cabbage, of which there had been such high expectations, had already provided a meal for some marauding insect and if that was not disaster enough the bloom on Smith's cauliflower had peaked a day or two too early. While any chance of success in our immediate group seemed highly unlikely (naturally no one wished to discuss their 'pièce de résistance'), it was only to be hoped that the wives with their flower displays and preserves did not suffer from similar misfortunes. So the spectators sympathized with each other. Even as they offered their commiserations, they could gleefully anticipate the astonished look on their neighbour's face when they showed their hand; after all, no one said they only had *one* marrow or cauliflower!

The park with its backdrop of Sandringham House, the church and Park House, presented an idyllic setting for a show which finds representation in various forms, such as fête, village fair, agricultural show, throughout England during the summer months. The Flower Show, which lent its name to the event, was housed in the largest marquee. The others were the Cottager's Tent where local people exhibited their home produce, fruit, vegetables, homemade pickles, cakes, preserves, and so on, and then there was the Fur and Feather Tent, where birds and animals were on show. The children needed no persuasion to take part. Diana decided to enter her guinea-pig and spent ages preparing Peanuts for his class. Her efforts were rewarded when she was presented with first prize in her section. One could almost imagine the proud look on Peanuts' face as he watched his certificate being placed against his cage. No imagination was required to see the pride on Diana's face. Charles entered his hamster, Mr Smith his produce from the vegetable garden; an amazing stroke of luck meant that another cauliflower had reached the required standard – and it won! Mrs Smith had prepared some marvellous homemade jam, an opinion shared by the judge who awarded her a prize. Charles's hamster was 'Commended', so all in all we had done well, helped along by the encouragement of Lord Althorp who liked to see us take part in local events.

There were several smaller exhibits including one from the Women's Institute, patronized by the Queen Mother who usually stayed at Sandringham House for these days in July to enable her to attend the Kings Lynn Festival to support her friend, Lady Fermoy. Her attendance at both these events was highly valued. Sandringham was a shooting estate, so it was only natural that in the afternoon one of the main attractions was a display of gun-dog obedience. Decoys were hidden and the dogs sent to retrieve, guided only by the sound of their masters' voices. Alert, intelligent, tails wagging in their eagerness to show their capabilities and to please. Most of the dogs were yellow or black Labradors, many had the Sandringham blood lines, bred from the Queen's kennels in West Newton. There were a few springer spaniels, liver and white or blue-black and white. Their thicker skins afforded them an advantage over the Labradors, enabling them to go fearlessly into dense and often prickly undergrowth. Their disadvantage, as in the case of Jill, was that many of them were too scatty to train to reach the high standard of obedience required for the gun. Lord Althorp often extolled the virtues of his previous gun dog, a spaniel, but Bray, still young, did her best to please him. Diana tried to persuade her father to enter the gun-dog competition but he was not satisfied that Bray had enough experience and in such a setting there were many diversions.

Two other country pursuits drew the crowds and both were represented. One was work orientated, the other more for pleasure. An impressive display of 'one man and his dog' was always popular. With a whistle as the only means of command the shepherd would put his faithful border collie through his paces, herding the flock from one pen to another, round, through and over obstacles on the way, the dog proving just how capable he was of dealing with the vagaries of sheep who always seemed hell-bent in life on suicidal missions, whether it was getting themselves trapped in fences or drowned in ditches. The skill that master and dog displayed and the loving devotion that shone in the eyes of the collie as he looked to his master for praise for a job well done were, in the eyes of many visitors, one of the highlights of the show.

At three o'clock we heard the call of the hunting horn as the West Norfolk Foxhounds, the local hunt, called their hounds to heel and prepared to ride from the far end of the park towards the main area. In those days not many people were anti-hunt, most regarded the humane killing of foxes as a necessity and farmers welcomed the hunt on their land. In our household, as in so many, opinions varied. Sarah loved to hunt and was therefore supportive, able to voice all the positive points, Diana was against anything that might threaten the well-being of animals and did not approve. Her lack of knowledge on the subject made it hard for her to voice her opinions as well as Sarah. For or against, it could not be denied how splendid they looked that day in the park. The horses' coats gleamed, their tack shone, the huntsmen were resplendent in their red jackets surrounded by the foxhounds, their tails upright, wagging like a mass of masts in the wind. The horses were restless, their ears pricked, and they were aware that the sound of the horn meant, 'Away!' Champing at their bits, ready for the chase, they were not conscious that the warmth of a July afternoon made for unusual hunting conditions, which are more of frost on a chilly autumn morning. Right or wrong, hunting is a tradition that is part of England, reminiscent of country houses, riders mounted on their horses, stirrup cup in hand on a clear winter's day waiting to move off. It is a scene that has graced many a book on English country life and, as such, is not easy to dismiss.

The crowds stood back and watched as the huntsmen made their way sedately up the park until they reached the top, where they called their hounds around them and had a photo call. Cameras of all shapes and sizes recorded the event. The huntsmen were not the only people to provide a splash of colour. The women in their light flowery dresses, men in shirtsleeves – obviously some devout Country and Western fans judging by their shirts – their thinning hair and bald patches protected from over-exposure to the sun's rays by summer trilbies, their winter flat caps put away for a few more weeks, all helped to add to the profusion of colour in the park. A final call on the horn to announce time for home; the foxhounds realized this was it. There was to be no thrill of the chase, no eager sniffing to pick up scent, just a walk up the park and back. What a disappointment, but surely an exercise that could not upset even the staunchest hunt saboteur!

The crowds began to thin as people started on their journeys home. For the lucky ones, it just meant a walk across the park, others faced car rides of varying distances. For the children and I, a few paces and we were back in our own grounds. We persuaded Diana that enough people had now seen what a worthy exhibit Peanuts had proved to be and it was better to bring him home along with Charles's hamster. After such a long day I was sure they would appreciate the comforts of their own cages.

Immediately after the flower show we had the Kings Lynn Festival to look forward to. This was a festival of music and art, founded by Ruth, Lady Fermoy, the children's maternal grand-mother, who was herself a talented concert pianist. She founded the festival in 1951 to celebrate the opening of St George's Guildhall which had been restored. It then became known as the Fermoy Centre. Lady Fermoy was chairman of the festival, but her friend, the Queen Mother, to whom she was a lady-in-waiting, was the festival's patron. Her presence at both flower show and festival demonstrated what close links the people of the area had with the royal family.

The children had all taken after their grandmother with their love of music. Sarah and Jane both played the piano. Diana enjoyed 'tinkling', but did not start lessons until she was fourteen years old. There were some programmes in the festival suitable for children although the majority appealed to an adult audience. Lord Althorp went through the programme of music events with me and together we decided on two suitable matinée performances to which I could take Charles and Diana. Sarah and Jane attended as many concerts as they were able to get tickets for and I was pleased to be invited to join them twice. It was during the intervals of these evening performances that I had my first opportunity to meet people of my age who lived locally. The festival itself lasted only a few days and made a wonderful change from normal, everyday life, but it was during that time that I met the people who, over the years, became good friends. They were very smart occasions and I loved the opportunity to dress up and mingle with so many elegant people, all deriving great pleasure from the concerts. Kings Lynn was very fortunate in having someone as well respected and influential as Lady Fermoy, who could entice such talent to the relative back-water of Norfolk.

Tickets were sought after and sold out quickly. Unfortunately, Lord Althorp was only able to get tickets for one matinée performance. Still, it was with excitement that we looked forward to this unusual way of spending an afternoon and determined to make the most of it. As with all children, Diana and Charles grew so quickly that they only had what can be classified as one smart outfit at Park House. In any case, there was little opportunity to dress-up. I felt very proud when we left, Charles with a tie neatly knotted rather than the open-neck effect he usually favoured. Diana's hair was groomed until it shone, hanging down to her shoulders instead of looking (as it normally did) as if it could do with a good brush. She was a meticulous little girl, but she was always so busy rushing everywhere that her hair, which she preferred to wear loose, constantly looked as if it needed attention.

The children sat quiet and well behaved throughout the concert. I let them have an ice cream when we went outside in the afternoon sunshine for the interval, but warned them to take great care not to spoil their clothes by letting any of it drop on to them. No accidents occurred and we returned for the second half. I could sense as it was drawing to an end that they were beginning to get restless. Charles was too young to be expected to enjoy a whole afternoon in this fashion, and once the bonus of an ice cream at the interval was over and the novelty of the entertainment had worn off he looked forward to getting home, changing into old clothes and having time to play before bed. Diana, who had just had her tenth birthday on 1 July during the school term, was always rather restless and fidgety. She did enjoy music and there had been a great variety, but she was looking forward to getting in the fresh air and started jiggling about on her seat. I nudged her and told her, 'It won't be long now.' Diana whispered to me, 'What time does it finish?' I told her and from then until the end watched her casting covert glances at her watch. They later told their grandmother how much they had enjoyed the concert, and I think for two-thirds of it that was true. I greatly enjoyed the outing with the children but I too was pleased I was given the opportunity to attend the evening concerts as there were times when I missed the company of adults and felt rather cut-off from a normal life. This did not often happen and once I had made the introductions – not through either Jane or Sarah, but simply because people at the concerts had been so friendly and introduced themselves – from that time on, I felt that I had made a niche for myself in North-West Norfolk.

Chapter Ten

J ane left Park House at the beginning of August, to return to her mother for the rest of the holiday which would be spent between her two homes, in Sussex and London. Farewells were said. I was sorry to see Jane leave, she was such a calm, steady person and her presence made the family seem complete. Diana and Charles knew they would soon see her again, when they too joined their mother. After the flower show and the festival, we were all pleased to have the opportunity to spend time quietly at home. It was nearing the middle of the holidays and several friends came to visit Lord Althorp. We rarely saw these visitors unless they had children, in which case they were brought to join us in the garden or the pool, weather permitting, or in the nursery should the rain have forced us to stay indoors. Usually outside, I used to tease Diana and say she would grow a tail like a mermaid as she spent so much time in the water. The children, left with us, were treated to a display of Diana's skills as soon as she realized they could not swim to the same standard as herself. This was usually the case as few of them would have Diana's opportunities to swim and were completely shadowed by Diana's proficiency. They would splash around for a short time and then rejoin their parents. Lord Althorp was very generous in letting others benefit from the pool that he had built knowing his children's love of swimming and wishing to provide them with something special to look forward to when they came for the holidays. He knew how lucky his children were, but at every opportunity he was pleased to let others share in that luck. Diana and Charles were not spoilt children and they did not mind in the least that others should share the pool. However, unless they knew the other children, they were basically shy and Diana hid her shyness behind a show of pool bravado.

Many would have considered that she was showing off but that was not the case. On the other hand, if the spectators were people she knew she could not resist a chance to flaunt her skills, often encouraged by her father who was so proud of her. The feat of hers that made him so nervous was the dive executed from the top of the slide. It really terrified him and yet Diana only had to beg to be allowed 'just once' and he acquiesced. Diana cared so deeply for her father and was so sensitive to his feelings. I was always surprised she persisted with this. I did not approve and would never allow Diana to do it when we were on our own.

Throughout childhood, teenage years and adulthood, Diana retained an affinity towards her father which was mutual. In December 1978, Diana wrote to me. It was during her father's first major illness, but by that time he was recovering. She told me that the night before her father collapsed with a cerebral haemorrhage, she had dreamt that something would happen to him – 'very strange – but then I am'. This is not a statement to be taken out of context and analysed as many seventeen-year-olds imagine themselves different from anyone else. They regard their opinions and beliefs to be individual and original and themselves to be unique. There can be no doubt though, that there always existed a closeness between Lord Althorp and Diana. He was a major prop and support to her and this was strengthened as Diana's marriage deteriorated. His death, although it naturally affected all the children, was felt particularly keenly by Diana. With his experience of the royal establishment, he was upset during the last two years of his life to see the unhappiness that this beloved daughter was suffering. As well as he knew her, even he did not allow for her tenacity and although her childhood dreams and aspirations had been publicly destroyed, she was not prepared to drift into a backwater and live her life as a sham. He could not imagine how there could be any escape for her, nor that it would be Diana who would set such a precedent in the monarchy.

The Queen Mother stayed at Sandringham House during her summer visits, but other members of the royal family often chose to stay at the smaller, more homely, Wood Farm at Wolferton. Princess Alexandra, who would become one of Prince William's godmothers, used to visit Park House during the summer. She was such a smart, elegant but natural person, always so pleasant and capable of putting people immediately at ease. I can easily appreciate why she is one of the most popular members of the royal

Diana's parents in happier days. Viscount Althorp and the Hon. Frances Roche on the day before they were married in Westminster Abbey in May 1954. (*Hulton-Deutsch Collection*)

A private snapshot of the young Diana outside Park House
during the time I was working there.

Diana returning to her prep school Riddlesworth in 1989. She is chatting to her former headmistress, Miss Ridsdale. (*Press Association*)

Top: Raine, as Countess of Dartmouth, (*left*) at around the time she became friendly with Lord Althorp. (*Press Association*)

Bottom: Diana's mother – now Mrs Shand-Kydd – at her daughter's wedding in 1981. (*Hulton-Deutsch Collection*)

family. She and her husband spent time with Lord Althorp and came to the poolside to be introduced and to watch the children swim for a few minutes, long enough for Diana to do her party piece. It was all so normal and relaxed, it was only after they left that Diana told me I should have made some show of a curtsey. I had never been introduced to anyone from the royal family before so it had not entered my head. I was pleased that Diana had pointed out my gaffe as I did not wish to appear discourteous and Lord Althorp would never think to remind me about this aspect of etiquette. I made a mental note that next time I was introduced to royalty I would try to remember to curtsey.

A few days later, on a Sunday, I was lying on my sunbed by the swimming pool, with Gitsie lying underneath, in case, in her view, I needed protection. It was still quite early in the morning and the children had not yet ventured to the pool, but were playing nearby, in the garden. It was really peaceful. I could hear the church bells and felt a little guilty that we did not go to church but we had had a few days of rain and it was wonderful to have the opportunity to bask in some sun. Everywhere looked so fresh and green. Smith had cut the lawns the previous evening and the air was scented with freshly cut grass. Suddenly Gitsie started to growl and beyond the sound of children's voices as they played I could hear the murmur of adult voices in the background. They grew louder as people approached us across the lawn.

I knew we did not expect any visitors and that mid-Sunday morning was not the normal time for anyone to call. Lord Althorp was working on papers in his study and Sarah was playing music and reading in her room. I turned my head and saw Lord Althorp and Sarah walking towards us with some guests – the Duke and Duchess of Kent. We knew they were staying at Wood Farm. They were friends of Lord Althorp – the Duke of Kent is Jane's godfather – and had been to church at Sandringham that morning and decided to call round afterwards to make arrangements for us all to take the children to the funfair at Hunstanton.

I wore only a bikini. When Gitsie alerted me to the approaching company and I realized immediately who they were I glanced round wildly for my blouse only to discover it had disappeared. Lying contentedly in the distance, asleep under a tree, was Amina – on my blouse. Sarah later told me that as they walked over the lawn Lord Althorp had said to the Duke and Duchess of Kent, 'That is Mary, she helps me with the children', to which the Duke of Kent supposedly replied, 'Oh, yes, we've heard all about her.' It transpired that Lord Fermoy, following his visit by helicopter, had been so surprised at the sight of 'the nanny', he had repeated the story later. At least when he had dropped in on us so unexpectedly, I had been wearing shorts as well. As they drew near, I thought to myself, 'Act naturally.' I got up and called the children over. Lord Althorp conducted the introductions. The children politely shook hands. The Duchess of Kent, so charming and kind, gently made them feel at ease. I remembered Diana's advice, that I should curtsey on such an occasion, but the few times I had practised a little bob in front of the mirror had not qualified me for the experience of executing a curtsey in a bikini. In a flash I decided it would be too ridiculous for words and thought the better option would be to look ignorant on such matters again and that next time I would try to get it right! So I simply shook hands, spoke a greeting and tried to appear as nonchalant as possible – as if this was the sort of thing I did every day! Lord Althorp excused us all for being so unprepared for visitors.

They returned to the house to finalize plans for the outing to Hunstanton a day or two later. The group was hardly out of earshot before Diana, who had been standing so meekly and coyly, burst out laughing as she recalled my obvious embarrassment. 'Why didn't you curtsey, Mary?' she asked unnecessarily. 'You know the answer to that perfectly well, Diana,' I replied. 'Can you imagine anything that would have looked more stupid?' I rescued my blouse from Amina who was completely oblivious to the consternation she had caused me and decided I would change at least into a skirt and blouse in case anyone else appeared. I had suddenly lost my enthusiasm for sunbathing! The children came with me to get drinks and biscuits from the kitchen. Mrs Smith had witnessed the whole episode from the window of her flat and joined us in the kitchen where the picture of my discomfort caused a great deal of good-natured laughter. Later, at lunch, Lord Althorp said to me, 'They certainly caught us on the hop, didn't they, Mary?' which I thought was a fine example of the Englishman's mastery of understatement. He told me it had been decided that we would go the next day to the funfair and that the Duke and Duchess of Kent would meet us at Park House with their children, 'when we will try and be better organized'.

Diana and Charles were excited about the excursion. It was a travelling funfair with all the added excitement of real atmosphere created by the travellers of the road who make a living by constantly being on the move, while simultaneously giving pleasure to the people who live in the different areas where they make their base, perhaps for a few days or a few weeks. Sarah and I too looked forward to the outing, it was an unusual treat for all of us and age can never quite blunt the appeal of a fair. I told the children how as a child I eagerly looked forward to the fair that arrived every Easter in Great Yarmouth, the next destination after it had taken over the old cattle market in Norwich. There was also a permanent funfair on Great Yarmouth sea front, owned by one of the old, well-known Yarmouth families. Every year it would be updated with even more daring attractions, but for all of that, in my mind, it could never compete with the atmosphere and thrill of a 'real fair'. The fair travelled from Norwich to Great Yarmouth through all the small villages and as we could hear it approaching, we, along with all the rest of the village children, would rush down to the main road to watch the gaily painted caravans go past. In all probability it was a difficult life for those involved, but how I used to envy the brown, grubby children their freedom, how they could always be on the move. My ideas, when I was a child, did not entertain thoughts of cold, wet weather and hardships endured. Diana did not share my romantic views. She said she felt sorry for the children; they would probably love to have a secure, steady home. I agreed with her but teased her by telling her that they did not go to school as regularly as she had to. Even that factor did not convince Diana it was a good life, she did not like the idea of always being on the move at all. Stability mattered to her.

The Kents arrived at the appointed time with their two eldest children. The youngest son, who was still a baby, was left at home with his nanny. This time we were prepared and got it right. Betts answered the front door and saw them into the drawing room where we were all gathered. We shook hands and finally I got my chance and executed a little bob. I could not resist glancing at Diana at the same time, to make sure she was watching to see that at last I got it right. We smiled at each other, then she immediately

139

looked down to hide the grin on her face. What two different types of people she epitomized – one shy and retiring, someone who would not appear to be capable of saying boo to a goose and the other one, extrovert and full of fun, someone who challenged and who would dare to try anything.

It was a very relaxed atmosphere and I noticed at once how Diana and Charles were at ease. The more time they spent downstairs with their father, the more relaxed their home became and this was quickly having positive effects on them. The children greeted each other, but in the presence of adults they retreated into silence. We decided to leave at once. I checked the children had everything they needed, money and coats in case it became cooler. Hunstanton is on the North Norfolk coast and I knew that even in summer it would be chilly as afternoon gave way to evening. I looked at the Duchess of Kent, so quietly spoken and calm, and at the same time noticed the piercing ice-blue eyes of her husband. She made a totally innocuous statement and I was appalled at the sharp response. It sounded so harsh to me and certainly did nothing to improve the impression I have of the attitude of men from the royal family towards their wives. The women of the royal family always seemed to remember their position and whatever feelings, inner turmoil or thoughts they might have, they retained a sense of equilibrium in public. Whereas in my inexperienced view, some of the men often spoke without first thinking of the embarrassment that certain announcements might cause to their partners, who in the face of any strains managed to appear undaunted and calm. To me, they often seem to be working on parallel plains that never meet, implying that in private there is a very different face to that displayed in public and it is left to the women to rise above any insinuations that thoughtless comments might cause. The men who have actually acted in a manner that is to be applauded are those from beyond the royal circle. Lord Snowdon and Mark Phillips are two examples. As the marriage of Diana and Charles progressed, he too seemed to fit into the mould of the insensitive husband. How often he made cutting asides to Diana, not quite quiet enough for them to be ignored, rather than offer a word of support to boost her morale and confidence. An example of this took place in Canada when Diana felt faint. 'Do you have to make such a spectacle of yourself?' he muttered audibly. Just the sort of comment a young wife needs during difficult times!

Whether the Duchess was used to this manner – perhaps it might be normal – or whether she was just so experienced that she could act as if it was normal, I do not know, but I can remember the exchange taking place as we were leaving the drawing room and stood by the grand piano and I realized how surprised I would have been if my father had ever spoken to my mother in that way – which I am sure he never did as it would have been quite out of character.

We set off in high spirits taking two cars. Lord Althorp's Jaguar was given a chance of an airing. It was cooler on the coast, as I had predicted, but at least it was dry and sunny. The fair, although not as large as the one I had spoken of at Great Yarmouth, still had a good selection of rides. There were many people already there but it was in the evenings when it became crowded. Some had come from the local villages, but mostly they were holiday-makers. The hustle and bustle enfolded us as soon as we arrived. The music from the various rides competed with the cries of the different stallholders as they tried to entice punters to try their luck. Sarah and I, put in charge of the younger children, started on the most harmless of rides at the fair, but the one that I told them had been my favourite as a child: the carousel, with its galloping horses, that under mechanical control could be ridden by the most inexperienced horseman. Diana said that was the closest she intended to get to a horse again. The gentle up and down and round and round on the brightly painted horses provided a gentle introduction to some of the more hazardous amusements on hand. Lord Althorp and the Kents stood and watched while Sarah and I were pleased with the excuse to ride the carousel as we had to keep an eye on the children. Encouraged to show our skill with the air rifle, we all successfully shot at the metal bars, knocking them down, each of us collecting a prize, not once being persuaded by the stallholder to 'have another go'. I expect he was pleased to see the back of us! Diana and Lady Helen, the only two who did not attempt the shooting, instead tried their skill at acquiring a goldfish. To achieve the desired result, they had to lob a table tennis ball into a glass bowl. I did not show them the easy way, which would

141

be constituted as cheating as it does involve leaning forward over the rail, thus making it easier to place the ball in the bowl. Even without my guidance Diana managed to become the proud owner of a goldfish whose first home was a plastic bag. Unfortunately, it suffered the fate of most fair-won goldfish – premature death. This time, not due to over-feeding, ignorance, a strange environment or pure pig-headedness on its part, it was not given a chance to show the tendency of its breed and to float on its back on the top of the water. Marmadude, the cat, had other ideas – an easy, fish course starter was the fate that befell the aptly named Goldy the very next day.

Passing the goldfish to her father for him to take care of, Diana asked me to take her and Lady Helen on a ride that not only involved going up and down and round at the same time, but also at a terrific speed – the Waltzer. In a moment of sheer lunacy, I agreed. The ride seemed to go on for ever. It was like being on a boat on a very rough sea, the only redeeming feature being that you knew it had to end sometime. Meanwhile, the girls loved it and between their shrieks, I was given an insight into the secrets that lay behind the immaculate turn-out of her mother – the Duchess of Kent – by her daughter. Until I assured her that not every woman receives such beauty treatments she had assumed that her mother's lifestyle was normal. Eventually, the ride ground to a halt and we staggered off with Diana requesting that we have another go. I refused. During the time we were on the ride, some of the other visitors to the fairground realized that they were in the company of royalty. It was interesting to notice that as so little fuss had been made and they were there incognito we had been able to move about so freely. Now though, once the whispers had started and we kept hearing, 'look who's over there', we were conscious of the recognition and the visit was no longer the same. I expect the Duke and Duchess of Kent and their children were used to such intrusions into their privacy and would hardly notice the attention paid to them, but for us, it was a new experience and Diana, at her impressionable age, really rather enjoyed the reflected glory of being associated with people so well-known. Sarah and I tried to appear nonchalant, taking our example from the Duchess of Kent – and failing. There was after all a little bit of Diana's reaction

142

within us. As for Charles, he really could not care less, his main aim was to get us on to the dodgem cars.

No fair is complete without a fortune-teller and this was no exception. Sarah expressed the most interest to visit. I was rather sceptical as to just how good the soothsayer would prove to be but was also fascinated to find out if she was authentic. Diana, anxious to know what the future held for her, wanted to visit with Sarah, but I told her she was too young and would not agree to it. If I ever told Diana she was not allowed to do something, she never tried to cross me by asking her father the same question in the hope that he might say 'yes'. Sarah disappeared inside the tent to learn what the future held in store for her and I complied with Charles's wish and we all headed for the dodgem cars. With an adult and a child in each car, we hurtled round the track. Diana shared my car, she had control of the steering wheel and was intent on slamming into as many cars as possible. I operated the pedals and was therefore in the stronger position to achieve my aim – to avoid as many cars as possible. When the ride finished Sarah met us and was immediately plied with questions from Diana as to what she had been told by the fortune-teller. At first, to antagonize her inquisitive young sister, Sarah said it was all a secret. Diana would not give up so easily. Always intrigued by the future, she thought such people could answer all questions and help the individual to plot their journey. Interestingly, in adult life Diana has often relied on astrologers and their predictions – possibly more accurate than the old gypsy at the fair. At Diana's continued persistence Sarah admitted that fame, fortune and a good, though volatile marriage – based, I suspect, on her red hair – was the forecast, one that was probably repeated several times a day, but on this occasion possibly with some accuracy considering the company her client kept.

Two hours after our arrival we left the funfair. We had ridden all the attractions we were brave enough to tackle, tried our luck at most of the stalls and eaten enough junk food, popcorn, candyfloss and ice cream to ensure we all felt a little delicate and would not need much dinner that evening. We said our farewells and left for our separate destinations. A few days later, Sarah, obviously mesmerized at the thought of looking into the future, acquired an ouija board. Much to Mrs Smith's disapproval, we sat down in the laundry room – which used to be the schoolroom – along with Isabel whom Sarah had invited to join us in this exploration into the future. Charles and Diana were playing in the nursery. The questions we asked the board were harmless but the accuracy of the answers concerning myself, answers which no one could have known, were quite unnerving. Diana came to see what was happening and wanted to have a go, but I refused. It was only meant to be a bit of fun, but it was quite frightening and I was disturbed enough not to allow Diana to get involved. I also advised Sarah and Isabel to leave well alone. To dabble, even in fun, with unknown forces is not to be recommended.

There were only a few days of the summer holiday left before I was to take the children to join their mother and Jane in London, from whence they would go to the Sussex home and spend some of their time sailing. This made an excellent contrast for the children, for of all the activities they enjoyed in Norfolk they did not sail. They adapted very well to wherever they happened to be. Never once did Diana or Charles express any desire to me that they wished they could be elsewhere, they made the most of the facilities on hand. I would imagine this attitude was maintained when they were with their mother. Lord Althorp decided we would go to London two days early and spend some time at his house there. We had spent a wonderful summer at Park House. Lord Althorp had given me a free rein to arrange the outings for the children and to spend the days in any way we wished. Often he was away and on those days the five of us continued to eat in the dining room. They were fun lunchtimes and conversation flowed easily. The children complemented each other. Jane was a great peace-keeper, perhaps in sub-conscious preparation for her future role as wife of the Queen's private secretary and sister of the Princess of Wales. We all really appreciated the beautiful room with its outstanding views over the park. Betts continued to serve us, barely managing to conceal his irritation that an established system had been upset by such an upstart – me! After lunch, we moved to the drawing room, dominated by its lovely grand piano which Sarah and Jane played for us. Sarah played from memory as she always seemed to have lost her sheet music. She went on to study music in Vienna, one of her first tastes of freedom after boarding school and a Swiss finishing school. She would ask us for requests, always from the classics. How I loved those occasions, seated in such a peaceful setting, having happy, relaxed children with me and listening to beautiful music played so effortlessly and in such a light-hearted way. Even as it happened, I realized that these would be some of the memories that would remain with me always. There was a poignancy in the music that touched the very soul and epitomized the beauty and solace that we derived from our surroundings. Jane played well and she did not lose her music but to my inexperienced ear her music did not hold for me the haunting evocation of that played by her older sister. Diana always provided the finale, a pounding rendering of one or two pieces that she had learnt by heart. I could see the grand piano almost shudder at the music Diana forced it to produce. It did however mean that we all joined in the after-lunch entertainment.

I chose to ignore much of the pettiness displayed by Betts during the absences of Lord Althorp. I could understand and sympathize with his antagonism to a certain degree, but as the summer wore on, Betts's small-minded comments became more obvious and intrusive and eventually they upset me so much that I determined to have a word with Lord Althorp on his return. I wished to explain to him that I was not prepared to put up with aggravation every time he went away. We were a small household and I did not feel it should endure discord amongst the staff and without doubt Betts tried to cause unnecessary gossip and upset in an otherwise happy home. I spoke to Lord Althorp immediately on his return, making as light of the situation as possible. He had been away on business and it could not be pleasant for him to return and find problems at home when all he wanted was peace. That was all I wanted too, so it was necessary to put an end to the unpleasantness. I told Lord Althorp, as we stood in the butler's pantry, that, sad as it would make me and I did not want to let him down, but that if I kept having problems with Betts I would have to consider leaving the house. He absolutely did not want that to happen and neither did I. The children were happy, which was the main thing, and generally the house ran well. Lord Althorp promised me he would talk to Betts and the other staff and make sure that the air was cleared and there would be no further problems. He kept to his word and from that time on, there were no more difficulties. The main issue was really the attitude of some members of staff towards me. On the one hand they were pleased to see the children so happy, on the other hand some were perhaps put out that a total outsider had come into the system, changed so many of the old established ways with such ease and quickly formed a good relationship with the children, even with Diana, who previously could sometimes be difficult. Now she was happy and settled, her unmanageable days had become a thing of the past. It was apparent, too, that I had Lord Althorp's approval on the ideas I mooted for the well-being of his children and his readiness to fall in with any new suggestion also irritated some of the older staff. He was always on my side and protected me from any such indignation as his greatest concern was for the happiness of his children. If my ideas helped to achieve this he would certainly agree to them. In the short time I had been there, I had already proved my loyalty to the children and to their father so it could not be doubted that I had their best interests at heart.

The children often saw their maternal grandmother, Ruth, Lady Fermoy, who had her Norfolk home nearby at Hillington, but their paternal grandmother who lived at Althorp was not such a regular visitor. Never once, during the time I worked at Park House, did Lord Althorp take his children to Althorp to visit his parents. He and his father, the Earl Spencer, did not get on well and I do not think he wanted the children subjected to the rather difficult atmosphere that prevailed at Althorp. I was told this was the reason we did not visit. However, Lord Althorp's mother, Cynthia Countess Spencer, came every summer to Park House to watch the annual cricket match when the President's XI played against the local cricket club. She, too, had been a lady-in-waiting to the Queen Mother and her visit coincided with the Queen Mother's visit to Sandringham. Countess Spencer was a 'real' lady. As soon as I met her I realized the difference generated by breeding. However adaptable the person who marries into an old family of the gentry may be, however hard they try they can never quite achieve that indefinable quality that is bred into an aristocratic family that has existed for generations. Lady Spencer was a warm, caring person with an air of serenity. Natural and friendly, she was loved by all the local people. Diana has inherited many of her

146

qualities. Although they did not see her often the children were very fond of their grandmother, they were always at ease with her and she was greatly missed when she died of cancer in the autumn of 1972.

We were lucky again with the weather for the cricket match, organized by Julian Loyd. Lord Althorp invited a number of friends to Park House for the day. Sarah, along with some of the older children who accompanied their parents, organized the tennis. During the summer, Sarah and I had played together quite often as it meant that I could stay in the grounds and keep an eye on the younger children as opposed to riding which would take me away. The tennis court had proved to be an unexpected bonus to my job and tennis was my favourite sport, after riding. Diana and I also used to knock a few balls about and I would help her to practise her strokes. We used to try to persuade Charles to be ballboy often unsuccessfully. Diana still had not started to play seriously. Although she had a good eye for the ball her capabilities were still limited and she quickly became bored because we could not keep the ball in play for long. Diana was constantly aware that she had two older sisters who were good at both academic subjects and sport and a brother who, although three years younger than she, was not far behind. At every opportunity, I tried to reassure her about her own worth and give as much encouragement as possible.

Diana's very raw approach to tennis did not prevent her from trying to persuade Sarah to let her play with her and her friends. Sarah quite rightly refused as she would have spoilt their games, but Diana did not take kindly to the rebuke. 'Don't be so mean, Sarah', was one of her favourite expressions but it never revoked Sarah's decision. I told Diana to offer to act as a ballboy if she wished to stay with the older girls but also suggested she might be better off with Annabel and Alexandra who were happily playing in the den. Diana had no intention of playing second fiddle to her sister and chose to take my advice and spend time with her contemporaries. In their company she soon forgot how put out she had been by Sarah's refusal to let her join in. From a very early age, the relationship between Sarah and Diana contained all the elements and emotions that exist between two sisters who have very

147

individual characters. Competitiveness, affection, protectiveness, envy, jealousy and finally, as adults, acceptance of each other on equal terms and gratitude for the support afforded to each other.

It would be difficult to picture a more perfect English summer afternoon. I sat with Diana, Charles and Countess Spencer watching Lord Althorp play for the President's team. Muted conversation, the low drone of insects, the sporadic clapping, the gentle drift of time when it seems a day will never finish – no-one wants it to – the distant shouts in the background from the tennis court . . . The best part of the cricket match – the interval for cream teas – came and we were joined by the tennis contingent. Play resumed again. I, too, did not want it to end but in the back of my mind was the knowledge that soon all this would just be a memory. We were shortly to leave the peace of Park House for the bustle of London and I was to face my first meeting with the children's mother since I had seen her in court. I did not think that it would be a very pleasant experience and planned to hand over the children as quickly and with as little fuss as possible. We still had two days left and I was a great believer in not crossing bridges until I came to them.

Diana and I found the cricket rather boring. Neither of us had a clue about the game but whereas I was content to take in the atmosphere and daydream, Diana was restless and could not understand how some of her friends could sit and look as if they were enjoying the match. Now that tea was over Diana would prefer to play in the den again. It had been no problem to persuade Diana to stay until the interval, the cream teas were a big attraction. I told Diana she could leave and do what she wanted but she was not to swim. Charles asked to stay so I chose to remain with him for a while longer. An hour later, he too had had enough. The tennis finished and I told the younger children they could join Sarah and her friends in the swimming pool if they wished, as it was their last chance for the next day we were bound for London. They needed no second bidding. Diana was out of the den, changed, and at the top of the slide within minutes. A sharp 'No' from me halted the speciality before it could be executed and the planned dive was converted into a gentle slide into the water. I let them play for a while and then announced that it was time to come inside. Lord Althorp and his mother had been invited out for dinner. Sarah, who was not coming to London with us, was out with friends, so Diana came to help me in the kitchen to get a hot supper ready as cook had taken the opportunity to have the evening off. She had been very busy during the summer and deserved the free time.

The next day we left for London. I went by train with the children. Lord Althorp went first to Althorp House, Northampton, and would join us later. Smith took us to the station. I read my book and the children had their comics, one of their treats when they travelled by train. We gazed out of the window at the countryside flashing past and talked very little, each of us immersed in our own thoughts as we recalled all that had taken place during the summer at Park House. We had made good use of our time. It had been extremely busy, full of new experiences and I was quite tired and looked forward to my own holiday. The children talked and discussed what they would prefer to do on the day we were to spend in London and wondered what activities had been planned for the time with their mother. There is no attractive way to approach London by train. Diana and Charles reiterated the very words I used to use as a child whenever we travelled to London, 'I can't imagine living here all the time'. The train pulled into the station. We checked to make sure we had collected all our luggage and stepped on to the platform. Above all the noise I shouted to the children to keep with me as we were carried along with the general flow. We followed the sign to the taxi rank. It did not take long before we were on our way to the London house, not far from Victoria in south-west London.

The taxi turned off the main road into a quiet mews and I saw for myself the contrast between my old terraced house in Norwich and this elegant town house. Built in three storeys with the main living area on the middle floor, it was beautifully furnished and decorated and made an ideal base for London living. Architecturally it was a complete contrast to Park House, but it was the first time I realized that it was possible to find an oasis of calm in the midst of a busy city. I could not even hear the sound of traffic when I was inside. A housekeeper was there to welcome us and later that evening Lord Althorp arrived from Northampton.

Diana and Charles had decided that they would like to visit their two favourite stores, Hamleys, one of the largest toy shops in the world, in Regent Street and Harrods in Knightsbridge. They had been to both shops several times before so it was I who was the stranger, only having visited Harrods once before. I usually considered its merchandise beyond my pocket and I had never been to Hamleys. This was our first port of call the next morning. I went alone with the children and after fifteen minutes I could understand why Lord Althorp had decided to relinquish the guardian role to me. It was the middle of the summer and London had many tourists. Some of them I expect were at Buckingham Palace, others perhaps at the Tower of London, but the majority I felt sure were visiting Hamleys. That is until we arrived at Harrods and I realized the remainder were there. Diana and Charles, both 'au fait' with the layout of Hamleys, tried to hurry me from one floor to the next – and there seemed to be endless floors – as they looked at games and toys that they might want to request for Christmas. Needless to say, what interested Charles was on a totally different floor to the items that Diana wanted to admire and she found it difficult to contain her impatience when I said we would look at Charles's choices first. On the other hand Charles was quite content to wait for Diana; he had much more patience than his sister. 'All good things come to those who wait.' It always annoyed Diana when I, or anyone, quoted such inane sayings to her as she was sure there should be a suitable reply and it frustrated her that she did not know what it was. With lists now prepared in anticipation of Christmas, we went on to Harrods and saw more toys but both children were also interested to visit the pet shop section. I have to admit that if I wanted to purchase a kitten, Harrods would not be the first place that would spring to mind. I would be more likely to visit the local farmer. In London Diana assured me that many people buy their pets from Harrods. As in Hamleys, both stores seemed to be crowded with well-dressed people, many from the Third World countries, laden with parcels. In sharp contrast were the Americans, the men dressed in brilliant coloured checked trousers with striped shirts and sometimes wearing stetsons. Comely, well-covered women in polyester dresses did not match up to Diana's idea of an American, mostly gleaned from pictures of Hollywood, and 'Isn't it bad manners for a man to wear a hat indoors?' I explained to them that ideas do vary from country to country.

In the afternoon, pleased to get away from shops, Diana and Charles decided they would like to visit Madame Tussauds, where we spent an enjoyable and interesting time discussing whether the wax models were good copies of the subjects. We all thought the last day had been a lovely way to end our share of the holiday and it had given us a great deal of pleasure. The next day, at the appointed time, I took a taxi with the children to Cadogan Place, the London home of their mother, kissed the children goodbye and wished them a happy time. As I had anticipated, their mother had very little to say and it was spoken to me via Diana – it had not been my wish to get embroiled in the custody case – and I did not think it was very pleasant for the children. As I could hear what was being said, I refused to let Diana get involved and repeat what was spoken so I answered her mother directly. Charles looked so bemused that I wondered if he thought it was a kind of game. Diana knew it was not and I was sorry, but hoped it would be quickly forgotten once I had left. I confirmed directly the time and date that I would collect Diana and Charles at the end of their holiday. I continued on my way in the taxi, turning to wave to the children as we drove away. I felt really strange and could easily appreciate why Lord Althorp did not like to see his children off. They both waved, Diana hesitantly, perhaps wondering if it would offend her mother, Charles quite gaily, oblivious to the underlying current, and then they turned to go indoors. The taxi dropped me off at Victoria station from where I caught the train to Gatwick airport and flew off to the sun. I was sorry to say goodbye temporarily to the children, but pleased to get away from the only bitterness of the holidays.

Chapter Eleven

During my four-week holiday, I thought often of the children and found myself looking forward to the time I would meet them again in London. I had quickly grown used to the way of life at Sandringham and after the initial break and relaxation without the children, I realized how much I missed them. I telephoned Lord Althorp as arranged, three days before I was due to go to London, only to be told to come straight to Park House as Diana and Charles would travel back with Sarah who had spent a few days with her mother. I was not unhappy at this change of plans as I did not look forward to further meetings with the children's mother.

I arrived at Park House in time to get unpacked and settled and saw Lord Althorp — there was no chance that he would pass the task of collecting the children to Smith or myself — leave for Kings Lynn station. I would like to have gone, but with all the luggage in the Simca, there would not be enough room so I had to wait at home. I was so pleased it was one of British Rail's better days and the train was on time.

I heard the car come down the drive and rushed out to meet them. Any strangeness or embarrassment was covered in the ensuing chaos, everyone speaking at once, dogs leaping everywhere, Smith trying to unload the car, Diana, for reasons best known to herself, perhaps she was hungry, relating in detail how 'delicious' the cake was that had been made by her mother's help. Mrs Smith, who had appeared in her quiet, and in my view slightly subservient manner to greet everyone, had her hackles raised within seconds and I could see her mind work as she determined to pass on this bit of information to cook. Why, *they* could both bake better than anyone else, everyone knew that. If I did not think Diana was too young to scheme so far ahead, I would have thought she spoke deliberately to guarantee a good cake supply to take back to school with her. Sarah rushed off to see 'darling Peppermint', to make sure she still had four legs after being parted from her for a few days and knowing that I too had been absent. Diana, having deserted Peanuts for much longer, hurried off to check on him, not content with Smith's reassurances. The euphoria did not last for long. We ate dinner together and the conversation was very animated as we caught up with each other's news, but the knowledge that the next day the children would go their separate ways at the start of a new school year hung like a shadow over us all. However much school is enjoyed, the actual parting is always a bit of a wrench. I knew that the next day would prove to be rather sad especially after such a long, happy holiday. I did remind Diana that at the start of her second year at Riddlesworth she was in a much stronger position than in the previous year when she went as a new girl. I told her, rather unnecessarily, to be kind and helpful to those who would start for the first time, reminding her how it takes a while to adjust to sleeping away from home and to try to help them to settle in, to remember how she had felt the previous year.

I continued to write often to Diana during the term. We had a hectic home weekend but it was cold and we spent most of the time indoors. As the days got shorter, Charles and I settled into life as it had been when I first started at Sandringham, spending a great deal of our time in the nursery by the bright open fire. I rode every day and about once a week friends came to visit me for dinner. Some were those I had met during the Kings Lynn Festival that summer.

That year it was planned for the children to spend the Christmas with their mother. Diana had just two days to stay with us at Park House while we waited for Charles to finish his school, then I took them to London by train. I was getting as used to the journey by this time as I was to the cold meeting that I expected would await me at the barrier. I was always sorry it had to be that way but I did not dwell on it or ever imagine that attitudes could change. My main aim was to hand the children over as quickly as possible with the sole intention of avoiding any confrontation that might upset them. As could be expected just before Christmas, most of the journey was spent discussing what presents they hoped to receive and whether any of their choices made at Hamleys during the summer holidays would appear. I believed that they would have their way. Christmas and birthdays were the two occasions when both parents allowed themselves to spoil the children. From the practical side of present giving there would be a selection of clothes and for pleasure and fun they would each receive a main gift, updates on bikes being ever popular, and for Diana, a weaving loom or a typewriter. There were also stocking fillers of books, jigsaw puzzles, board games, soldiers for Charles, a skipping rope for Diana, yo-yos, roller skates, a pogo stick. These are just some of the presents that I can remember. Computer games were yet to dominate the market. In this aspect of the children's upbringing they were treated no differently from the way in which many parents like to indulge their children.

Diana asked me what presents I hoped to get for Christmas. I said that now I was older I viewed Christmas through different eyes. The magic it held for me when I was a child was no longer there. Awareness of the commercialism had all but obliterated the real meaning of Christmas, and the magic had been replaced by knowledge that in the eyes of many people it was simply a marketing enterprise. She argued how lovely it was to see the shops so well decorated. I agreed with her and tried to explain to both Diana and Charles how much more effective it would be if they were not decorated until November rather than so many weeks beforehand, then the festivities could be condensed and thus more appreciated. I told Diana and Charles how I loved to hear the carol singers, and the different bands like that of the Salvation Army, singing in the streets just prior to Christmas and how their music added to the atmosphere. I told Diana that I thought the best part of Christmas was the opportunity to spend time with family and friends. It was the one time in a hectic year when we could be together. I chose not to describe the closeness of our family Christmases when John and I were Diana's age. How my father would work so hard until late on Christmas Eve when he would return from delivering the last box of Christmas goodies that had been assembled over the weeks by his customers and stored at our home to be kept a secret from their families until Christmas arrived. Or how I would not consider that Christmas had started until my father was safe in the house, his work completed. I always worried about him having a road accident. It was only then that I could allow myself to get into the true Christmas spirit.

Diana and Charles asked me how many days' holiday I had from school. I told them how lucky I was because I was at a private school, so I had nearly four weeks, whereas my brother at state school only had two weeks and I never let him forget it. 'I bet he was jealous of you,' said Diana. 'No,' I told her. 'John was never jealous of anyone.' I told them, though, that my father only had one day off, Christmas Day, as it was one of the few days in the year when there were no newspapers or post and we all made the most of it. Diana asked me where we went shopping for Christmas presents. I told them how we saved our pocket money and an evening was set aside when, after the shop was closed, we were allowed to go in to choose the presents we wished to buy for our friends and family. Diana loved to hear how we were allowed to work in the shop to earn extra money preparing the orders that the customers left us, ready for my father to deliver them and the weekly orders during his lunch break. I described how busy the post office became as Christmas drew nearer and that one of my jobs was to stamp all the cards that were posted ready for the vans to collect and take to Great Yarmouth. Diana asked me if I hoped to have a shop as a business one day as it seemed like good fun to her. I told her I did not want to be tied in that way. My great-grandmother had first had the post office, but when my father retired it would be sold. 'What will you do when you leave us?' she asked. I wondered if it was a trick question to see if I planned to leave. I replied that I had not even thought about the future as it was my intention to stay at Sandringham for as long as I was needed. They were not aware that I was employed just until Charles went to Maidwell, his prep school. It was a long way ahead and it was unnecessary for them to worry about me leaving.

We were met at the barrier as prearranged. Jane had already broken up and come with her mother to meet us. I was extremely grateful for that as Jane was as friendly as she had been at Park House. Already a person in her own right who, while understanding her mother's feelings, would not be influenced by them. Personally I had done her no harm, we had got on well during the summer and I was pleased that she still greeted me warmly even in the

155

presence of her mother. Amidst the greetings it was easy for any difficulty to be disguised and I could see the relief on Diana's face as it appeared that all was well. I was happy. Christmas, children's favourite time of the year, should be unspoilt. No time was wasted. Hellos and goodbyes were spoken simultaneously. I wished them a wonderful Christmas and said how I would look forward to hearing if their wishes had been answered when I came to collect them.

As planned, I spent Christmas with friends and family, catching up on news. I welcomed the break. My life away from Park House was such a contrast. Both lives had many qualities that I enjoyed. I looked forward to spending the second part of the Christmas holidays at Park House with the children. The holiday passed very quickly and it seemed no time before I was making my way to the station to catch the train to London. As usual I drove first to Park House and then Smith took me on to the station and would return to collect us a few hours later. It was very crowded with many people either returning home after visiting their families in Norfolk or, having spent Christmas and New Year at home, intending to spend a few days away before they had to return to work and the children went back to school. The train journey passed in a very pleasant atmosphere and even as I enjoyed it I wondered if it would be sustained in our group during the return journey. On the days I took or collected the children from London, it seemed I spent the whole day on the train. I arrived in London and anxiously scanned the crowds for familiar faces. My stomach churned. I instinctively knew this time there would be no Jane to help alleviate the fraught atmosphere that I had come to take for granted. On the journey, I kept telling myself, 'Don't worry, in another two hours it will all be over and we'll be on the way home.' I do not think anyone, unless they have experienced a similar situation, can appreciate the knotted feeling caused by tension when there is no choice but to face an unpleasant meeting that lies ahead, one made even worse when it is beyond the control of someone who just has to act as the unfortunate middleman.

I saw the group move towards me. Their mother, a tall, striking-looking woman, stood out in the crowds. Trailing behind, a mask on their faces, were Diana and Charles. Why were they trailing behind? Was it intentional to disguise any eagerness they might feel about their return to prevent hurting their mother's feelings? Perhaps they really did not want to come back or was it simply that their mother walked so quickly? It was the latter reason but I was so tense and wound up I assumed the worst just to add to my suppressed agitation. I would give no one the satisfaction of sensing my discomfort. 'Not long now, Mary, fifteen minutes and it will all be over.' Thus boosting my confidence, I moved forward to draw attention to myself, a smile on my face – no need for everyone to look miserable. I was right; although I continued to scan the crowds for sight of Jane, it was in vain, just a mass of strange faces with unseeing eyes rushing past to catch their trains. 'Here goes, five minutes', and I stepped forward. Politely I held out my hand to greet the Hon. Mrs Shand Kydd and promptly tried to pretend I had had a sudden impulse to do an arm exercise and allowed it to swing to my side again. 'Great start,' I thought to myself. Turning brightly to the children, I kissed first Diana who returned the affection in a very restrained manner, wary of upsetting her mother, yet not wanting to hurt me. Inside I felt like saying, 'Oh, don't worry, Diana, just be yourself, this is all for my benefit, she'll be all right when we've gone.' Of course, I could say nothing like that. I just had to have the good sense to understand Diana's reticence. That did not stop me from feeling angry that Diana could not feel free to act naturally. Charles stepped forward and kissed me, bless him. This farce was well over his head. He had had a lovely time with his mother, now here was Mary and he was going back to his father, it was all as simple as that for him. I hugged him, grateful for his natural approach. I asked their mother if there were any messages. 'You know what to tell your father, don't you, Diana?' 'Oh, one of those days,' I thought. There were a few more sentences of instructions to Diana. It seemed to me to put her in an invidious position. Much as I longed to say something I was not empowered to do so. If I spoke my mind I knew it might cause extra problems for their father. Diana was told, 'Don't worry, you'll be all right, you'll settle, don't forget what I said, please phone me', all subtly emotive remarks, in my view quite damaging for any child of that age to have to be baffled by. Diana always was all right as soon as the parting was over. If such phrases had not been uttered Diana would not have been affected at all at transition times. We got on so well and they were happy. How I hated these meetings. Still, every job has some bad points and this was about

157

the only one in mine. I just kept thinking to myself that soon we'd be on the train. Finally, we escaped; we had said our goodbyes and were aboard the train waiting for it to head towards Kings Lynn.

The conversation on the train as it pulled out of the station was very stilted. I felt my mood lighten as we left suburbia behind and the scenery gave way to open countryside. After the tension that had built up inside me on my journey to London and the subsequent meeting I was just relieved to have it all behind me and to be heading towards familiar ground and even if talk was difficult at the moment, I knew I would be able to get everything back to normal once those tensions had been given a chance to dissipate. Christmas soon provided animated conversation and I was not surprised to learn that Diana and Charles had both acquired the presents they had set their hearts on. Not spoilt children, I was pleased their wishes had been granted on this special occasion.

I chose to ignore the fact that communication was not as easy as usual and ploughed on with my incessant chatter about how I had spent the holiday, feigning indifference as to whether they were interested or not. I continued to speak to prevent silence and sulkiness creeping into the compartment, and my chatter provided a diversion from introspection. Little by little Diana relaxed. Charles, once all his immediate questions had been answered and he in turn had answered mine, took out a book to read. I had told them that although I'd had a wonderful break, I was really pleased to see them and we would make the most of our time together before school began again. I said I had seen their father and he too was looking forward to our return. In answer to this remark which I had reiterated to ensure that they knew a warm welcome waited for them at Park House Diana, glancing at me to judge my reaction, said how sad her mother would be now they had left as she would be all on her own. This seemed to be a popular theme for Diana as she had spoken similarly on our return from the Easter holidays. I forbore to mention that her mother's husband and friends would be with her. Diana was only testing me to see if I would make any disloyal remark about her mother and at that delicate time I could not be sure that Diana would not repeat it when she spoke to her mother on the telephone. I made a point to remain perfectly neutral about both parents and kept my thoughts to myself.

158

Charles, not so tactful and very used to his sister's dramatics, must have been listening with half an ear for he looked up from his book long enough to say to his sister in quite a disparaging tone, 'You know Mummy is not on her own, Diana, and you always say that about Daddy too.' His sister brought down to earth, he returned to his book. Charles was right, Diana always said how sad it was for her father every time they had to leave him on his own. These manipulative remarks were a result of a mixture of liking to imagine herself as an indispensable daughter combined with her rather melodramatic view, understandable though it was, that commuting between two parents should not actually be straight-forward and without problems. Sometimes Diana would fan the flames. Both parents loved their children and provided stable homes for them with all their familiar, special belongings to hand. 'Anyway,' said Diana, not to be outdone by her brother, 'I promised Mummy I would phone her as soon as I got home.' I agreed with her that was important and she must make sure not to forget. With such a reasonable statement there was very little point in Diana continuing to stir up trouble.

Once she accepted that she would not be able to get me to make any derogatory comments Diana changed the subject. Her moods could swing rapidly. Sadness and discontent were swept immediately from her mind and were now replaced with countless questions about my own holiday which confirmed my previous suspicion that she had not really listened to me before, such had been her determination to find a way to try to embarrass me. I breathed a sigh of relief. The worst seemed to be over. In all the time I spent with Diana, it was only during the train journeys that the less likeable side of Diana's nature was exposed. Although I found this unnerving, it did not upset me unduly as I appreciated that changing from one home to another could be unsettling and in a way I felt Diana was entitled to express a less affable side, rather than just let adults assume she could be shifted around without feeling any emotion. I also quickly realized that if I did not rise to the bait, Diana would soon give up and let her natural optimistic disposition re-emerge. She was much more interested in looking forward to the next experience than in dwelling on the past. The nearer we got to Kings Lynn, the more animated Diana became as she looked forward to being reunited with all the pets, her father and the Smiths. 'Were they all well, would Mr Smith meet us at the station?' Now she could not wait to arrive.

The familiar face of Smith was indeed at Kings Lynn station waiting to meet us. He was as permanent a fixture in the children's lives as anyone and was inexorably linked to Park House and Norfolk. He and his wife had represented a constant presence in Diana's life for as long as she could remember. When her father was not there, nor the mother, when the au pairs and nannies were constantly changing, there was always Mr and Mrs Smith. Diana never forgot them. They were an indelible part of her formative years. She invited them to her wedding and even after her marriage, when the Smiths had long retired and moved to Dersingham, Diana wrote and told me that when she stayed at Sandringham she had visited them in their cottage. I can imagine the intense pleasure this must have given them and depicts exactly the loyalty and sincere kindness that is part of Diana's character.

Smith said he met us as Lord Althorp was out but that he would be home by the time we arrived. We were all a little tired. It had been quite an emotive day, in different ways, for all of us. The children, sitting in the back of the car, answered Smith's enquiries as to whether they had had a good Christmas and then lapsed into silence as Smith concentrated on his driving and I made polite conversation with him. On arrival, we went straight to the nursery wing and within moments Lord Althorp appeared to see Diana and Charles. The happy, bubbly, excited Diana of the latter part of the train journey disappeared, to be replaced again by a shy, and I could not help feeling, somewhat deliberately withdrawn, demure child. In a confused way, Diana thought that if she appeared too excited to see her father he might think that meant that she was happier to be with him than with her mother. Too young to really appreciate just how fair-minded Lord Althorp was about his children, she did not realize this was a pointless exercise as he would not have placed such a connotation on her behaviour. He was always far too thrilled to have his children home again to concern himself with one-upmanship. It was also true that Diana probably thought she would get more attention and another chance to dramatize if she appeared a little subdued. Diana was always shy and reticent at initial greetings, quiet until she grew more confident. Charles was pleased to see his father and immediately fitted into the system as if he had never been away. Diana too greeted her father with affection and asked if Sarah was at home. Sarah was out with her friends. Lord Althorp, clearly very pleased and thinking he was about to give a treat to his children, a surprise, then told Diana and Charles that they had been invited by the Queen to Sandringham House, to a party with the young royals – Andrew, Edward and some other children.

I instinctively knew that Diana realized how much this meant to her father, the thought that he was offering them a treat, but in a confused way she felt that it was disloyal to her mother to appear so readily to fall back into Park House routines. She thought it would look as if she did not care, if, when she spoke to her mother on the phone, she told her that she was going at once to a party. Diana would normally love to have accepted but her feelings were of divided loyalty. It was a shame the invitation had to coincide with the day of their return. Diana pleaded a headache. It was the first time she had mentioned she did not feel well to me. Neither of the children had ever talked about headaches before. She said it was impossible, that she did not want to go, that she was not well enough and she was too upset. Much as she loved her father, she had thrown herself so whole-heartedly into this new melodramatic role, that she failed to see the look of abject disappointment on his face. He tried once again to persuade Diana and said she would feel fine once she was there, but Diana showed a trait that has remained with her in adult years, strength of will, and she could not be persuaded to change her mind. Charles, who had been perfectly happy to go along with the invitation, saw the line of resistance that Diana was taking and thought loyalty demanded that he agree with her. It was the only time during my stay at Park House when I really felt like shaking Diana and telling her to pull herself together and think of other people, which she usually did without any persuasion.

I did neither but I thought to myself how uncomplicated boys were by comparison to girls. Charles had been perfectly amiable up until that point. Girls seemed intent on making life more difficult, at times by over-reacting and dramatizing. I advised Lord Althorp, after his failed second attempt to coax Diana into changing her mind, to leave the subject and telephone to make our apologies. Diana, taken aback that she was not going to be given another chance to reiterate sorrow, upset, headache and so on, said she had to telephone her mother. I told her she had to wait until her father had finished his call, as we were already tardy in declining the invitation. Once the phone was free she must certainly ring her mother as she had promised. She could use the telephone in the nursery where she would be able to speak privately. I told Lord Althorp not to worry, that Diana would soon become her normal self. After the initial awkward start of the train journey, she had been really bright, I told him, and just to leave her with me. I felt so sorry for Lord Althorp as I watched him walk dejectedly away and angry that Diana felt it necessary to hurt him out of this misguided sense of loyalty. But if the departure from London had been less stressful, Diana would not have been put into such a position and would have felt free to accept the invitation with pleasure.

Now before all the psychoanalysts rush forward to condemn me for lack of understanding of the traumas young Diana was experiencing, let me emphasize that I understood everything very clearly. I was witness to the station scene, just as I was witness to the provocation of a very knowing little girl on the train and a witness to the immediate transformation when I did not take up her challenge. I saw how happy Diana was and excited at the prospect of the second part of her holiday. A child who was truly, deeply traumatized, would not be able to maintain the contentment Diana continually displayed, apart from those occasional hiccups, throughout the time I knew her. I have yet to meet a child, either with one parent, two parents, one happy home or two parental homes, who does not display some signs of obstinacy at one point or another. Diana knew exactly what she was doing. She had full control of her emotions and I let her work her way through it. I assured her father that, left to her own devices, she would soon become the sunny girl with the naturally bouncy spirit again. Perhaps he was naïve to have expected to see this immediately on her return.

I passed by the nursery door which was ajar, and heard Diana tell her mother she had a headache. I wonder if she received sympathy. I expect so. All Diana received from me was advice to go and lie down until she felt better. Within five minutes, the peace and tranquillity of Park House had washed over her, tension passed and the phantom headache was gone. 'Great,' I said. 'Now we've got over that, get the torch and we'll go and say hello to the dogs.' There was one last attempt at stirring. 'What about the party, Daddy wasn't angry, was he?' 'Of course not,' I said. 'You couldn't possibly go with a headache. He has phoned and explained.' With that, Charles, Diana and I, wellies on and well wrapped up against the cold, ventured out into the dark, to be greeted by warm muzzles and wagging tails – excited dogs battling to lick us in welcome. Perhaps, after all, Diana was right, this was more fun than a party. Amongst screams of laughter, I knew we were back on course. We were home.

Chapter Twelve

The royal family were in residence at Sandringham House, their winter home where they always stayed after a Christmas spent at Windsor. Their proximity made no difference to the Spencer family. For many years there had been ties between the two families, one from the very top drawer of British aristocracy, the other royal, and because their presence was taken for granted, there was no sense of awe amongst the Spencer children just because their neighbours happened to include the Queen of England. The families did not socialize frequently, although Lord Althorp was often invited on shoots on the estate, but the children, apart from the occasional party invitation, usually only met by chance in the park. It was pleasant, though, to think of the lovely Sandringham House inhabited sometimes as a family home, rather than just standing empty and ready only for inspection by summer visitors.

I have to admit, I was rather in awe of the neighbours even if the children were not. When I was a child my neighbours had been my Nan and Grandad and it took me a time to adjust to the grandeur of those that now lived next door to me. Unlike the children, who did not give it a second thought, I was always conscious that I might bump into one of them as I walked or rode in the park.

Early on one of the first mornings after our return to Park House, just as dawn broke, I decided to take the dogs for a walk before the day started. The children were still asleep and even when they woke, they would be happy to read or play in their rooms. The cold winter morning did not induce for them any wish to leave the warmth of the house to go outside. In the weak light between dawn and real daylight an eerie silence hung over the park and a soft steady drizzle fell, not heavy enough to make me wet but fine, leaving a clinging sense of dampness everywhere. The park was shrouded in mist and I walked along with my head bent to try to protect myself from the light rain. In the ghostly stillness it was easy to lose myself in my thoughts and become entangled in the gossamer web that enveloped and shrouded trees and bushes from human eye. The dogs chased wildly around, noses to the ground. It was a good morning for scent and soon rabbits were rushing in all directions, making for their burrows. We had been asked to keep the dogs under control so that the pheasants were not disturbed and driven to other land. A shortage of them would restrict the pleasure of the royal shoots. Usually I abided by these rules but so early in the morning and with visibility so poor I did not expect anyone else to be about, so I thought I would let the dogs have some freedom and give them a chance to let off steam. In any case they seemed more interested in animals than birds so I did not think they could do a great deal of harm. Actually I did not approve of shooting, so I thought 'good luck to them' if some game birds escaped to safer places.

Suddenly the peace and solitude was broken by the dogs who started to bark furiously. Walking towards me through the rain was a man, his head bent against the elements, he too apparently lost in thought. He was dressed in the essential country uniform of Barbour and green wellies and a hat pulled well down over his head. I immediately wondered if he was a gamekeeper or someone who would reprimand me for letting the dogs run loose. I hoped not, as I did not want any hassle or unpleasantness to upset my peaceful, reflective walk. As our paths met I spoke a cheery good-morning, hoping that a bright face would act as a buffer and deterrent against any rebuke. None was forthcoming. The man looked at me. His response of good-morning was not spoken in the voice of a gamekeeper. The dogs, their hunting suspended for a few moments, rushed around him. 'Don't worry, they are quite harmless', was my rather unnecessary statement, as their tails wagged furiously while they sniffed happily at his legs and did not give any indication of attack. Even as I spoke I realized who the man was – Prince Charles. Ever since the royal family had arrived at Sandringham House, I had imagined what it would be like if I met anyone of them while out in the park. It finally happened when I least expected it, but I was not really surprised and before it had time to dawn on me we had both continued on our ways. I called the dogs and returned to Park House, quite excited to recount the experience of my early morning meeting to Sarah and Diana. I did not expect young Charles to be very interested, after all, I was only talking about the son of his godmother.

I called the children. It was time to get up but, as I had guessed, they were already playing quietly in their bedrooms, not in any rush to go outside. Sarah, who had spent most of the holiday with her father and was already at Park House when we returned from London, came along to see what plans there were for the day. I described to them my meeting in the park with Prince Charles and how I had thought that he was the gamekeeper. Diana said, 'I bet you were embarrassed.' I denied this and went on to explain that I had not immediately recognized him as I had been preoccupied with the dogs. Sarah asked me to repeat the conversation. 'Hardly a conversation,' I told her. 'More just a passing pleasantry.' 'Didn't you say "Sir" when you spoke to him?' she asked upon being given an exact repetition of my words. I confirmed that I had not and said that I did not realize that I was meant to. I had fallen down on my royal etiquette. Diana jumped in to tease me about how remiss I was in the presence of those from next door. I reminded her I had not come up against these situations before and asked if, unless I was told, how I could be expected to know? 'Anyway,' I said, 'I was surprised *he* didn't touch his cap.' I had grown used to this form of basic politeness shown by the country men towards women and which I thought was a simple courtesy and in a way, flattering. It remains an old sign of good manners and one I still find very attractive and endearing. I teased Sarah and said if she had got up early enough she could have come with me and then I would have been able to copy her correct manners! Diana joined in the banter and added that then Sarah could have had a chance to chat to Prince Charles. Sarah responded by saying that she was not interested in doing that and then she turned the tables on Diana by reminding her she had lost her chance to speak with Prince Andrew by refusing to go to the party, 'just because you were being dramatic'. 'I was not, I had a headache,' retorted Diana. 'Now, don't start all that again, we're only having a joke,' I told them both firmly. That was what our conversation was, good-natured chatter about two princes whom none of us expected would ever feature in our lives, beyond reading about them in the newspapers. Perhaps we should have consulted the ouija board? But even if it had forecast the future accurately I am sure that none of us would have believed or paid any regard to its predictions.

Lord Althorp had been invited to shoot that day at the home of his niece, Elizabeth, whose husband farmed at East Rudham, about twenty miles from Sandringham on the road to Fakenham. Diana had been bridesmaid for the first time when her cousin had married Anthony Duckworth-Chad at St James, Piccadilly, in 1969. She had been about eight and had so loved the experience that she said that was why she teased her sisters to marry young so that she could repeat it. Jane finally complied with her wishes when she married Robert Fellowes in April 1978 at the Guards' Chapel in London. The reception was held at St James's Palace and attended by several members of the royal family including the Queen Mother. Diana was the chief bridesmaid and once again loved the experience which served to add to her ideals about love and marriage.

We were invited to join the party at midday for the shooting lunch of soup and game pie. The food was set out by household staff in the large kitchen and the girls assured me it was well worth while to go although Diana and I did not care for the shooting. Sarah accepted it all readily as being part of country life. Later when the family moved to Althorp, Lord Spencer wrote and told me that Diana had helped with the rearing of the baby pheasants, so she must have come to accept the inevitable. It was an integral part of her upbringing and later if it was demanded of Diana that she join a shooting party she would not refuse.

The lunch was as enjoyable as the girls had promised but it provided one of the only occasions during my time at Park House when I did feel alienated from the people around me. I had no idea of the form that a day's shooting took and was quite surprised and not pleased to realize that children and those in charge of them were expected to eat separately from the members of the shoot and the other adults. Had not Lord Althorp always treated everyone the same I should have expected that to be normal and so I now found segregation difficult to accept.

Hunting, another controversial subject, also played a part in our lives at Park House. Sarah belonged to the West Norfolk

Foxhounds. During term time, if the meet was within hacking distance, I would join for the day and take Peppermint just for the outing and the different riding country. It made a pleasant change and gave me a chance to see new faces and have a chat. I have always considered hunting to be a good training ground for young horses. It teaches them the social side of life. They go out with green ribbons tied to their tails to show that they are beginners and learn how to behave in company and how to stand still while the hounds are searching for scent. I find that part of hunting rather tedious. To sit still on the horse for sometimes quite long stretches can prove to be both cold and boring unless it is for this teaching purpose. However, boredom can be relieved by a hip flask full of a warming liquid and good company, and in any case it is instantly dispelled when the hunting horn blows. Horses' ears prick, excitement trembles through them and the chase is on again. I can well appreciate the exhilaration of the chase and understand why people become so addicted to the sport especially because on the days I was out, the fox always escaped.

Sarah planned a day's outing. Diana called her callous and cruel and was totally ignored. The meet was near by and they were all set to gather on the village green. Lord Althorp, Diana, Charles and I decided to go and see her off. The morning was crisp and clear and many riders turned out. The huntsmen looked just as resplendent as when they had paraded at the flower show on that bright summer's day in July. Today, I knew it would not be long before they and their horses were splattered in mud as they galloped across ploughed fields. I saw several people I had met on previous hunts, mounted, and for a moment envied them the chance to be out on such a good winter's day. Sarah, sitting on Peppermint, recognized many people and mixed freely, her grey horse standing out amongst bays and chestnuts. Peppermint was a wonderful hunter. She was well behaved and could be relied upon to jump any obstacles, hedges or ditches we met in full flight. Lord Althorp appeared to know the majority of people, both mounted and on foot, and it was a very convivial morning. Diana met one or two friends and I wondered if she envied them their nerve when she saw them mounted on quite spirited animals but I felt the subject was best left ignored. The hunt moved off and we went back to our cars. Lord Althorp wanted to return home but the children and I had a warm drink and then decided to get back in the car and see if we could follow the hunt for a time.

We met some people whom I remembered seeing earlier and they told us the direction of the hunt. It had travelled quite a distance. We followed their instructions then left the car and joined a group of old men who were leaning on a fence, talking animatedly and gazing across the field. They seemed to be more knowledgeable about the habits of the fox than either the huntsmen or the hounds. In quite sarcastic tones, when I asked where the hunt was, one of the party informed us that 'it' had 'gone that way', pointing with a wave of his walking stick. It was the emphasis he put on 'it' and 'that way', that encouraged me to ask, 'And which way did the fox go?' 'Aaah – he be going that way,' he replied with another wave of his stick in the opposite direction. At that moment the hunt streaked past us in the very direction prophesied by the old man, hounds racing ahead – it is a cardinal sin on the hunting field to call those four-legged creatures that bark 'dogs' – a quite magnificent sight, which we could appreciate all the more because I believed my informer and realized they had lost the fox. We began to move towards the car. 'Wait a minute, my dear,' said my advisor, who had grown much more amiable and was anxious to prove his second theory was correct. 'You and your children stay a minute and you'll see old Reynard.' Diana and Charles roared with laughter. I hushed them and doubted whether he would be able to see the old fox if his eyes were so bad he imagined that I looked old enough at less than twenty-two years of age to have a daughter of ten and a son of seven. I thought, 'I can't look that old,' and felt obliged to explain, even though the whereabouts of the fox was the all-consuming topic, not children, that they were not my son and daughter, I just looked after them. The old boy was not interested. My explanation was really more for Diana's benefit to stop her teasing me later. I told the children to be quiet so as not to frighten the fox just in case he should appear and within moments the old man's second prediction proved sound. The hounds, horses and huntsmen had long gone. We could no longer hear the sound of the hunting horn. There was a slight rustling in the thicket behind us and, breaking cover, out ambled the large burnt red, wily fox, as relaxed as you please. He cast a sly look in our direction. I could almost imagine that he winked at the old man to acknowledge his country wisdom. He knew we would do him no harm. He strolled across the road and into the field in front of us, turning to slope off in the opposite direction to that in which the hunt had rushed. We all laughed. The fox had appeared so nonchalant and unconcerned and he clearly intended to live to see another day.

We said goodbye to our fellow spectators and returned home for lunch. Sarah arrived later in the afternoon. There had been some good runs, but they had not seen any fox. Diana could not wait to tell her that one had walked past us, only a few yards away. Sarah did not want to believe her sister at first, but I assured her that for once Diana was not exaggerating.

At dinner that evening, Lord Althorp told us that he would like us all to attend church the next day. 'Why?' chorused Sarah and Diana in unison. 'We never go to church.' 'Exactly,' I said. 'That is why we are going.' Sarah, who knew the system better than I, was able to contradict me. 'I know why you want us to go, Daddy. It's because the Queen is here and it doesn't look right if we stay away.' Lord Althorp admitted that Sarah's reasoning was more or less correct. Diana and Charles were quick to complain. They did not want to go. I told them to behave, they were not asked to do much and they could fuss all they liked but they were going, so why not be quiet and accept it for once. My unexpected and unusual firmness quietened Charles immediately. As I pointed out to him, he never went to church and it would do him no harm to give up an hour for once on Sunday morning. Lord Althorp, having made his announcement, lapsed into silence and concentrated on his dinner, happy to sit back and let me deflect the complaints. Diana, even though she knew she was backing a loser, was still determined to have one last attempt to excuse herself from church. 'I have to go to St Peter's [the church attended by Riddlesworth pupils] every Sunday.' 'Good,' I replied. 'Then we can rely on you to help with the singing because you should know most of the hymns.' 'It's not fair,' muttered Diana, knowing her cause was lost. 'Do look on the positive side,' I said. 'At least I won't insist on you wearing your black walking shoes.' This was a reference to the heavy school shoes which the girls hated to wear. Twenty years later, they would be considered the height of fashion. I told them the subject was closed and asked Lord Althorp what time he wanted us to leave. It would only take two minutes to walk to church. The time arranged, I turned to talk to Sarah about the various people she had met during the day and recounted for Lord Althorp's benefit the story of the fox which immediately perked Diana up as she described the way he had looked at her. Lord Althorp heaved an almost audible sigh of relief that the matter of church attendance had been so quickly settled and with so little bickering. Like me, he wanted life to go along as calmly and peacefully as possible and would go to great lengths to avoid any unnecessary disruption, but sometimes it was necessary to be firm.

I had never even been inside St Mary Magdalen Church at Sandringham. During the summer I had witnessed the streams of visitors who had come to see this beautiful little church but as so often happens when a place of interest is on the doorstep, it is always easy to imagine there is plenty of time to explore it another day. In all probability, had we not been summoned to attend church that particular Sunday, I might well have left Sandringham and never gone inside.

Sunday morning found us dressing to look both smart and to keep warm, as my experiences of churches warned me that even in the middle of summer they were chilly. As this was in the depths of winter we would surely freeze unless we took adequate measures. Warm woollen tights, thick skirts, sweaters, overcoat, boots and a scarf and gloves for good measure. None of us looked as if we would grace the cover of a fashion magazine, but one thing was for sure, we would not freeze. Charles wore thick brown corduroy trousers and sweater under his coat. Suitably clad, we set off at the requested time.

We took the short cut across the back garden and entered the churchyard from the park entrance, thus avoiding the crowds who had collected to catch a glimpse of the royal family. Ten years later, there would still be crowds braving the fury of a Norfolk winter's day. The royal family present a never-ending spectacle, but ten years later, one of the main members of the family, the one whom most of the crowds wished to see, was the young Princess Diana, already in the early stages of her first pregnancy and thus already fulfilling her duty to present an heir for the throne of England. The crowds who gazed on her then would be totally unaware of the illness and misery those first months of pregnancy gave her and how she did her best to disguise it in front of those who had grown to adore her. Diana wrote to me when she returned to London from Norfolk, 'I am still feeling and being ill, well into my fourth month.' To the crowds though, who stood outside the church ten years before on that cold winter's day, we were unknown as far as they were concerned, probably just locals. We resembled a family group of a tall, well-built man, with a sturdy young boy by his side, obviously his son, and three girls, all slim, his daughters. One had long blonde hair, another a few years younger had long, thick, wavy red hair and the youngest girl would have looked about ten years old and insignificant with her shoulder-length, mousy brown hair. A pleasant enough looking little girl, but not one who would attract more than a passing glance.

We entered the church and moved to the front where the family had its own pew. Sarah sat down first, I sat next to her. Lord Althorp sat next to the aisle and Charles and Diana sat between the two of us. The church is small and quickly filled to its capacity. The children were very well behaved. Diana's weekly visits to church with her school had proved beneficial and taught her the necessity to sit still for an hour. The few minutes we had to spare before the start of the service were spent checking out the hymns and whispering 'I know that one,' or, 'I like that one,' thus confirming that the rector had at least chosen hymns which would ensure we could all have a good sing-song. The Queen's land agent, Julian Loyd, whose home, Laycocks, was a short way down the park, and whose wife had provided my first invitation out with the children in the previous Easter holidays, sat with his family in the pew behind. Diana risked a covert glance behind to acknowledge Alexandra's presence and then turned quickly back as I gave her a nudge. Wedged between her parents I doubt Alexandra would have even raised an eyebrow in Diana's direction. They appeared a close-knit family and were certainly very supportive towards Lord Althorp, but I was always conscious that they regarded our arrangement with its relaxed, easy-going routines as slightly bohemian. They could not criticize it as the children always appeared happy and when it mattered, like now, we got it right, the church outing proving a perfect example of this.

There are many Sundays in the year and perhaps we should have been more conscientious about church attendance but, after

172

all the girls did go to church at school. Charles and I read stories from the children's Bible and we said prayers before bed. Diana joined in these during the holidays and we regarded that to be enough of an introduction to religion at their age. Lack of pressure meant they would not be alienated nor would it prejudice them from making their own choices and decisions as they grew older. Later when we all collected in the dining room for lunch after the service Sarah cynically commented how she was sure people realized we only went to church when the royal family were in attendance. The family pew, situated as it was at the front of the church, was very conspicuous, Sarah's view may well have been shared by all who sat behind and who religiously supported the church throughout the year. Diana added, 'Alexandra is so prim and proper, she wouldn't even *look* at me before the service.' I reminded Diana that, guarded on either side by a parent, Alexandra probably had no intention of risking a rebuke and her lack of acknowledgement had nothing to do with being 'prim and proper', just sound judgement.

The congregation were all seated. The organist continued to play until the service began. I could hear shuffling from behind. Sarah, to my left, stood up. I followed her example bending to whisper to Diana, who passed the message on to Charles. 'Stand up'. The royal party entered the church and walked down the aisle to take their seats in pews set at right angles to our own. There was quite a contingent that day. The Queen Mother, the Queen, Prince Philip and all four of their children. The service started almost at once. Now I had a chance to look around and could appreciate how truly lovely the church was with its bright, rich colours in the stained windows. There was also a marvellous, solid silver altar. The marble font which had been given by Edward VII stood at the base of the tower and it was here that Diana had been christened on 30 August 1961. Diana had an impressive list of godparents, but she was the only one of the children not to have a godparent from within the royal family.

We all enjoyed the singing; for some reason tone always seems to improve when it is accompanied by an organ. I expect the sermon and prayers were topical with a relevant theme but I have to admit I did not pay much attention. The whole experience was so unusual for me. I wanted to try to memorize as much detail as

173

possible so I could repeat it later to my parents. I had never before sat in church, or sat anywhere, in the presence of the Queen. I remembered all those years studying in history at school, learning about the monarchy through the ages. Even the houses at our school had been named after royal houses, each identified by a prime colour. Plantagenets, Tudors, Stuarts and finally Windsor which was represented by green. The monarchy was something to be read about, studied, written about in exams. It was, literally, academic until that Sunday when 'them' met in the same place as 'us' and somehow the distance and distinction between the two would never be quite the same for me again.

An even stranger experience was at the end of the service when the strains of the national anthem rose from the organ and filled the church as we all stood to sing, 'God Save The Queen', and there the Queen was, just in front of us. As we sang, I glanced at her. She stood absolutely still and looked straight ahead with a serious expression. How many countless times, in how many different places she must have stood to the strains of the national anthem.

The Queen radiated a quiet confidence, a sense of continuity and solidarity. It would have been impossible to imagine her innermost thoughts as she stood with her family in the little church on her Sandringham estate. I was pleased Lord Althorp had insisted we all go to church that day for I suspected that it would be a unique experience for me. How could I have ever imagined that nine and a half years later, I would stand in Wren's splendid St Paul's Cathedral, light years away from that time in the lovely little church of St Mary Magdalen, Sandringham, and again sing the anthem in the presence of the Queen at the wedding of her son and the girl who on the previous occasion had stood at my side.

A monarchist through and through, I have sung the national anthem throughout the following years many times and in many different places. It never fails to bring tears of emotion to my eyes and a tug at my heart. In the furthest corners of the world, in the most backward, remote places, when I am asked, 'Where do you come from?' I reply, 'I'm British' and I am then bombarded with questions about our royal family and the beautiful Princess. Even if they cannot read English they have seen the pictures . . . Diana in her blue suit taken on her engagement day. Diana wearing the

Spencer tiara in her regal wedding splendour, her decorated and uniformed husband beside her. Diana, mother with her two boys. . . .

Throughout her working life, the Queen has commanded respect. She has ruled with dignity, putting duty to the nation before personal pleasure. She exemplifies the ideal part that the monarchy can play in life.

The Queen has shown what the monarchy stands for in terms of public probity, moral rectitude and correct behaviour, now largely destroyed by some self-centred 'young royals' who have chosen to put personal happiness before integrity and duty. They have destroyed or at any rate threatened so much in their refusal to stick to the path they are obliged to follow, which is their duty and their work. So many who are 'ordinary' folk do not enjoy their work, and their dislike of it affects their home life, but they do not give up, they do not say 'I don't like it so I'm not going to do it any more.'

Most 'ordinary' people cannot afford to take this attitude so they have to face their problems, discuss them and settle for a compromise because there is no other way. Eventually, the compromise becomes acceptable. Not for the 'ordinary' people does the luxury of the affordability of an 'opt-out' clause exist. Most people would, I think, agree with this, which is why so many despise the weakness that has been portrayed within the royal family and which has diminished their standing. Conversely, all over the world Diana has come to represent beauty, youth, hope, a dream and as even the colours on the posters fade, let us hope they are never fully aware of the truth, of the sadness that lies behind the story of their fairytale princess. It is just these people, the socially, physically and mentally disabled whom Diana can inspire and help so much. It can only be hoped that justice will overcome prejudice and that there remain people who are confident enough in themselves, with voices strong enough to be heard, who will continue to acknowledge the asset within the family that is Diana. Let them turn negative thoughts into positive thoughts and cast aside unworthy grievances that would only further diminish the respectability of 'The Firm' and instead act in such a way as to start on the restoration of credibility, of an image that has been so severely damaged.

A mockery has been made of the monarchy. It has become a subject for ridicule lowering its standards to the level of that of the most insignificant soap opera. Some of its members have adopted a mentality that equals the most second-rate actors. It is twenty-two years since I sat in the peace of Sandringham Church. Then our monarchy was still envied and revered throughout the world. It is twelve and a half years since I sat proudly in St Paul's Cathedral to watch the fairytale marriage that seemed, then, set to continue the proud heritage. Is it not now time for a mature and confident approach so that fulfilling, suitable roles are carved for all parties in the family? It is time to stop all squabbling and bickering, to accept that both Charles and Diana have a tremendous amount to contribute towards the future, if not together, then separately. To quote one of the inane sayings, that Diana hated me to use, 'Two wrongs do not make a right.' Let the special people take a leaf from the book of the ordinary ones, face the problems head on, accept there exist differences of opinion. I feel strongly that with sensible discussion an acceptable compromise could surely be reached. In January of last year, 1993, during the early weeks of Diana and Charles's separation, while it was still the main topic of many people's conversation, most of whom expressed amazement that such a situation could have been allowed to develop in this unprecedented way I wrote to Sir Robert Fellowes, 'Anger is my incentive to write to you. I feel that no situation, particularly one as important as this should ever be written off as a lost cause.' I strongly felt that Diana had never received the guidance, sympathy and support that would have helped her so much from within the royal circle and court. In Sir Robert Fellowes's reply to me he wrote that whereas the death of Earl Spencer was a great personal tragedy, more than that it was a tragedy 'in the knocking away of a great prop and stay to the Princess of Wales at a vital moment'. He realized how badly Diana needed such support and must have recognized how desperate his sister-in-law was in her unhappiness, but his powers to help were limited by his own position, loyalties and responsibilities. I cannot help but consider whether the actors and their supporting casts, each with their own backs to cover, are big enough to accept the challenge. In latter years it has nearly always been the women of the royal family who have shown strength and fortitude. Sometimes I wonder now if time may have

176

helped the initial bitterness felt by both parties to subside. As each partner shows they are mature and capable of carrying out their individual duties and bearing in mind their common interest and concern for the welfare of their children (both parents have consistently shown fairness in time shared by them) and with the apparent support and backing of the Queen and Prime Minister for Diana, it is hoped that eventually a working partnership can again be established with respect proffered to each partner.

The service was over and the Queen and her family left the church. We all filed slowly out, talking animatedly now. Once outside the church, we were confronted by a large crowd that had waited during the service in order to see the royal family again. Reporters were on hand to record the colour combinations of coats, dresses, suits, worn by the female family members, no one the slightest bit interested in the men's clothes. Youngsters rushed forward eagerly to present their little posies, their patience during the long wait suddenly made worthwhile by the gracious acceptance of their offerings. Lord Althorp asked me to take the children home and told me that he would return in time for lunch but to ask cook to delay it for half an hour. I was quite taken aback at this cluster of loyal subjects. I was so pleased that, although cold, the day had remained dry and it drew my attention to how easily I took for granted my surroundings and the nature of the life I lived. Recognition of just how supportive the masses are towards the royal family also served to bring home to me just how privileged I was that, even for a relatively short period, I could share in a life experienced by so few, a lifestyle that in years to come will have disappeared completely.

We walked home briskly, taking our private route across the park. We looked forward to the warmth of Park House. I told the children I would ask cook for some chocolate biscuits to keep us going until lunch and then I went to give her Lord Althorp's message. We changed into warm, more casual clothes. I lit the fire as I realized that much of the remainder of the day would be spent indoors and by four o'clock it would be dark. In Norfolk the days do not lengthen noticeably until the middle of February but psychologically once the shortest day, 21 December, has passed I always illogically feel we are going forward and happily acknowledge every new spring flower brave enough to show its face. Diana picked a bunch of snowdrops for me before she returned to school. I thanked her but told her that superstition has it that it was bad luck to have snowdrops in the house so I placed them on a windowsill by the back door where I said I would see them every time I passed by and be reminded that spring would arrive one day soon.

I took the biscuits and hot drinks to the nursery. Sarah had disappeared to her room. We had nearly two hours to ourselves before lunch. The children played quietly and I sat and read and wrote letters. I was an avid writer and made sure I kept in regular contact with friends, several of whom lived abroad. I stressed the importance of written communication to Diana and Charles who willingly wrote their thank-you letters with very little prompting from me. I used the well-worn line as an added incentive, 'If you don't write to say thank-you, you can't expect to be invited out again' or to receive another present. They sat at the table in the nursery to write, Diana covering two sides of paper in her large rounded hand, while Charles would struggle to fill one side with his small upright style.

Everywhere was so quiet. Sunday has a certain indefinable feel and aura that seems to impregnate itself into the atmosphere regardless of surroundings. On this particular Sunday the silence was broken by a knock on the front door. Lord Althorp had yet to return and Betts had the morning off. I went along the passage, calling to Sarah that someone had arrived. She said she would go and see who it was and ran down the front stairway leading into the hall with Diana racing down behind her. I stayed upstairs, as I did not consider it necessary for a reception party to greet whoever had turned up so unexpectedly. Sarah opened the door to be confronted by Princess Anne who had decided to call by after church before returning home. I hurried back along the upstairs corridor to the nursery to ask Charles if he had any idea where his father had gone. He did not have a clue but as luck would have it, just as I was wondering what to do next, I heard Lord Althorp's voice in the hall. Meanwhile Sarah, with Diana tagging along behind, had shown Princess Anne into the drawing room. I ran down the back stairs to be met by Lord Althorp on the way to the wine cellar in the basement only to find the door leading to the basement locked. I asked, 'Where is the key?' He had no idea; only

Betts knew and of course today there was no Betts. Once I had got over the surprise that my employer did not even know where the key to his own drinks cellar was kept, I said, 'I've got a good idea. I'll ask the cook if she's got any sherry.' Sherry was duly produced and cook saved the day. I could not believe that such a household would not even keep one or two drinks readily available for emergencies such as this. I took the sherry to the butler's pantry and poured it into a decanter to try to hide the fact that it was cheap stuff, mostly used in trifles, and placed it on a silver tray along with some glasses in what I hoped was the correct fashion, and carried it into the drawing room. There were times when I could understand why our household might have been considered not quite normal. The 'nanny' does not usually enter a drawing room bearing drinks and then proceed to pour them! There was a very relaxed atmosphere. Charles by this time had joined us and both he and Diana sat quietly, as I did, while Sarah, her father and our royal visitor conducted a lively conversation. Princess Anne did not stay very long. It was nearly lunchtime when she left, but her visit had been welcome and interesting. Lord Althorp told us later that the Queen had expressed disapproval that her daughter had, in her eyes, acted without decorum by arriving without prior invitation. I, conversely, thought it sad that an impulsive act that caused no offence at all should give cause for a reprimand.

Our household, on the fringes of the royal circle, made allowances for occasional surprises, but it appeared there was no room for such lassitude within royal circles, not even in the immediate family, and I thought that such strictures must prohibit a great deal of fun. I did not envy them their life but this incident afforded me a little insight into the enormous adjustment Diana had to make when she married. How difficult it was to be for her to be continuonscious of and to abide by the rules imposed upon her when she took the step from aristocracy to monarchy. She was still so young and if sometimes she kicked up the traces, surely her occasional lapses should have been understood and forgiven?

We had plenty to talk about during lunch, a lively meal as we discussed the service, or at least the people who had been in church. We debated whether we should just go on special occasions to show a face or whether that was being hypocritical. I stressed how pleased I was that we had gone: I for one would not have wanted to miss the experience. Diana agreed with Sarah. She was sure everyone knew the real reason we had put in such a rare appearance. I told her that it did not matter at all what anyone thought, it was up to us to make our own decisions. We discussed our surprise at Princess Anne's unexpected visit and joked how unprepared we always seemed to be when any members of the royal family appeared. Lord Althorp told us that several people were guessing that Princess Anne's engagement to Mark Phillips, who was a house guest at Sandringham, would soon be announced, although it was still being strenuously denied by the Palace. 'That,' said Lord Althorp, 'doesn't mean anything.'

Lunch over, the rest of the day was spent quietly. After the excitement of the morning, the afternoon was a bit of an anticlimax. Charles and I prepared his clothes for school as his new term started the following day and Diana was also due to start school that week. We had all enjoyed our winter holiday at Sandringham. I found it difficult to believe that I had now lived at Park House for nearly a year. The time had passed so quickly, but in many ways it seemed longer than a year.

Our life was to continue in the same way for some time, but always drawing nearer on the horizon was the date that Charles would leave his school, say goodbye to daily life at Park House and start at boarding school. My life at Sandringham would end then, although I would continue to visit in the future and remain in contact with members of the family for many years.

Chapter Thirteen

The terms of my employment were as companion to Sarah and Jane, to look after Diana and Charles and to prepare Charles for the new period in his life, attendance at prep school. As I started the second year of my employment at Park House already there seemed to be an air of change. Lord Althorp spent more time away than he had done previously. I assumed this was because he was more confident that the children and household would run happily, even in his absence. He was aware that in September Charles would leave Park House, the last of his children to go and that this departure spelt the end of the early childhood years. The empty house would seem large during term time without the noise and clatter of the children. Only for a few weeks during the holidays would the peace of corridors be pierced by the sound of their voices.

As if in preparation for the times ahead most of Lord Althorp's days were spent in either London or Northampton so that eventually when September arrived his transition to the other homes would not seem strange. It would be another three years before the children's grandfather, Earl Spencer, died on 9 June 1975 at eighty-three. The death of the old Earl meant that the family would have to leave Park House forever but when the time came they adapted well to their new home, Diana, perhaps better than her older sisters for she was always able to make the best of a situation. She did however write to me not long afterwards, 'We all miss Norfolk terribly . . .'; she added, '. . . but it's lovely here' and, ever honest and realistic, 'especially at the moment as the stepmother is away.' It was always Park House that retained a special place in their hearts. It was the place that Diana always regarded as her true childhood home. When Diana came home from school at the end of that summer term in 1975 and saw all the packing cases in Park House, she could not bear the sight of them and what they symbolized – the leaving behind of happy childhood memories. It all looked so gloomy. She felt desolate so she raided the larder with her friend Alexandra Loyd, took all the peaches she could find and the two of them disappeared to the hut at Brancaster Beach for the day. It was to be the last time that Diana ever went to the beach hut. Shortly after the start of those summer holidays, the move to Althorp Hall was completed. Not only did the death involve a major move, it also meant that the children's titles changed. The girls changed from 'Honourable' to 'Lady' and Charles had a total change from the Honourable Charles Spencer to Charles, Lord Althorp, his father relinquishing the title as he inherited that of Earl Spencer. I was the last person employed to care for the children. Lord Althorp invited me to return during the school holidays if I was free and in the country. When the final summer holidays ended and the girls went back to boarding school and Charles started at Maidwell, I did not leave feeling that the departure was final as I was confident that we would meet up again. There was no special sadness beyond that which I usually felt when I said goodbye to them. Certainly there were no emotional farewells. I was ready to leave. From the time I started, I knew when my contract would end and life offered so many possibilities it was time to move on. I had loved every moment of my time at Sandringham, but nothing lasts for ever and I was ready for new experiences. I was also confident that the girls were happy at their schools and knew that once Charles had adapted to boarding school life, he would do well. This hunch proved to be accurate. Six years later, Charles wrote and told me, 'At Maidwell, my prep school, I had a wonderful time. I became head of the school in work . . . I played for the cricket and rugby teams getting my colours in the latter.' I was satisfied I had done the job to the best of my ability and knew we would all meet again which we did when I joined them for the winter holiday at the end of Charles's first term at Maidwell, but after that time I moved to Istanbul to teach advanced English, typing and shorthand in a finishing school and to do the administrative work involved in the fashion side of the school for the shows it presented both in Turkey and Europe. The girls were all so self-sufficient now that they could look after themselves and their young brother. Naturally the house staff were retained for the home had to be run, whether there were people there or not.

Already during my first year, Charles and Diana had both changed considerably. Charles had grown more outspoken and extrovert; his balanced comments proved him to be a deep thinker, who was considerate in all his actions. He performed well at school, consistent, clever and serious, but as his confidence grew so he took more of an active part in conversations, expressing his views and opinions in a concise, thoughtful way. He remained a self-contained, easy lad to care for. He was happy to please me and never contradicted anything I asked him to do. This willingness to help did not mean he had no spirit. My requests were always, I think, reasonable and we all did our best to ensure the household rolled along as smoothly as possible. Antagonism was seldom expressed. The days passed quickly in a routine that rarely faltered, changing only between holidays and school time.

The change in Diana was very noticeable. There had by now been an enormous transformation from the shy little schoolgirl with the downcast eyes I had first encountered at Riddlesworth to the fun-loving but still polite girl, a year later. Attendance at the school had been a major contributing factor to this change, but also the knowledge that a secure, happy home awaited her in the holidays served to annihilate much of the uncertainty that had dogged her since her parents' separation. As time passed, Diana found it easier to accept the separate homes of her parents. Love, security and happiness were there in both while her growing maturity helped to dispel any self-doubt that might still lurk in the shadows. She was surrounded by people both at school and home who encouraged her to fulfil her potential and who heaped praise on her efforts. Gradually her self-confidence grew. Diana established a more mature approach, both towards her work and to the people around her.

The move to Althorp Hall in the summer of 1975 upset all the family. Sarah and Jane, both by now with their own homes and work in London, were less affected, but Park House had been their base too for many years. Diana was not happy about the move to Althorp but she accepted it for there was no choice. She was always an adaptable girl and threw herself into the change of environment, making the best of the inevitable. For Sarah and Jane the move to Althorp simply meant that they spent more time at their London homes and Diana who was now at West Heath would often stay with one or other of her sisters in London during her free weekends. Jane had by now bought a flat in Warwick Square in Pimlico. When she had successfully completed her A levels at West Heath she had gone to Italy for six months to study art and history of art in Florence. On her return to London she took a secretarial course and then joined the magazine, *Vogue*, as an editorial assistant. Sarah had bought her flat in Elm Park Lane, Chelsea. She had spent time at a finishing school in Switzerland after the rather abrupt end to her schooling at West Heath. From Switzerland, she went on to Vienna to study music before taking a secretarial course in London. She obtained a position in Savills estate agency in Berkeley Square, London. It was from this office that Sarah found the flat that Diana eventually bought four years after the move to Althorp, at Coleherne Court. Money for it had been released from a trust left her by her American great-grandmother, Frances Work.

Diana, from the first year I met her, developed – as she grew older – a sensitivity about what mattered to people, not only those within her family circle, but to others she later met in her working life. This genuine caring has stood her in good stead for her future role. When Diana's friendship with Prince Charles became public, gossip mongers searched hard and unsuccessfully for scandal and past affairs. Their search was in vain, there was nothing, no dirt to dish. She enjoyed her growing-up years in the main but she always kept a portion of herself apart. She bore an aura of naïvety that attracted people, who none the less were unable to penetrate the cloak it provided. There can be little doubt that the experience of her parents' divorce established in her a wish to keep her own life as steady as possible.

Instilled within her was the certainty that emotional entanglement led to uncertainty and upset. She tried to avoid any confrontation that spelt 'pain'. Diana always mixed well and enjoyed the company of a likeable circle of friends, several from her Norfolk days. While academically she was never going to be a high-flyer her lack of formal qualifications does not portray her in the correct way. Like many teenagers Diana could be lazy, particularly about subjects that did not interest her.

Her teenage years found her as popular as she had been as a child. She was energetic, fit and healthy and concentrated on sport, swimming and her ballet which gave her more pleasure and satisfaction than school work. From an early age she liked to help people and did not waste an opportunity to help those not so well off as herself. She enjoyed a round of community service encouraged by her school. Not until after her marriage did illness start to dog her. Before that, if she had been unhappy, as she was during her stay in the Institut Alpin Videmanette at Château d'Oex near Gstaad, her finishing school, Diana could do something about it and escape. On that occasion constant outpourings in letters about her misery to her parents persuaded both of them to allow her to leave. On the matter of her finishing school, Diana was consistent in her feelings. Several months later, she wrote to me, 'I went to a finishing school for three months which I hated . . .' No amount of letters, though, could ever provide any form of escape or cure for the unhappiness experienced from early on in Diana's marriage. Only as she became more and then more trapped in a marriage that daily grew increasingly devoid of love did the feeling of helplessness engulf her and manifest itself in bulimia illness. Diana became ill because of the helpless anger and hurt that struck after recognizing she was not loved. As she came to realize this and acknowledge that the abiding ambition she had nurtured from the time I knew her as a young girl, indeed which we spoke about during our first car journey together, that of a happy family life filled with love, was never going to materialize with the man she loved and married she was shattered. Many people find themselves in situations like this, I know, but for Diana it was more awful. For to escape from her husband and perhaps give herself another chance at family love and happiness in her position was unthinkable and without precedent. Indeed impossible.

Diana had faced and coped with her parents' divorce and had changed quickly from a shy, sad child into the lively, mischievous little girl I knew. She was helped by the other people around her and the environment we established. She handled the transition from girlhood to teenager with competence, helped by the love of both parents and the support of her older sisters, choosing at times to be the liveliest member of a party or to keep herself to herself, depending on her mood – and all teenagers have moods. She grew from being an ordinary teenager to a woman of the world with very little help from anyone, drawing only on her own inner reserves of strength laid down from the early days of her childhood and her determination to do her best. Later she was determined to make her husband proud of her.

I watched the transformation from child to teenager, to girl-about-town, to Princess. In her last months of freedom Diana had her own car but during the week found it quicker to use her bicycle. She, like her flatmates, led busy social lives, but they went out in a group rather than on individual dates. None of them smoked or drank much. They enjoyed giving dinner parties at home or eating out in reasonably priced restaurants. There were special outings to theatre and ballet, but Diana's life was no different to that of most girls of her age who lived in London. She did not much like parties and loathed nightclubs, feeling more confident on home ground surrounded by her friends and music. She loved to shop at Harrods and Harvey Nichols and her flat that she shared with her friends was tidier than most because Diana loved to clean. I met Diana in London with Sarah and she was just a happy, ordinary girl, never involved in any serious romance. She loved her jobs, caring for Patrick Robertson, a little American boy, and her work at the Young England Kindergarten. She was, in every way, a typical example of a contented girl from an upper class family, learning to stand on her own two feet with a loyal, trusted circle of friends. I felt for Diana every step of the way as she was drawn more and more into the public eye. I admired the way she tackled the challenges and grew in confidence. It was always there, even as a child, the determination and will that she had to display, to establish and retain her identity. I like to think that the talks and guidance I gave her earlier helped her on this path. When the world knew that there was a strong possibility Diana and Charles might marry I wrote to Diana advising and encouraging her to be true to herself, and to examine the sincerity of the depth of her love: 'Although you have known of Charles for so long, you have had so little time to really understand him. It must be very difficult when you are always in the public eye. Your hopes were always to fall in love and marry, be sure this is not infatuation because of who he is and remember you will never again be a private person. You are not just marrying a man, but taking on a whole new way of life, duty and work. I want only for you to be sure you are in love and then to be happy. It is such a big step from which there can be no turning back.'

I then joked with Diana about her childhood dreams being answered in such noble fashion, making her think again of the seriousness of the situation. I imagine it was inconsequential in the course of events whether I wrote or not, but I felt it was my responsibility to play my part to try to ensure Diana's happiness and that she entered this liaison with her eyes open. However presumptuous it might have appeared on my behalf, to be true to myself, I had to write. I told her, 'If you are absolutely sure, then I offer you my congratulations.' When the engagement had been announced, Diana wrote to me from Clarence House, the Queen Mother's home, and thanked me for my letter and said how much I had helped her 'to bring all this about'. It has to be said that sometimes now I wish that I could have advised her more, but it was not possible. I knew Diana so well and perhaps could have guided her but to me Charles – apart from that early morning meeting in the park so many years before which hardly qualified me to make any substantial judgement – was an unknown quantity. I suppose, like Diana, I rather naïvely assumed he would marry her only if he loved her. I reasoned he could marry whom he chose so he was hardly likely to consider a marriage without love. I did not take into consideration that as Diana fitted all the other criteria, love was incidental in Charles's eyes. Had I realized there was no love, I would have done everything in my power to try to dissuade Diana from such a disastrous step, which was to lead to the betrayal of her childhood dreams as well as his wedding vows. Diana, had she ever suspected that such a possibility existed, would never have put herself in a position where there could be no turning back.

As the childhood years had seen one major change, that of Diana's parents' divorce, so there was another in Diana's teenage years. After the upheaval of the move to Althorp during the summer of 1975, an even more daunting development was the marriage of Lord Spencer to Lady Dartmouth – Raine – in July 1976 at Caxton Hall in London. It was a quiet affair with only two witnesses, but not his elder daughters. Sarah and Jane, twenty years and eighteen years old respectively at the time of their father's remarriage, did not get along with their new stepmother. Diana, who had already had to adapt to so much and had a much more forgiving nature, tried to put up with this unwelcome addition to their household. Diana never accepted Raine, but she was honest enough and cared so deeply for her father, that she could see how happy this woman, whom they dubbed 'Acid Raine', made him. There were such phenomenal death duties to pay on the death of their grandfather that Lord Spencer on his own would have been left wondering about the best way to tackle them. Charles, of course, was far too young to be able to advise and help his father. A few years later, he could have done so with some perception. The children have criticized many of the then new Lady Spencer's ideas but had she not been there to help and advise it is quite possible that Charles, who today is 9th Earl Spencer, could have been left with even less of the famous treasures of Althorp. For however much they might deride her, Lady Dartmouth was a forceful, formidable character, a clever woman who applied her boundless energies and her interest in art and architecture to restoring Althorp's grandeur – but it has to be admitted, in my view, not always in the most tasteful fashion. The sale of some of the treasures was necessary to cover the massive death duties imposed when the old Earl died. It is always sad when long-held treasures have to be disposed of but the indisputable fact remains that Lady Dartmouth brought Diana's father happiness, ending his lonely years, and by 1978 Althorp Hall was again solvent. She achieved this by cutting back staff and the household budget and opening the house to the public, apparently much to the children's disdain. Sarah, when first questioned about the frequent presence of Raine at Althorp, replied icily, 'She is helping my father open the house on a commercial basis. In my grandfather's time he did not care for the idea of the public walking around his house.' When Lord Spencer married Raine, he was left in no doubt as to the feelings of his children towards his new wife. They did not attend the wedding. Indeed there were only two witnesses at Caxton Hall in London, one of whom was Raine's half-brother, Glen McCorquodale. No one else knew. Raine phoned her mother, Barbara Cartland, afterwards and said, 'Hello, we're married,' in a style that could have come straight from one of her mother's novels.

From the start, when the children set eyes on the new woman

in their father's life, it was apparent the two parties would never get on. The first time Lord Althorp brought her to lunch at Park House and to meet the children was in the summer of 1972. I joined them for lunch with Sarah, Jane, Diana and Charles. As visitors now often came to Park House there was little reason for us to suspect that this was anything other than another friend. Raine was then Lady Dartmouth, who had been married for many years and had four children. She did various public works in London where she obviously had grown to know Lord Althorp. The children had beautiful manners and I never had any qualms that they would behave anything other than perfectly when we sat down with visitors in the dining room. Children are, however, intuitive. Sarah and Diana were no exception. Deeply protective towards their father, they jealously guarded his time and affection. Their mother had remarried in 1969 and they liked their stepfather, Peter Shand Kydd, finding him easy-going and fun to be with, but they were wary of any new woman coming into their father's life, anyone who might upset the gentle existence we had established at Park House. Nothing however can stand in the way of the winds of change and nothing, as it turned out, could stand in the path of the formidable Lady Dartmouth.

Sarah eventually told me that there had been murmurings that her father spent a considerable time with Lady Dartmouth. They shared several interests. I told her that there were always gossip-mongers and as her father was unattached, there would always be people trying to connect him with a woman. I reminded Sarah that it was inconceivable there could be anything other than friendship as Lady Dartmouth was married. The dark mutterings were sufficient, though, to place doubts in Sarah's mind and she wasted no time in telling Diana what she had heard about 'this woman who is coming for lunch'. Diana in turn questioned me and repeated what Sarah had said. I told her it was all total rubbish and that for once it was Sarah whose imagination had run away with her. However, enough had been said for me to feel extremely nervous about the forthcoming luncheon and not to be as confident as usual that the children's manners could be relied upon. Lord Althorp left his children in no doubt that they were the centre of his world. This was the way they liked it to be and they were not prepared to take any chances that this might change. Diana felt, too, that rather confusing sense of loyalty to her mother. Now and again she asked me if it was possible that her father might marry again. I told her I had no idea. I did not give it a thought, it was of little interest to me. He seemed so wrapped up in the world of his children and work that I did not even consider the remotest chance existed. In any case he was hardly likely to discuss such a personal subject with me. Diana was reassured by the natural surprise I expressed at her questions and went on to add that she was pleased this was the case as it would not really be fair to her mother. When I pointed out to Diana that I did not really understand her sense of reasoning because her mother was, after all, already married again, Diana regarded that as an irrelevant issue. Basically, the children wanted no competition in the affections of their father.

It was none the less with a feeling of trepidation that I entered the dining room for lunch. I felt tense and nervous and for the first and only time during my stay at Park House, wondered if I was capable of keeping the children under control. My only hope was that they respected me enough not to upset me by showing any lapse in their good manners. My main concerns lay with Sarah and Diana. Under unnatural circumstances Diana could easily be influenced by her sister and become giggly simply to alleviate tension.

We were the first in the room. Betts had placed Lady Dartmouth on Lord Althorp's right and Sarah opposite her on his left. Charles sat next to Sarah with Jane on his left. I sat opposite Jane with Diana between me and Lady Dartmouth. I felt strategically placed to shoot warning glances at Sarah without being observed by our guest and in a position to nudge Diana, if I felt she was about to explode with mirth. For a moment, I allowed myself the hope that perhaps I was being unreasonably cautious and that my fears might prove to be ill-founded. I should have known better than to allow such a ray of optimism to cloud my basic instincts. I knew this lunch was not going to be a relaxed affair. Lord Althorp and Lady Dartmouth entered while Betts was telling us where to sit. Lord Althorp carried out the introductions which passed off smoothly and we all sat down. The sight of Lady Dartmouth had already proved a source of astonished amusement to Diana. I knew her mother was Barbara Cartland, renowned equally for her hugely successful pick-me-up, put-me-down, light romantic novels (although I never read them myself) as for her whim always to dress in pink. I suspected her daughter might also be a bit different. However, nothing prepared me for the woman who appeared in the dining room that day and who was later to become a permanent fixture in the lives of the children and their father. It was quite an experience to meet such a person. She was immaculate, every hair on her carefully coiffured head set rigidly in place, stiff with lacquer. Her well-applied make-up accentuated her porcelain-type skin. She wore high-heeled shoes and was dressed in a smart, well-cut suit that did justice to her trim figure. Later I read that one of her former colleagues on the Greater London Council said of her, 'She's not a person, she's an experience.' A statement to which I could easily relate. She looked as if she belonged to another era, as if she had walked straight out of the pages of one of her mother's novels. The rather irrelevant thought crossed my mind as to how on earth she managed her hair when she went to bed. Diana found her whole persona overpowering and even before we sat down, she had to struggle to suppress her giggles. A very sharp nudge from me, backed by a tap on her foot for good measure, enabled the first potentially embarrassing moment to pass, helped by the diversion of the food being served. When the family ate alone we served ourselves from the heated trolley, but when we had guests Betts sprang into action. I consciously avoided any eye contact with the children sitting opposite for I was not sure how strict a control I had on myself or whether I would be able to keep a straight face should I catch their eyes dancing with barely concealed amusement. It was not my place to initiate conversation, merely to guide the children through lunch and help them out if they got in a muddle.

I must give Lady Dartmouth credit. It must have been an extremely daunting situation to be confronted with four hostile children, so protective of their father that they could barely conceal their antagonism towards her. Sarah and Jane were perceptive enough to know that in the future, however unlikely the idea seemed now, Raine might prove to be a threat to their family happiness. Lady Dartmouth, although charming and attentive, had no intention of being demoralized by unspoken aggression from these children, whom she considered far too liberated. She did her best to be amiable to the children and to include everyone in the conversation. Her iron will and ability not to let anything stand in

191

her way or intimidate her was apparent from the outset, as was the enormous gulf in the different personalities between herself and her future step-children. The lunch neared its conclusion. I began to relax. It had, after all, not been as bad as I had feared. It is one thing to make condemnations in private, but good manners had won the day. Sarah alone had ventured one or two risqué comments which I had quickly parried by bringing Jane into the conversation. She could always be relied upon to keep the talk on a safe level.

I relaxed too soon. Sarah realized she had nearly run out of time to make an impression on the guest which would clearly express her dislike and contempt for her. Some of Sarah's less gracious comments, when not deflected by me, had been brushed aside by Lady Dartmouth in such a way as to imply that 'this child's comments are not worthy of a reply'. Sarah felt she was left with no alternative but to resort to outright rudeness. She burped. Diana giggled. A shocked Lord Althorp said, 'Sarah!' to which she replied, 'In the Arab countries it is recognized as a sign of appreciation.' He was so appalled he did not bother even to comment on this explanation, but told his eldest daughter to leave the table. A stunned silence fell across the room as Sarah abruptly pushed back her chair, which luckily defied gravity and did not fall over thus adding to the drama and walked out. Sarah knew her father would never have taken such a line if the guest had meant nothing to him but, of course, if that had been the case, Sarah would never have acted in such a way. None of us had ever heard the father speak so sternly, it was quite a shock for all of us. Lady Dartmouth could try as hard as she liked in the future to gain their affection, but from that very first day the assurance of failure was sealed, she had no chance of success.

Diana, propelled into action by this unprecedented dismissal of her sister, promptly overcame all shyness and tried to defend her against such unjustice. 'But Daddy, Sarah did not mean to be rude, she couldn't help it!' 'That's enough, Diana,' said her father as I tried to hush her, while he, unwittingly, ensured another condemnation against his guest. Diana though, with the passage of time and her forgiving nature, while she never warmed towards the woman who would become her stepmother, did accept her more readily into the family than did her older sisters. Even Diana, when she wrote to me in later years, said that she did not now spend much of her holidays at Althorp and preferred to stay with either Sarah or Jane in London. When Diana did visit Althorp the staff appreciated the easy-going girl who provided them with light relief after the absolute correctness of the Countess. Casually dressed, with no make-up, the complete opposite to her stepmother, she gave herself no airs or graces, she was always natural and at ease with them and they with her. She would not stand for any indifference and was meticulous about the 'correct' way to behave. She would always wear evening dress for dinner and expect others to do the same even within the family. She rarely went outside for the fresh country air, preferring to work in bed until midday, when she would appear, perfectly groomed. She held herself distant and aloof from the staff, while Diana was warm, talkative and friendly.

Diana out of consideration for her father eventually accepted his new wife, but that first lunch, with Sarah's empty chair so glaringly obvious, as a reminder that Lord Althorp had spoken in such an unusual manner not only to Sarah but then so abruptly to Diana, was all too much for her. She mumbled that she did not feel well and asked permission to leave the room. Not one person there believed her for a moment but neither were any of us inclined to question the validity of her request, with which Lord Althorp readily complied. I am sure that he was as grateful as the rest of us that the discomfort and stress of the lunch was coming to an end. Betts, who had been party to the scene, had wasted no time in repeating the incident in the kitchen. Mrs Smith later told me that the general consensus was that should Lord Althorp ever meet someone in the future whom he wished to marry, the woman would find it nigh impossible and an unenviable task to gain the approval of his children. Certainly at that time it never seriously entered our heads that Lady Dartmouth could possibly be a contender for the title of the Countess Spencer.

During the first year of Diana's marriage she wrote and told me that she had taken her husband to Althorp for a weekend. Prince Charles accidentally damaged a chair. Raine, so fanatical that everything had to be just right, did not for once know what to say and Diana thought her confusion was really funny as she could well imagine what Raine would like to have said if the person had been anyone other than the Prince.

So in the last year of my contract, Lady Dartmouth breezed into the children's lives, reminiscent of a galleon in full sail. During the summer holidays Lord Althorp made enquiries as to some of the other children who would start at Maidwell with Charles and we invited George Courtauld to stay for a few days so that when Charles started he would not be completely alone. Diana had gone to Riddlesworth knowing some people and that had been a great help to her. Lord Althorp wanted to make sure that Charles was given the same sort of help. Charles, though, was different from Diana. By the time he left for school, his trunk packed, and after several days of me sewing name-tags on his clothes, including a seemingly never-ending supply of socks, he had become, as Lord Althorp had hoped when he employed me, a quietly confident, capable lad, well able and prepared to cope with boarding school life. He later wrote and told me how much he had loved Maidwell where he did well academically, allowing him confidently to enter Eton. When Diana left for her school her parents' divorce and mother's remarriage were not so far in the past. By the time Charles went away, life had jogged along securely and he left behind a much stronger secure base. Lord Althorp wrote that I had indeed helped to achieve this during my employment and in providing stability for Diana when she came home for holidays and exeats. He added, 'I would like to thank you for what you did for the four children while you were at Park House. They have each derived lasting benefit from your companionship and interest.' And further in the letter, 'Very many thanks again for all you have done for the family during your nineteen months with us. It has been great fun having you here and I hope you were happy . . .'

Chapter Fourteen

There can only be a conclusion to my story, for I do not believe that the story of the history of the monarchy can be concluded for a very long time. It was only ever my intention to describe one year in the life at Park House, for the passage of each year usually follows a similar pattern to the one before, with only the participants ageing, while the setting remains timeless. The main addition to the normal course of events in the second year was, as I described in the previous chapter, the arrival of the future Countess Spencer. Life rolled on through term time and holidays with laughter, fun and much happiness. We worked as a unit, as a team. We respected each other and from that grew love and affection. Ours was a charmed life, reflecting a way of living that most can only dream of. Traditions that are part of an established way of life are still played out in beautiful homes around the country.

This experience, combined with the challenge to succeed in my work towards establishing a secure and happy home, full of laughter, that would always supply a base for the children, had a great influence on my own life. It taught me that no matter what the environment for the upbringing of children the most important thing is to encourage them to set a code of behaviour, to make their own standards and always to adhere to them throughout life. The time I spent at Park House opened my eyes to another world, flawed only by unpleasant meetings at train stations, which I felt was a small forfeit to pay for such reward. I considered myself lucky to live in such a household, where I was made to feel so at ease and never felt any great social divide. Massively larger than my own family home it may have been but basically the same ideas of what constitutes a good family life pertained. On so many occasions, I drew on my own experiences of childhood and family life and put them to good use at Park House. I used to joke when

I left Park House that academic qualifications, although an asset if they can be acquired, are not a necessary ingredient for success or job satisfaction. I felt then, and I still do, that two of the biggest accomplishments required – besides the rare commodity of common sense – to be in a position to meet interesting people and visit places, are the social accoutrements of riding and tennis. There is no doubt that my ability to ride served me in very good stead at Sandringham, indeed was one of the requirements of the job.

Sarah's horse, Peppermint, had given me so much pleasure and in a way it was fitting that as the time drew near for me to leave, Lord Althorp asked me to organize the sale of the horse to a good home and he would borrow a horse for us during the summer holidays. As Sarah would be away so much in the future he decided it was better that he borrowed hunters for her, if and when the need arose, rather than keep a horse permanently at home. I advertised Peppermint for sale in the local paper and received several replies. I chose, without hesitation, the first people who came to see her. George and Pauline were an older couple who lived quite near my parents so over the years I would be able to see Peppermint now and again, but the most important reason for my choice of home was that I knew they would keep her for the rest of her life. They did. They loved and cared for her in a home that could never have been bettered. Only two years ago I wrote and told Sarah that after a life of kind care, old age had finally necessitated that she be put down.

During the years that followed, I visited Park House a few times but I never went to Althorp until I attended Sarah's wedding. Contact was spasmodic as all of us moved on in our own worlds, but we still kept in touch through letters. Occasionally I read about one or other of the children in gossip columns in the newspapers and we managed sometimes to meet in London when I could hear the true story. It often amused me to read an article when I knew the facts which lay behind it but I was busy with my own life and paid little attention to the gossip columns. The years flew by, filled with so many different experiences and spent in so many different countries that gradually my life at Sandringham began to seem unreal to me. I happened to live in London for the two years leading up to Diana's marriage and then we met more often and caught up with the news, some of which I already knew from the letters written. Diana always wanted to work with children, but like me, several years earlier, she lacked any relevant qualifications. Like me, that did not daunt her, but unlike me who had struck so lucky with my first job, Diana was less successful. She wrote to me, 'I started testing my maternal instincts by looking after a 3 yr. old in Hampshire, one of Sarah's boyfriend's sisters, so to start off the whole thing was a failure.' Diana did not let this rather inauspicious start detract from her love for children. She continued, 'Then I went to help my cousin for 3 wks to look after her 3 small ones, all under 6: I loved that.' Diana's abbreviations in her letters show either she wrote in a hurry and out of a sense of duty and loyalty, or she had still to learn that it is incorrect and considered poor taste to not write in full. I was always pleased to receive her letters however they were written. When we met in London, I saw just how rapidly the shy young girl I first set eyes on was beginning to show signs of future beauty. Those meetings, in restaurants or at Sarah's house in London, served to remind me how wonderful was the life we had shared at Park House. When I began to write this book I became increasingly grateful that such a story could be shared by others as I tried to give an insight into why the Princess of Wales is so popular with ordinary people. It is because she was an ordinary girl, with the type of childhood shared by many children. It was only the setting that was not quite so ordinary. Through the challenge, the ups and downs of the formative years, through the euphoria of falling in love and subsequent marriage, through the sadness of total disillusionment, she retained the ability to communicate with people. I watched it all. One morning as I packed in my hotel room on the island of Kauii – I had been in the Hawaiian islands for a five-day travel conference, four islands in five days and still time to get a suntan – I switched on breakfast television and there, all those thousands of miles away, was Buckingham Palace, as reporters excitedly talked about the Royal Wedding two days away. It took considerable mental effort to accept that from the little island in the Pacific Ocean I would take the island plane to Oahu and then change planes and fly via Alaska to London. I did and it seemed that in no time at all I was in a taxi on my way from Victoria station to the office in Mayfair, driving past the very palace I had seen on television. I was the manager of the tour operating division of our travel agency. We had several offices including one in Los Angeles with which I liaised and where I spent much of my time. It was for me to negotiate rates with the airlines and deluxe hotels in the States and prepare an American portfolio to market those hotels in Europe and the UK. Besides doing the negotiations, I also wrote the portfolio and helped with the sales and marketing. An exciting, fulfilling job which entailed a great deal of travel and challenge, but none of the journeys had ever been as exciting as my return from Hawaii for Diana's wedding.

It was the most glorious Tuesday afternoon so crowds had already started to collect near the palace. The air was charged with excitement and happiness. It was so infectious. I could hardly believe that after such a trip, the next day I would attend the very wedding they waited to celebrate. The wedding of the girl I had heard them talk about on the television as I prepared for the flight back to London. I wanted to share my feeling of pride with everyone – not vanity that I had been invited to attend a royal wedding – but pride because the girl I had cared for, who had shared her childhood dreams with me, had succeeded in fulfilling her ambition and in such a style. A few years later I experienced other emotions that I wished to share, those of anger and sorrow as I read and watched with growing dismay the total and public disintegration of Diana's marriage. Then there was so little that I could do, but I could not rest until I had expressed my feelings to Sir Robert Fellowes, the Queen's private secretary and Jane's husband. I wrote of the unacceptable manner in which Charles coped with his young wife's behaviour.

> He ran to Camilla Parker-Bowles who knew Charles long before Diana came on to the scene. When Charles went running to her, knowing his wife's feelings about the woman and how threatened she felt by the friendship, she in her position of confidante should have told him to grow up and sent him packing, back to his wife.

Sir Robert Fellowes guardedly replied, 'I would like to say a proper thank-you for putting so much thought and care into a most interesting analysis of this sad situation.'

From the time leading up to her marriage and afterwards, I had received several letters from Diana. They were full of excitement and optimism. A wedding that was to be broadcast all over the world and which would be shared by millions still presented similar problems to one in the smallest household. Diana wrote and told me that to be 'engaged for six months is quite something and definitely to be avoided'. She went on to say that 'all the family are in complete over-drive and a lot of "non-speaks"'. These letters helped to make me feel close to the preparations for the greatest and most important day in Diana's life.

The day I received the invitation to the wedding, sent by registered post, and from then on, one of the questions most of my friends asked besides 'What will you wear?' was 'What will you give them for a present?' The latter was an extremely difficult decision. Finances were a major consideration. Mortgages, a young son, working and living in London, meant money was quite tight and I was faced by the same obstacles which confront everyone who genuinely wants to give something special but has to abide by financial restrictions. I had lived in Istanbul and travelled frequently to Turkey. Over a period of time, I had bartered and bought kilims – the Turkish wall carpets. It was one of these I chose to give Diana and Charles as a wedding present. I am realistic enough to guess that it probably never saw the light of day again but it was very precious to me and I was happy I had something special to give. I followed instructions for the delivery of presents and went by taxi from my office in Mount Street to Buckingham Palace. It was only to a back entrance, but I found it very exciting to pass through even a very minor gate, it made me feel very much part of an historical event.

Dear Diana wrote me a lovely personal thank-you letter saying, 'how typical it was of you to give such a wonderful present'. I thought how typically kind of her to write this when she obviously received thousands of presents. She went on to say how well 'the antique rug would go in "the nest"'. When Diana left Highgrove after her separation and I read in the paper that Charles was putting out many of her belongings I had an urge to write and ask him that, rather than throw it out, he could return it to me. Naturally I did no such thing, but I bet others who gave presents must have wondered if their gifts had been relegated to the rubbish tip. I have absolutely no idea what happened to the rug. It was lovely, before, to hear how happy she was amidst all the preparations. Now and again after her marriage I heard from her. Sometimes just a note, other times a more 'newsy' letter. She seemed to cope so well with the enormous changes in her life. I read about Diana in the papers and I was so proud of her and the way she was learning and all the time becoming more and more beautiful as her confidence grew and she acknowledged her growing popularity with the people. It was not so long, though, after her marriage that gradually I noticed a change in her letters. I had received one from her in which she sympathized with me on the fact that my husband had gone to work in Uganda and she knew I would not be able to see him so often. I had not wanted to tell her that we were contemplating separating knowing how much she hated such a thought especially amongst people she knew. Separation and divorce were subjects that Diana never wanted to get involved with and which she thought would never happen to her. She did not like the shadow of other people's reality cast over her when she was so happily married. So I kept my counsel. Later on I did not even explain how amicable was our separation and that several times a year I travelled to Uganda with our son so he could see his father and I could teach English in the city school in Kampala. I would like to have told Diana that for I knew she was interested in children in the Third World countries, in fact Diana was interested in all children, but I said nothing.

In the same letter of condolence Diana went on to say 'how hopeless I would feel if my other half went away'. Not so long after that letter, the change in the tone of her correspondence became more apparent. The lightness was missing. Just six months after her marriage she was already learning the score – she now knew that she would have to give a great deal more than she could take. She wrote, 'I might even have to learn to ride a horse, Mary, as it is the only time I will ever see my husband on his own.' That reference to riding was a standing joke between us ever since the day she had her fall. Diana hated riding. I felt for her so deeply as I re-read the letter several times and realized the little she said embraced so much left unspoken. She had already confronted problems which she had not even anticipated. The dawning of a realization that she could not expect a cosy twosome which most newly married couples take for granted, and most of all that she would have to learn to be very flexible if she was to achieve any of her ideals. Diana seemed beyond reach. I did not have the audacity to pick up a phone and ring her. In any case I doubt I would have got through to her. Perhaps it might have been better if she had had older, experienced, outside friends to turn to, people who could view the situation without prejudice. But she might not have taken advice, caught as she was in the folds of the establishment, relying on them to advise her until, as she grew wiser, she realized what a closed hierarchy she had entered.

Diana's maternal grandmother, Lady Fermoy, to whom she had grown quite close in her teenage years, did venture to say to her that she doubted if Palace life was suitable for her and in her capacity as lady-in-waiting to the Queen Mother she spoke from years of experience. Diana, young and in love, like countless young brides before her thought that for her, love would make all the difference. The young are very self-assured, thinking that they know everything and that older people who try to advise using the knowledge gained from their own experiences do not really know what they are talking about. The Countess Spencer, the serene and dearly loved paternal grandmother, might have added her voice to the doubts expressed by Lady Fermoy had she still been alive and then history may have been different. History books, though, are not written on the strength of 'if'.

I continued to write, but now we were worlds apart. Diana replied, letters that said nothing and spoke volumes. Her every public move was watched by me and millions of other people. I saw the air of innocence that she retained up to her marriage disappear. I suppose that is only natural. It was the speed of change that startled me. Motherhood, too, brought its changes. Diana looked more beautiful than ever, the innocence subtly replaced by a glowing maturity. The attractive girl grown into a fascinating woman. Gradually though, despite her confident beauty, the freshness and sparkle disappeared. Looking from afar it seemed that after just five years the carefree girl had gone for ever, replaced by a woman who at times looked as if fifteen not five years had passed by. Her face, so often a reflection of inner thought, caught unawares, seemed so pensive. I wrote to her, 'Diana, are you all right?' I did not really expect an answer, I do not for one minute think she ever got that letter. Again I wrote and received no acknowledgement, not even from a lady-in-waiting. It was only later we learnt of the battles she had to fight alone.

Her beauty returned as she grew more confident in her own worth, as little by little she accepted and acknowledged the terrible mistake she had made and tried to work towards a solution. As Diana strove so hard to succeed, why did it not occur to anyone in the family or at court that she had to have a real reason for turning against her husband? He did his duty physically, but not emotionally. She had made a success of her work and has never lost the 'common touch' that has made her so popular. No one can ever accuse Diana of not trying – her reward was to be made a scapegoat because of the inadequacies of her husband, a man who did not waste an opportunity to put Diana down mentally. Charles was ever ready to criticize, but hardly ever prepared to offer a word of praise as she struggled to come to terms with the enormity of her position. It is an acknowledged fact that a weak person who is cleverer than his stronger but not quite so cultured partner, a person who feels internally inadequate, will use his mental prowess to abuse and blame that partner and try to demean them. Continually, but only in public, Diana rose above such mental torture. In private, she tried to hide her grief at the destruction of her dreams and to maintain a happy home for her sons, a promise she had made to herself from childhood. But the struggle and fight against impossible odds became overbearing. Diana became ill.

There is absolutely no doubt in my mind that Diana would never have married unless she was absolutely certain, not only that she was in love, but that she was loved. She would never have contemplated marrying anyone who she was not quite sure returned her love just as deeply. Frankly, the idea that Charles was not in love with her, which he now admits, would not have crossed her mind. Charles knew her family. He was a man of the world. He knew how naïve and innocent Diana was and how important love and family life were to her but he cheated her, knowingly and cynically in my view. When he told her he had never loved her as separation became inevitable a part of her died. I am in no doubt about the tremendous pain and hurt she must have endured when she realized she had never been loved by him. Diana faced an unenviable battle. She had tried so hard to please him and to make him proud, to win his love, but as her suspicions about another woman proved to be more and more accurate, she saw her chances of winning the outright love of her husband as impossible. After all, why should he bother, he had everything he wanted? He saw no reason to change his life just because he was now married. It was for Diana to make all the changes. Charles was, after all, simply following in the footsteps of the royal men before him. It was regarded as an unwritten prerogative of former princes and kings to be allowed their mistresses. It was more or less expected of them and they were not rebuked for this assumption.

The woman chosen for a royal wife had to have many qualifications to be regarded as suitable for her future position as Queen, but love was not one of the requirements. A wife was necessary to produce children on the right side of the blanket and to ensure that the monarchy continued. By maintaining a relationship with his mistress Charles, who had plenty of examples throughout history to refer to, was acting in a manner that many considered quite acceptable for a royal prince. Such an arrogance was not something that Diana could ever accept and she would never have dreamt that she would be expected to condone such behaviour. In this conviction, she did not intend to change. The accumulated factors of the strain of her position, with so much to learn and adjust to, a husband who was not easy to please and the emergence of 'that woman', whose position Diana would never accept ... The resultant stress caused Diana's illness.

Instead of questioning the reasons for her illnesses and why Diana behaved in such a dramatic manner, instead of trying to help, instead of wondering if it could possibly have had anything to do with him, Charles wallowed in self-pity about being misunderstood and thus became increasingly irritated that fate should deal him such a poor hand in the form of his young, unstable wife. He did not try, because he did not care, because he was too wrapped up in himself. Charles chose to ignore how much Diana had done for the monarchy. He ignored how diligently she had worked. He ignored how she had brought life into a monarchy that had become drab and colourless. Many others have already advanced the view that Charles was jealous at the speed with which Diana learnt her duties, the adeptness with which she carried them out and how loved she was by the people. A stronger man would have been proud of the efforts made by his young wife, but Charles would not even accept that some concessions on his part would have made a world of difference to Diana. He did not want to face the unpalatable truth. It was in his power to make Diana happy, but that would have involved some tiresome alterations to his lifestyle. Instead of facing what lay at the root of all the problems, he acted like a spoilt little boy, wallowing in self-pity, and turned to the woman he knew would understand him. So closed a vicious circle which Diana could never break.

Diana's sense of betrayal as she reflected on the qualms and pain she had suffered due to 'that woman' was quite justified. Further, to discover that people she had regarded as mutual friends had deceived her by lending their homes for his dalliances, must have been like a knife turning in her heart. It must have seemed to her that so many were against her and she was fighting against insurmountable odds. This crisis, though, was the turning point. Slowly Diana's love and respect had faded, a natural enough progression if love is not returned and it becomes obvious that it never will be. Eventually Diana's strength of character and sense of self-preservation stiffened. That did not obliterate the sadness or fill the void of what might have been. From the time Charles and Diana became engaged, Diana felt she could trust Charles, she could belong to someone whom she could love completely without fear that he would leave her. He was, after all, one of the few people in the country for whom marriage *had* to be permanent. He had said the same thing himself six years earlier. 'In my position, obviously the last thing I could possibly entertain is getting divorced.' Diana wrote to me after her marriage, 'I adore being married and having someone to devote my time to.' It was all she ever wanted. How bitter was the pill for Diana to swallow that there can be nothing certain in life.

In fairness it has to be recorded that Charles did express reservations to friends before his marriage. He enjoyed his bachelor life. His physical needs were catered for. There was this need for an heir, but why rush? However as he tended to be a ditherer no one paid much attention to his protestations. This Lady Diana Spencer who had no past, on whom there was no dirt to uncover, would be the ideal wife, or so he was advised. No wonder, when asked during the interview after their engagement was announced, what they shared in common and when urged further, 'And I suppose you are in love?' Diana immediately replied, 'Of course!' while Charles agreed but added, 'whatever "in love" means'. In an earlier interview one of the qualifications he had stressed for a wife was, 'Essentially you must be good friends, and love, I am sure, will grow out of that friendship.' Diana was a friend. Charles did not regard it as important that he was not 'in love'. Certainly it was not a consideration in his marriage stakes, and as for Diana's feelings, well, who on earth would stop to consider them? Charles was weak and should have confronted his fears more honestly or better still, instead of voicing them to others, he should have had the strength to approach Diana herself. It is believed that even his mistress urged him to go ahead with the marriage, thinking she had nothing to fear from such a quiet, shy girl, assuming her to be meek, mild and pliable. Had Charles tried to understand his future wife at all, he would have realized these had never been Diana's attributes. To Diana, Charles expressed no doubts. Diana never had any aspirations to marry a prince, only to marry for love. Charles did not confide in the one person who would have released him from the sham of a loveless marriage – Diana herself.

Diana was used as a pawn by the establishment, some of whose members would even now like to brush the entire episode under the carpet and pretend she does not exist.

Diana, though, does exist. Maturity has given happiness in the form of her sons and a growing awareness of her own worth. It has also brought much pain, grief, sorrow and disillusionment. Most importantly, maturity has brought her wisdom. Her husband, envied by the male population the world over for his choice of wife, a woman desired by so many men, will not now stand by her side to share and appreciate the way she has struggled and fought against such adversity. This is no wonder; it is said that Charles cannot bear to be in the same room as his wife. It is never pleasant to be reminded of personal failure and have to look it in the face.

Diana is such an asset to the monarchy and she does not deserve to be relegated to the backwaters, that is no reward for her achievement. Let it not be forgotten that she is mother to the future King of England. The part of her heart that died when she learnt how she had been deceived by her two-timing husband can gradually be filled, not with love aside from that which she receives from her children and her own friends and family, but love of work she so willingly undertakes amongst the deprived and ill people of Britain and within the world, to whom she may always be seen as their Princess.

I strongly feel that the establishment should acknowledge their part in the destruction of the dreams I knew Diana harboured from the days of childhood and, small recompense as it might be, try to make some amends and give her the backing and support she needs. She deserves to be fulfilled. Everyone does. She has had to accept it will not be in the way she had always imagined, but she is strong enough to turn second best into triumph. Her pleasure will transmit itself to her sons and they deserve to benefit from her happiness. Let the confidence she worked so hard to acquire, that has been knocked so badly, be fully restored. Let Diana follow in the footsteps of so many royal women before her who put duty before personal happiness as she wants to.

Amends can be made if there is courage. The tabloids can be deprived of tales of continual animosity and references to acrimonious proceedings. Time should be allowed to heal the damage done to the monarchy and to Diana. Time heals many wounds, but when love has been betrayed and the heart broken it can never be replaced. Lessons can be learnt, good can come from bad, a different happiness can take its place.

Ironic and incredibly sad that both Charles and Diana wanted the closeness that can be achieved with love, marriage and a family. He after his lonely childhood, Diana more especially because of her parents' divorce, but together they could not answer the other's needs. His weakness, lack of understanding and caring, led to the destruction of one girl's dreams – the girl I once knew.

Conclusion

What of the future?

For Diana, maturity brought wisdom, the ability to survive, intuition to get out when there is no longer hope, to cease harbouring expectations of what might have been and instead concentrate efforts on constructive plans for the future. Towards the end of my book I wrote that Diana did not deserve to be relegated to the backwaters, that her considerable talents should be utilized in the area closest to her heart – the underprivileged, in both health and monetary terms. Before Diana allowed herself the luxury of pursuing her favoured course, she took again the example of her mother-in-law, cast aside the hurt her husband had caused and tried to put duty first by complying with the wishes of the Queen, the nation and what she instinctively felt that duty insisted was the best course: to seek a working reconciliation with Charles, even going so far as to suggest Charles returned to Kensington Palace and that they worked as a team for the sake of the monarchy and their children. The offer was dismissed out of hand by Charles, who, for all his good intentions, has failed to make a solid impression on the hearts and minds of the nation. It was rebuffed with alacrity prompted by the thorn long inserted in his side, that he has allowed to get under his skin and to fester rendering him incapable of making any sound judgements. Diana had managed successfully to cast aside that same thorn before it too further destroyed her and all sense of reason. In the same way, Charles must take radical measures to free himself before he makes further irrational decisions. The thorn, Camilla Parker-Bowles, was a major factor in the breakdown of the marriage, and she thwarted any hope of reconciliation between Charles and Diana. It would appear the word 'duty' does not rate as highly in Charles's vocabulary as should be expected from the heir apparent. Clearly his dictionary is written back to front, placing the three 'l's, loins, love, lust, before the two 'd's, devotion (to the Crown) and duty.

Diana could do no more, she had tried everything. Every relationship, be it personal or working, has to have a fair degree of give and take. Diana was prepared to give up any idea of an alternative career and any hope of a more fulfilling personal relationship, in order to work together with Charles for their country. Diana always hated the way in which she was perceived to be in competition with her husband. She never was a competitive individual, preferring always to work together in team situations. The media chose to photograph Diana in any number of varying engagements, rather than those attended by her husband. This did not mean that his appointments were less significant, it simply meant that Diana sold more newspapers, created more revenue, and that is the prime motivation of any business. That Charles chose to blame Diana for what makes good common sense is a failing that he should accept as his problem. It was clear, however, that the sacrifices Diana was prepared to make were not to be reciprocated. Charles would agree with nothing that Diana suggested. A separation? 'No,' he said. She acquiesced. He then decided that that was exactly what he wanted. Diana did not wish to withdraw from public life initially; Charles wanted her to. When she told him later that was exactly what she intended to do, he could not understand why she should take such drastic action. Charles always said divorce was out of the question, now he states that he would like a divorce. Diana must have wondered if she could ever please him.

After much private thought and consultation with people whose advice she respected, Diana decided to retire from centre stage, to rest, devote more time to her children, to wait awhile in the wings and leave the stage to her husband, no longer able to blame failures or lack of interest in his ventures, on all the attention given to his alluring wife. She, like a flower that has bloomed so long in the sunlight, eventually needed respite in the shade, to be replanted and grow strong again, away from the weeds that tried to strangle her and the relentless glare of public attention, on the one hand so necessary and on the other so slowly destructive. She will use her time away to strengthen her roots and to re-emerge more powerful and positive than ever, in an even more fulfilling role, which will combine her acknowledged attractiveness and position in a way that will prove advantageous to the causes closest to her heart. A hands-on job which will provide a greater sense of achievement and worthiness – and Diana needs and deserves this for herself. Ultimately it will provide more satisfaction than the role she initially married into. Far into the future, Diana may even be given the chance of personal happiness again, but much as she would have loved more children, this is a long way down her list of priorities. The happiness of her two sons is at the top of that list. Unless something unforeseen happens, William will one day be king and he needs all the guidance and strength possible from his mother to provide a secure, stable childhood that will form the basis of his character as he matures, to enable him to serve his country with the same sense of duty and selflessness as that portrayed by his mother and grandmother. Charles, meantime, can now have the full attention of his advisors as they are given free rein to find him a suitable role; his mother can clearly see now that there is no happy alternative but that she continues to sit on the throne for her lifetime, hoping her children sort themselves out so that her demise does not spell the end of the monarchy.

Charles must do something and if that could be combined with trying to reinstate his credibility in the eyes of the nation, all to his advantage. It is an unenviable task that faces those who would help. Charles's esteem has been severely damaged, most of it self-inflicted, so he has a long way to climb. By the time he might even hope to begin to achieve this, Diana will have re-emerged and unwittingly will probably again draw the focus away from her erstwhile husband, unless he finally makes some sacrifices and tries to help himself. Unless he does this, all the help and influence in the world will be to no avail. Well, he has a choice. He can either follow his wife's example – highly unlikely – and put that woman out of his mind and life, or he can forget any hopes of ascension to the throne. It displays an incredibly condescending attitude towards his people – 'they won't mind, in time my acts will be accepted' – to imagine they will condone such an unethical form of behaviour. It would require expert marketing to make acceptable the fact that a divorced man could ever be king – it was for this very reason that Charles used to say he would never be able to contemplate divorce. The monarch is leader of the Established church, Defender of the

Faith. Times are changing so perhaps, but . . . Charles, though, truly lives in a world of make believe, if for one moment he imagines that the people would ever accept the woman who brought so much pain to their princess. There does not exist the marketing expertise in the world to bring about this transformation of attitudes. Just because Charles is Prince of Wales, he cannot imagine he can bend the rules to suit himself. The established code of etiquette must be adhered to in order to retain any degree of respect and if he feels unable to accept this situation, he would be best advised to return to the weeds and plants of Highgrove and leave the future running of the country to his son William, who with the guidance of his mother, brighter than any bloom Charles might hope to find in his garden – something he always failed to recognize or accept – and with the expertise of others at court, should have a much better chance of success than his well-intentioned but weak, indecisive father. The restoration of the credibility of the monarchy lies in the future King William.

Index